ESSENTIALS
of
CHRISTIAN FAITH

ESSENTIAL CHRISTIAN DOCTRINE
VOLUME I

ESSENTIALS
of
CHRISTIAN
FAITH

Steve Burris. Editor

COLLEGE PRESS PUBLISHING COMPANY • JOPLIN, MISSOURI

ESSENTIAL CHRISTIAN DOCTRINE

VOLUME I

Essentials
of Christian Faith

Authors

Bales · Castelein · Cottrell · Hall · Kurka
Leggett Lowery · Newby · Paris · Pressley

Editor

Steven E. Burris

College Press Publishing Company, Joplin, Missouri

The views expressed in this book are those of the individual authors. They do not necessarily reflect the views of the publisher, editor, or other authors.

Library of Congress Catalog Card Number: 91-77273
International Standard Book Number: 0-89900-822-4

Contents

_____ *Preface* _____

In today's pluralistic environment a clear sound must be heard concerning the essentials of faith and practice. The Restoration Movement has not readily accepted a "systematic theology" throughout its history. This volume is not an attempt to provide a systematic theology. It is intended, however, to provide a solid base from which the serious Bible student can build. Therefore, it is foundational, not exhaustive.

It is necessary that we go back to foundational matters at this point in our history. We live in an instant culture. We have come to expect instantaneous answers to all of life's questions, including questions about God, the church, and the Christian life.

No culture is shaped in a vacuum. We have a view of life that carries us along much like a stream. We step into a stream (worldview) that is already flowing and the current naturally carries us along, whether we understand its origin or its logical destination. And as we see so clearly in First Corinthians, the problems of the culture find their way into the church.

And yet, the Christian is summoned to be salt and light in the world. As salt we preserve the world. As light we illuminate situations and expose their meaning. As Paul addressed the Corinthian church, he charged them, saying, "*We are* destroying speculations and every lofty thing raised up against the knowledge of God, and *we are* taking every thought captive to the obedience of Christ."[1]

> Most Americans don't know how to think biblically any more. Public schools forbid it, churches ignore it, and families are too busy to make it stick.[2]

As in the Corinthian Church, the effect on Christianity in the 1990s is unmistakable. The same accommodation and tolerance, relativism, personal autonomy, morality, authoritarianism, totalitarianism, relativism and consumerism that is prevalent in society can be found in the life of the church and Christian as well.

> Anxiously awaiting major overhauls of our perspectives and experiences, we tend to dismiss the minute, tiny adjustments going on about us as insignificant. We have missed the fact that the cumulative effect of these minor alterations has resulted in changes in our world that in reality are far greater than the single, big bang that we have been so steadfastly awaiting. What is happening is more like Chinese water torture, with the water slowly eroding, one drip at a time, the foundations of our Christian culture.[3]

Without laying all of the blame here, much of what has occurred has come through educational systems, both sacred and secular. Education maintains a central role in either maintaining or changing the worldview of a culture. Christian institutions are affected by the encroachment of secularization as surely as any school. The pressure from societal influences, parents, even well meaning Christian leaders, to compromise the founding vision is enormous. In short, even in some Christian institutions — whether they be seminaries, universities, Bible colleges, Christian schools, or Sunday schools, clear Bible teaching is systematically watered down by socially acceptable values.

It is past time for Christian leaders to become pro-active in this struggle. If we can understand what is happening around us and to us we can make a difference. By understanding the streams that carry us along, and have profound influence in our churches, our function as salt and light is enhanced. We can re-direct the stream, we are better able to preserve the world, and we bring life and freedom, truth and visible good to the world around us.

This series is written believing that with God's help change can be effected. Volume One *Essentials of Christian Doctrine*, and Volume Two *Essentials of Christian Practice*, are an attempt to return to the basics. It is an effort to see essential areas, not as fragmented parts or subjects unto themselves but as a part of a larger whole. Unless our doctrine is lived (incarnated) out each and every day in the life of the Christian and the church it is ineffectual.

The individuals writing these chapters represent an exceptional group of Christian scholars. They have prepared themselves academically to address their assigned topics. They were chosen because of their demonstrated expertise. Some are familiar to the reader. Others may be new. Each provides a unique perspective. No one will agree with every position advanced in this book.

This book is an attempt to spade up essential doctrines. It is an attempt to integrate our belief in God's infallible and inerrant Scripture. It is our only rule of faith and practice. Therefore, careful exegesis of Scripture is applied to each subject. It is intended to provide the Christian leader with the four or five essential components of each subject. It is our aim that these pages will inform and stimulate the reader to consider these essential matters again.

We dedicate these volumes to Don DeWelt, whose life and ministry incorporated both sound doctrine and practice. His dedication and inspiration lives on in those touched by his preaching, teaching, and writing.

Stephen E. Burris, editor

Camarillo, California
February 1992

ENDNOTES

1. II Corinthians 10:5, NASB.
2. Bob Slosser, *Changing the Way America Thinks* (Dallas, Texas, Word Publishing, 1989), p. 7.
3. George Barna, *The Frog In The Kettle* (Ventura, California, Regal Books, 1990), p. 24.

The Word of God

Jack Cottrell

Everyone reading this book owns dozens if not hundreds of other books on a wide variety of subjects. Many of them probably have to do with religion, especially the Christian faith. Several of the latter are no doubt copies of what we call "The Bible."

Someone may say, "It's true. I own quite a few books, and I also own several Bibles. But I don't think of the latter as just another part of my library. *The Bible is not just another book*; it is in a class by itself."

This is quite correct. One of the most fundamental essentials of Christian doctrine is that the Bible is different from every other book that has ever existed. What makes it different is not its theme, and not even its message. Its uniqueness is due rather to one basic fact having to do with its origin, i.e.,

11

the Bible is not just the words of men but is also *the Word of God*. This can be said of no other book in the world; this is why the Bible is truly in a class of its own.

In this chapter our purpose is to explore the meaning and the implications of the fact that the Bible is the Word of God. We will do this in two steps. First we will examine the Bible's claims about itself. Then we will summarize the reasons why these claims can be accepted as true.

I. WHAT DOES THE BIBLE CLAIM TO BE?

When we are confronted with any book or document, the first thing we need to know about it is *what it claims to be*. Who is its stated author? What is its stated purpose? Does it claim to be fact or fiction? How does it desire or intend to affect our lives? It is important that we ask such questions about the Bible, and that we understand from the beginning what it claims to be. These claims have been traditionally summed up in the terms *revelation* and *inspiration*.

A. Revelation

The most pervasive assumption that runs throughout the Bible is the reality of God. When we open the Bible to practically any page, we are immediately confronted with a world view that revolves around the being and doing of God. He is without question the central figure in its pages; his presence there is so common that we usually take it for granted. He is a *God who is*.

God is pictured in the Bible as the sovereign creator and ruler of the universe. He made this world and everything in it,

including the human race. The fact that he deliberately created the world and ourselves shows that he has a purpose for it
all; he wants to accomplish something, especially through his
relation to us human beings, who are uniquely made in his
own image. A part of this purpose, expressed both in the original creation and in the final redemption, is to share his goodness with us. We are intended to enjoy eternal fellowship with
God while at the same time honoring him in sincere worship
and service, to the praise of his infinite glory. This has been
God's desire and God's plan from the very beginning. Thus
he is depicted in the Bible as a *God who plans*.

God is seen in the Bible not only as one who has a plan
and a purpose, but also as one who acts to carry out this purpose. Throughout the Bible he is pictured as doing things in
relation to this world. He initially brought it into existence out
of nothing. After the first human pair sinned against him, he
has responded with countless deeds of both wrath and grace,
as recorded in both the Old and New Testaments. Of primary
importance are the many things he has done to redeem his
people from the consequences of sin. This includes especially
his interaction with the nation of Israel in preparation for the
Redeemer, the coming of the Redeemer himself to work the
works of salvation, and the giving of the Holy Spirit to inau-
gurate the church. In these and many other ways, God is seen
as a *God who acts*.

But none of this would mean anything to us, and would
scarcely even be known by us, if it were not for the fact that
God at specific points in history has spoken to certain repre-
sentatives of the human race and through them has told us all
these things in human language that we can understand. Thus
he is a *God who speaks*. Herein lies the reality of revelation.

That God should desire to communicate with the creatures

made in his own image is not surprising. Indeed, that is the very reason he made us in his image, as *persons* with whom he could commune and communicate. From our side this is all that is needed for God to be able to speak to us in understandable language; we are "programed," so to speak, to receive and understand messages revealed by him. And certainly from God's side there is no reason why he cannot speak to us on our level. After all, being infinite in his knowledge and wisdom, he knows how to reveal truth even to finite creatures.

That God has revealed truth about himself, his will, and his works is one of the basic claims of the Bible. Sometimes God spoke directly from heaven to a large audience, as in the giving of the Ten Commandments. The account of this event begins, "Then God spoke all these words" (Exod. 20:1); afterwards God said, "You yourselves have seen that I have spoken to you from heaven" (Exod. 20:22). At the baptism of Jesus God spoke these words: "This is My beloved Son, in whom I am well-pleased" (Matt. 3:17).

More often God spoke directly to a chosen individual, who then delivered the revealed message to other people. Such a person was called a *prophet*, a term which basically means "a spokesman, one who speaks on behalf of another." Hebrews 1:1 says that God "spoke long ago to the fathers in the prophets in many portions and in many ways." Sometimes the message was revealed in dreams and visions, and sometimes in a kind of vocal, "mouth to mouth" speech (Num. 12:6-8).

After receiving a message from God the prophet often took it and spoke it orally to its intended audience. In this way Nathan the prophet delivered God's words of judgment to King David: "Thus says the LORD God of Israel" (II Sam. 12:7).

At other times, however, the prophet recorded the revealed message in written form so that all future generations could hear these words of God. Much of the Bible represents itself in just this way, namely, as revelation from God recorded in writing by divinely-chosen spokesmen. David himself, who wrote most of the Psalms, said of them, "The Spirit of the LORD spoke by me, and His word was on my tongue" (II Sam. 23:2). The great prophet Isaiah begins his book thus: "Listen, O heavens, and hear, O earth; for the LORD speaks" (Isa. 1:2). Jeremiah introduces his message in a similar way: "Now the word of the LORD came to me saying" (Jer. 1:4). The message to Jeremiah included this instruction: "Thus says the LORD, the God of Israel, 'Write all the words which I have spoken to you in a book'" (Jer. 30:2). Ezekiel 1:3 says, "The word of the LORD came expressly to Ezekiel the priest." Hosea 1:1 begins, "The word of the LORD which came to Hosea." The Apostle Paul said to the Corinthians, "The things which I write to you are the Lord's commandment" (I Cor. 14:37). Such examples could be multiplied hundreds of times.

Thus the Bible claims to be about revelation from God. It is based on revelation; it reports revelation; at least in part it IS revelation from the very mind of God to our minds. No writing could make a more significant claim than this.

B. Inspiration

When God uses a spokesman or prophet to deliver a message to other people, this process takes place in two distinct steps. First, God places the message in the prophet's mind in some way. This is the act of revelation. Second, the prophet delivers this same revealed message to others, either orally or in writing. In this way the content of revelation given to us in the Bible originates with God but is mediated to us by a human being.

This raises the question of the accuracy of the mediated message. Certainly we can trust God to have revealed the message correctly to the prophet in the first step, but how can we trust the prophet to have accurately passed it along to us? More importantly, how can God himself trust the prophets to remember everything he has told them and keep everything straight and make no mistakes as they transmit his message to others? After all, even though God is infinite in his knowledge and power and is infallible in all that he says, human beings are finite and limited and are capable of memory lapses and mistakes. How can God be sure that his words are mediated accurately?

The answer lies in what is commonly called *inspiration*. We usually say that the Bible is inspired, or given by the inspiration of God. This is something quite distinct from revelation. Whereas revelation is God's action in the first step of communicating his message through spokesmen, inspiration is his action in the second step. In this second stage, when the spokesman is in the process of passing the message along (either orally or in writing), God is exerting a power or an influence upon that person in a way that guarantees that what he says will be what God wants him to say. This influence is what we call inspiration.

At this point we should note that not everything communicated to us by the writers of the Bible can be called revelation. Large portions of the Bible are revealed by God and could not have been known in any other way. But some parts of the Bible consist of information or data of various kinds that were not revealed by God but were known to the writers by some other means, such as existing documents, personal experience, and personal investigation.

For example, Joshua 10:13 relates something "written in the book of Jashar" (see II Sam. 1:18). Luke says that he wrote his gospel after "having investigated everything carefully from the beginning" (Luke 1:3). Since he accompanied Paul on some of his missionary trips, many of the events Luke records in the book of Acts were things he experienced personally (see Acts 20:6-7, 13-15). In his writings the Apostle Paul sometimes included references and greetings to his personal friends (see Rom. 16:1-23).

The fact that this sort of data is included in the Bible leads us to ask once more, how can we trust this material to be true and trustworthy? The answer again is inspiration. It really does not matter whether the material in the Bible came to the writers by revelation or by experience or by some other means; all that matters is that when they wrote it down, they were writing under the divine influence of the Holy Spirit. This is what guarantees that their message was exactly what God wanted it to be, and it is the basis for our accepting it as accurate and trustworthy.

Inspiration has thus been defined as the supernatural influence exerted by the Holy Spirit upon prophets and apostles which enabled them to communicate without error or omission those truths, received through revelation or otherwise, which God deemed necessary for our salvation and service. What this means is that some parts of the Bible are revealed and some are not, but *all* of the Bible is inspired. Thus it all has God's "stamp of approval."

Even though *inspiration* is the English word most commonly used to describe this supernatural influence, its literal meaning does not necessarily match the Biblical concept as defined above. Our use of this word is no doubt based on the

King James translation of II Timothy 3:16, "All Scripture is given by inspiration of God." This word occurs only one other time in the KJV, in Job 32:8, where it obviously means "breath." In II Timothy 3:16 it is based on a Greek word that also includes the idea of breathing, *theopneustos*, which literally means "God-breathed." The NIV accurately translates this verse thus: "All Scripture is God-breathed." The reason why this does not literally match the word *inspiration* is that this English word means "to breathe in," while *theopneustos* or "God-breathed" means "to breathe out." Thus even though we will all no doubt continue to speak of the Bible as "inspired," we should remember that we mean by this that the Bible is "God-breathed" or breathed out by God.[1]

The fact remains that II Timothy 3:16 makes one of the most profound Biblical claims regarding the nature of the Bible as a whole. It does indeed affirm that "all Scripture is God-breathed" (NIV). Exactly what does this mean? It means that when the human authors of the Bible were engaged in the process of writing their message, whether revealed or otherwise, the Holy Spirit was so guarding their minds and their hands that the result was as if their message had come from the very hand of God. When they were putting their words down on the original parchments or paper, the Spirit was in such control that whatever they wrote was as accurate and trustworthy as if it had been breathed out of the very mouth of God.

This does not tell us anything about *how* the Holy Spirit was doing this. We greatly err when we try to impose one particular mode or method of inspiration upon the Bible. A very few Christians have thought that inspiration means that God actually dictated every word to the human authors, who wrote them down while in a trance-like state. Critics of the Bible often present this idea, in a derogatory way, as the standard Christian belief. But this is not a proper understanding of inspiration, nor is it what most Christians have believed. It may well be that some parts of the Bible, especially the revelation sections, were in a sense dictated; but this most certainly does not apply to most of the Bible. We need not speculate as to the specific manner in which the Spirit worked, knowing that in his infinite power and wisdom he could do whatever was necessary to ensure the sufficiency and accuracy of what was written. This could range all the way from dictation to a general kind of supervision or superintendency.

Other passages of Scripture besides II Timothy 3:16 affirm this divine influence and the inspired nature of its result. For example, II Peter 1:20-21 says that "no prophecy of Scripture is a matter of one's own interpretation, for no prophecy was ever made by an act of human will, but men moved by the Holy Spirit spoke from God." The word "interpretation" is not a good translation, for it usually refers to how the *readers* of the Bible interpret or exegete it. This is not the meaning of the original, however, which is actually referring to how the *writers* of the Bible came up with their material. The NIV puts it more accurately: "No prophecy of Scripture came about by the prophet's own interpretation." In other words, Isaiah's prophecies are not just his own interpretation of things; nor did someone like David or Amos just sit down and decide on his own to write a book of the Bible. Rather, the Holy Spirit was in control of the writing process. Peter literally says that "men spoke from God as they were carried along by the Holy Spirit" (NIV).

Other such testimony to inspiration abounds. For example, Matthew 22:43-44 says that David wrote Psalm 110:1 while he was "in the Spirit." Acts 28:25 says that "the Holy Spirit rightly spoke through Isaiah." Also, Isaiah 7:14 was "spoken by the Lord through the prophet" (Matt. 1:22). Hosea 11:1 was also "spoken by the Lord through the prophet" (Matt. 2:15). God "spoke by the mouth of His holy prophets from of old" (Luke 1:70). Acts 1:16 refers to prophecies "which the Holy Spirit foretold by the mouth of David concerning Judas." Jesus promised that the New Testament would be written under the full inspiration of the Holy Spirit (John 14:26; 16:12-15). Paul declared that he, along with other apostles and prophets (see Eph. 2:20) spoke "not in words taught by human wisdom, but in those taught by the Spirit, combining spiritual thoughts with spiritual words" (I Cor. 2:13).

Thus the Bible claims to include words and messages actually revealed by God. It also claims that the written record of these revelations, along with the record of God's acts and dealings with his creatures in history, along with the description of the basic historical circumstances within which all these things occurred—i.e., "all Scripture," is inspired by the Holy Spirit. When we combine these ideas of revelation and inspiration, the result is a Bible that claims to be of *divine origin*.

C. Your Bible

How does all this relate to the Bibles that average Christians use in their everyday lives? Most people reading this book will have one or more English versions of the Bible; people in other countries have Bibles in many other languages. What can we say about these Bibles we actually use? How are they affected by these divine works of revelation and inspiration that happened thousands of years ago?

1. The History of Our Bible.

We must acknowledge that only the original writers of Scripture (Moses, David, Matthew, Paul, etc.) actually received revelation from God and were inspired by the Spirit when they wrote down the original text of their books of the Bible. Thus only the original text can technically be described as inspired.

Because these writings were immediately recognized as having infinite significance, they were copied and distributed and translated and quoted hundreds and even thousands of times. Thus even though the original *manuscripts* (the actual parchments and paper) of the Bible disappeared long ago, the original inspired *text* of the Bible was preserved in these many copies and translations.

Because the fallible copiers and translators were not inspired as the original writers were, it was inevitable that some minor scribal errors and omissions would appear at various points in their copies and translations. This does not mean, however, that we have no way of knowing what was in the original text of Scripture. Through a careful and painstaking comparative study of all the available copies and translations—a process known as textual criticism—we are able to work our way backwards to a reconstruction of that original text in the Hebrew and Greek languages. In a few cases where the existing manuscripts differ, we are not able to decide which was the actual original; but we know where these places are, and no significant teaching is left in doubt.

It is from these reconstructed original Hebrew and Greek texts that contemporary translations are made into other languages such as English. The English Bibles we use every day are all based on such a text, though in some cases where alternative readings cannot be decided on with certainty, some translations favor one reading while others opt for another one. This produces some minor differences in the actual content of our English translations. Most of the differences, though, are just differences of opinion as to what is the best way to translate the original text into English.

We can safely say that all such differences are in the end minor, compared with the overwhelming consensus as to the original text and to its meaning when translated into English. Thus we may say that for all practical purposes (with the few exceptions being noted in the footnotes of a good reference Bible), the English Bibles we use every day accurately represent the original text.[2] To the extent that this is the case, we may speak of our English (or French, or Rawang) Bibles as revealed and inspired in the senses explained above.

2. The Nature of Our Bible.

Insofar as our Bible accurately represents the original text, it has the very same nature as the original writings that came from the pens of the apostles and prophets. For all practical purposes we can speak of it in the same way as we would the latter. Its doctrines and prophecies are truly revealed by God, and it is in its entirety inspired by the Holy Spirit. Because of these two facts—revelation and inspiration—the Bible we use today may be described as follows.

First, the Bible is *the Word of God.* Any part of the Bible actually revealed by God is obviously his own words, but what about the parts that are not revealed as such? By virtue of the fact of inspiration, they also are the very words of God. *All* Scripture—every part of it—is God-breathed (II Tim. 3:16). Because of this supervisory influence of the Holy Spirit, nothing has been written that does not have his full approval. The writers spoke "not in words taught by human wisdom, but in those taught by the Spirit, combining spiritual thoughts with spiritual words" (I Cor. 2:13).

In Mark 7:10-13, when Jesus quoted the writing of Moses (Exod. 20:12; 21:17), he called it "the word of God." Whether God said it (Matt. 15:4) or Moses said it (Mark 7:10) makes no difference as long as Moses was writing under the influence of the Holy Spirit. In Romans 3:2 Paul describes the Old Testament with the very significant phrase, "the oracles of God." The NIV gives the specific meaning of this phrase: "the very words of God." In view of passages such as I Corinthians 2:13 and I Thessalonians 2:13, we may properly describe the New Testament in the same way. Thus our Bible is not only "the Word of God," but "the very words of God."

Second, the Bible is *infallible*. We often hear the Bible described as "the infallible Word of God," and properly so. The term *infallible* means "incapable of erring or making a mistake." Because the Bible is indeed the inspired Word of God, it *must* be infallible. This is true because God is not capable of error; he "knows all things" (I John 3:20). Neither is he capable of deceit; he "cannot lie" (Titus 1:2).

Third, the Bible is *inerrant*. The inerrancy of the Bible is not equivalent to its infallibility, but rather is the result of it. The term *inerrant* means simply "without error." Certainly whatever is incapable of error (i.e., infallible) will also be inerrant, or without error. Thus again, because the Bible is indeed the inspired Word of God, it *must* be inerrant. Insofar as the Bibles we use today accurately represent the inspired original text, they are inerrant.

This is how the Bible represents itself. As we have seen, because of inspiration, the Bible is properly called the Word of God and even the very words of God. Psalm 12:6 tells us that "the words of the LORD are pure words." Proverbs 30:5

declares, "Every word of God is flawless" (NIV) or "Every word of God proves true" (RSV). Speaking to his heavenly Father, Jesus sums up this idea thus: "Thy word is truth" (John 17:17).

The most significant Biblical claim to inerrancy is the declaration of Jesus in John 10:35, "The Scripture cannot be broken." In an impromptu debate with hostile Jewish leaders Jesus quoted a verse from the Old Testament (Psa. 82:6) to make his point and then affirmed that "Scripture cannot be broken." This is an implicit use of the logical form known as a syllogism: no Scripture can be broken (major premise); Psalm 82:6 is Scripture (minor premise); therefore Psalm 82:6 cannot be broken (conclusion). It is also an example of deductive reasoning. That is, Jesus begins with a statement about the nature of the Bible in general and then applies this to a particular part of the Bible.

What does Jesus mean when he says that Scripture cannot be broken? In light of the context (i.e., quoting a Bible verse to establish or prove his point), we can see that he means that whatever Scripture says about any subject will be true and thus final. Whatever the Bible says is true, just because it is in the Bible. We can put our complete trust in the Bible because it cannot be broken, questioned, refuted, denied, found faulty, found untrue, challenged, or disproved. It is unalterable, indisputable, indestructible, unbreakable in its truth.

Fourth, the Bible is *authoritative*. Authority is the right to establish the norms for truth and conduct. Only God has such authority inherently, and he expresses his authority to us in the words that he has spoken through the prophets and apostles. Since the authority of one's words is no different from his authority as such, the authority of God's words are the same as his own inherent authority. Since the Bible is the very words of God, there is no difference between its authority over us and the authority of God or of Christ. Our submission to the authority and Lordship of Christ is measured by the degree of our submission to his words. This is seen in Jesus' question, "Why do you call Me, 'Lord, Lord,' and do not do what I say?" (Luke 6:46).

Our commitment to the authority of Scripture is expressed in the familiar slogan, "The Bible and the Bible alone is our only rule of faith and practice." The word *rule* means "authoritative norm." That the Bible is our rule of faith means that we believe whatever it says; that it is our rule of practice means that we obey whatever it commands us to do. Its authority requires no less.

Finally, the Bible is *sufficient*. Because the Bible is the infallible, inerrant, authoritative Word of God, it is the one sufficient source of knowledge for all our spiritual needs. It is sufficient to show us how to be saved. Paul refers to "the sacred writings which are able to give you the wisdom that leads to salvation through faith which is in Christ Jesus" (II Tim. 3:15). Referring to his gospel and its accounts of Jesus' miracles, John says that "these have been written that you may believe that Jesus is the Christ, the Son of God; and that believing you may have life in His name" (John 20:30-31). See Romans 1:16.

The Bible is a sufficient source of truth on other subjects besides salvation as such. As II Timothy 3:16 says, it is "profitable for teaching" or "profitable for doctrine" (KJV). This is important, because God not only "desires all men to be saved," but also "to come to the knowledge of the truth" (I Tim. 2:4). The Bible is our only authoritative norm for true doctrine.

The Bible is also sufficient to show us how to live a holy

life. Because all Scripture is inspired or God-breathed, it is also "useful for teaching, rebuking, correcting and training in righteousness, so that the man of God may be thoroughly equipped for every good work" (II Tim. 3:16-17, NIV). As David said, "Thy word is a lamp to my feet, and a light to my path" (Psa. 119:105). Because of this he could also say, "O how I love Thy law! It is my meditation all the day" (Psa. 119:97).

Finally the Bible is sufficient to show us how to construct and conduct the church in our day. Paul says that the church is "built upon the foundation of the apostles and prophets" (Eph. 2:20). This can refer only to the *teaching* of the apostles and prophets, which is available to us only through their written word. The term *prophets* here refers to New Testament prophets (Eph. 3:5), which includes all the non-apostolic writers of New Testament books. This is why we strive to be a "New Testament church." We must never forsake the Old Testament and its authoritative doctrinal teaching and instruction in righteousness, but we realize that the New Testament is our special norm for the organization and practices of the church of Jesus Christ.

II. WHY DO WE BELIEVE THE BIBLE'S CLAIMS ABOUT ITSELF?

It is one thing to understand and explain what the Bible actually claims for itself; this is what we have tried to do in the previous section. But it is quite another thing to accept these claims as true. Other documents, such as the Koran and the Book of Mormon, may make the same or similar claims. Why should we accept the Bible's claims rather than those of these other writings, or why should we accept any at all?

The point here is that once we have understood the Bible's claims for itself, we must then ask whether there are good and sufficient reasons for believing that they are true. We must be careful not to argue in a circle, i.e., not to *assume* they are true just because "the Bible says so." We must be able to present *specific reasons* for believing the Bible's claims about itself. Once we are confident that there is indeed sufficient evidence for the truth of these claims, then and only then will we be able to say that we believe whatever the Bible says just because "it's in the Book."

We do not have space here to do anything more than summarize the major evidences for the truth of the Bible. They are usually categorized as *internal* evidences and *external* evidences. The former are certain characteristics or phenomena of the Bible considered in itself that are so unusual and remarkable that the only cause sufficient to explain them is the divine inspiration which the Bible claims. The latter is evidence from outside the Bible that supports or verifies specific claims made by Scripture especially in the areas of history and geography.

One point of internal evidence for the Bible's inspiration is the unity of its content. What makes this so remarkable is the great *diversity* of the circumstantial characteristics of the Bible. It is comprised of sixty-six units written over a span of about fifteen hundred years by around forty authors in three languages. Its types of writing include history, law, poetry, prophecy, biography, and letters. Yet, despite this diversity, these sixty-six parts fit together into a single unified book that develops a single major theme: redemption from sin. This is one story with a single unfolding plot, a planned drama with a beginning, a middle, and an end. In light of its diversity, how can we explain this remarkable unity? Neither chance nor ordinary human intelligence could have produced it. This unity requires a single mind behind the production of the whole Bible, and that can only be the mind of God.

Another element of internal evidence for the truth of the Bible's claims about itself is the pattern of fulfilled prophecies woven into its fabric. Its writers record numerous detailed predictions of events that later actually happened. Such successful prophecies can only be of divine origin, for only God has infallible knowledge of the future (Isa. 41:21-26). This confirms our belief that Scripture is the Word of God.

One other point of internal evidence is the Bible's remarkable self-consistency or lack of internal contradictions in matters such as doctrine, ethics, and history. If only human authors were responsible for the Biblical writings, we could expect numerous inconsistencies and discrepancies. The Bible's freedom from such things supports our belief in its divine inspiration. Of course, critics who give the Bible only a careless once-over and who are looking for reasons not to believe it have always tried to identify certain alleged contradictions within it. More careful study shows that these are only *seeming* contradictions, however, and can be reasonably explained.

The external evidence for the truthfulness and accuracy of the Bible usually comes through the wealth of data uncovered by historical and archeological research. In the nineteenth century and earlier, before such research was common, critics attacked many of the Bible's historical claims as being completely false. They asserted, for example, that such people as Abraham or the Hittite nation never existed; or that the book of Acts was a fictional narrative with no basis in fact. Much to their embarrassment, however, a steady stream of archeo-logical discoveries has swept away such unfounded attacks and has shown the Biblical accounts to be reliable and true.

Though we have only been able to touch the surface of these evidences here, we have at least made the point that the Bible's claims to be the inspired Word of God are not some-thing we accept on "blind faith." We believe these claims are true because there is good and sufficient evidence to support them. Thus when we submit ourselves to the full authority of the Bible, we can do so with the utmost confidence.

III. CONCLUSION

Why is it important to take seriously the Bible's claims to be the inspired and inerrant Word of God? Why is it impor-tant to fairly evaluate the evidences that undergird these claims? Because the total message of the Bible is the only truly consistent and truly optimistic world view. It is the only body of knowledge that can make earthly life peaceable and eternal life possible.

Because it alone comes from the transcendent and all-knowing God, the Bible is our only source of absolute truth about the things that matter most in life. It is the basis for true knowledge about the nature of God and man. Its message of creation and redemption gives meaning and purpose to our lives. It is the source of our knowledge of true morality and true worship. And above all, it is our only guide to salvation and hope. It tells the truth about sin and death, and it shows what God has done to save us from them. It shows us how to receive this salvation: how to get right with God and stay right with him. It shows us what we can expect in the future—beyond death and in eternity—if we do receive it.

The Bible is not an end in itself, and should never be idolized or venerated as such. The true end or purpose of our existence is our right relationship with our God. As our only source of knowledge on how to find this relationship, however, the Bible is an indispensable means to this end and thus is one of the most precious gifts God ever gave us.

Endnotes

1. The reason we do not change the English word is that the term that literally means "breathed out" is the term *expired*, which we usually associate with dying or passing away. We simply do not care to say that "all Scripture is given by the expiration of God," or that the Bible is "expired." Thus we stick with inspiration.

2. Although no single English translation is perfect, some do a better job of accurately representing the original text than others. My personal preference for studying and teaching is the New American Standard Bible.

The Fatherhood of God

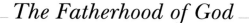

Norman Bales

A Sunday School teacher observed a young student working feverishly to complete a drawing. Her curiosity was
aroused so she asked, "What are you drawing?" He said, "I'm
drawing a picture of God." The teacher informed the student,
"But Johnny, nobody knows what God looks like." Johnny
replied, "They will when I get through."

Most of us have probably wished we could have a picture
of God, maybe even a television transmission from heaven
with God making himself available for an interview. At times
we may be frustrated by our awareness that our picture of
God can only be drawn from the inspired pages of the Bible.
We see the results of his handiwork in nature, but we can only
know of his character and his nature from the revelation of
Scripture.

Perhaps there are times when we would like the privilege of engaging in a two way, audible conversation with God. You might want to say something like, "Lord, do you really mind if I stay home from church this Sunday? I'm sure you've seen how tall the grass is in the yard; the drain pipe in the bathroom's stopped up and the house is a mess. You know how hard I worked this week. I'm sure you've noticed that I put in fifteen hours of overtime and my in-laws are coming next week to spend two weeks with us. I was just wondering if it might be all right to skip church this one Sunday and take care of my ox-in-the-ditch kind of problems."

You can ask the Lord a question like that, but you cannot expect him to come back with a voice from heaven that says something like, "I've been giving due thought to your request and even though many of your problems stem from poor stewardship of your time, I'm going to relent this one time and let you stay at home. Just don't make a habit of it."

We cannot deal with God on that basis. What we know about God and his will for us is on the pages of the Bible. While it's not possible to sketch a two dimensional picture of God or converse with him on the telephone, we do have some word pictures in the Bible.

The Bible writers used various techniques to enable us to develop powerful mental images of the kind of being that God is. In describing himself God draws from our own experiences. He uses words, names and descriptions which are familiar ones to tell us about himself. Perhaps the most graphic word description in the entire Bible occurs when God reveals himself to us as "Father."[1] The term encompasses God's authority, his protective care and his desire for closeness with people who have been created in his image.

Previous chapters have been devoted to concepts of transcendence. The transcendence concept tends to emphasize the distance between us and God. God is also immanent. Immanence refers to the presence of God in creation. It is through God's immanence that he deals compassionately with the human condition.

> A God transcendent, like some consummate painter, adorns with his brush the lilies of the field; but a God who is immanent breathes into the lilies and they become the expression of himself. A God transcendent, like some master-craftsman, fashions the fowls of the air for flight; but God who is immanent lives in every bird, and breaks the eternal silence in their song. A God transcendent, like some mighty sculptor models with his deft hand the human form; but a God who is immanent looks through human eyes, and thinks in the thinking of the human brain.[2]

It is necessary to establish the transcendence of God in order to properly appreciate his holiness, but then if transcendence is not balanced with a sense of immanence, we run the risk of leaving the impression that God is so distant we can never hope to establish a meaningful relationship with him. To dispel that mistaken notion, we now consider him as our Heavenly Father. The Bible does not describe him as the CEO, the Manager, the General, the Commandant. He's our Father. We can believe that we actually are capable of having a family relationship with the Creator of the universe.

THE USE OF FATHER IN RELIGION

Addressing deity as Father is not unique to the Judeo-Christian tradition. It shows up in pagan religions. The Greek god, Zeus, was called the "father of men and gods." The

Greek philosophers who came under the influence of Plato spoke of the "fatherhood of God."[3] The Bible writers did not borrow the concept of God's Fatherhood from the pagans, but the concept was not alien to pagan experience.

THE FATHERHOOD OF GOD IN THE OLD TESTAMENT

The Christian use of the Father image is actually derived from the Old Testament. It is a mistake to claim that the Fatherhood of God does not occur in the Old Testament. In fact it has been suggested that "Nowhere is the personhood of God more evident than in his Biblical description as Father." That motif is clearly presented in the Old Testament. Isaiah wrote a significant statement of praise in Isaiah 63:16.

> But you are our Father, though Abraham does not know us; or Israel acknowledge us; you, O LORD, are our Father, our Redeemer from of old is your name.

In a later portion of the same praise section he wrote, "Yet, O LORD, you are our Father. We are the clay, you are the potter; we are all the work of your hand" (Isa. 64:8). One of the great grace passages appears in the 103rd Psalm.

> As a father has compassion on his children,
> So the LORD has compassion on those who fear him;
> For he knows how we are formed;
> He remembers that we are dust (Psa. 103:13-14).

Even though many references to God as Father are included in the text, the portrait of God, as an intimate and personal parent, is generally missing from the Old Testament literature.

34

God is a Father, but in terms of his personal relationship with individuals, there's still a certain distance.

He is portrayed as Father of the Hebrew nation. God instructed Moses to go before Pharaoh and say, "This is what the LORD says: Israel is my firstborn son" (Exod. 4:22). Through the prophet Hosea, God recalled, "When Israel was a child, I loved him. Out of Egypt I called my son" (Hosea 11:1). God maintained a special father relationship to the kings of Israel. Nathan's message to David included the following assurance. "I will be his father and he will be my son. When he does wrong I will punish him with the rod of men, with floggings inflicted by men" (II Sam. 7:14).

How Israel Benefitted from the Fatherhood of God.

1. Protection. God's relationship with Israel as a Father meant that he would protect Israel. "The LORD your God, who is going before you, will fight for you, as he did for you in Egypt before your very eyes, and in the desert. There you saw how the LORD God carried you, as a father carries his son, all the way you went until you reached this place" (Deut. 1:30-31).

2. Discipline. God's role as a father also involved the discipline of Israel. "Know then in your heart that as a man disciplines his son, so the LORD your God disciplines you" (Deut. 8:5).

Israel's Responsibilities.

Although God regarded the nation as his children, he made it clear that they would experience the blessing of being in his family only if they responded as obedient children. Being the children of God placed Israel under an obligation to be a holy people.

> You are the children of the LORD your God. Do not cut your-selves nor shave the fronts of your head for the dead, for you are a people holy to the LORD your God. Out of all the peoples on the face of the earth, the LORD has chosen you to be his treasured possession (Deut. 14:1-2).

If everything had gone according to plan, the history of Israel would have been a story of unbroken prosperity and happiness, but it didn't happen that way. Israel often forgot the responsibilities that go with being God's children. Isaiah's first message to Israel from God lamented the rebellion of God's children.

> Hear O heavens! Listen, O earth! For the LORD has spoken: I reared children and brought them up, but they have rebelled against me (Isa. 1:2)

Through the prophet Malachi, God said, "'A son honors his father, and a servant his master. If I am a father, where is the honor due me?' says the LORD Almighty" (Mal. 1:6). Christian parents, whose children have disappointed them, ought to consider the implication of these verses. Even though God himself was a father to Israel, he could not keep the nation entirely faithful to him. Once he granted them the privilege of free moral agency, they were then free to rebel and some of them did. It wasn't that God did anything wrong. Israel failed to behave responsibly. The nation was responsible for its own behavior. Some Christians seem to think that Proverbs 22:6 is an ironclad guarantee that every properly trained child will remain faithful to God from the cradle to the grave. If that were so, then the free moral agency of the child would be circumvented. Do we believe the individual has a free will or not? If God could not control Israel throughout its history, what makes us think we can control our children for an entire lifetime? It's true that many of us make mistakes with our children and sometimes those mistakes do affect the spiritual direction a child takes. But there also comes a time when children are responsible for their own behavior. If God cannot be held responsible for the disobedience of his children then why should Christians be forced to bear some kind of stigma of guilt when their children walk down the wrong path?

God's Continual Love for His Children

Even though God was sorely disappointed with his children, he kept coming back and showing his love to them again and again. In Jeremiah 31:20, God said,

Is not Ephraim my dear son, the child in whom I delight? Though I often speak against him, I still remember him. Therefore my heart yearns for him; I have great compassion for him.

Hosea's home was a picture of God's compassion for Israel. Hosea had taken a wife who was not faithful to him. She left his home and brought shame to the family. Years later Hosea bought her on the slave market and returned her to his home. Hosea is the champion lover of the Old Testament. But the story of Hosea is more than a tragic tale of Hebrew family life. God's love for Israel was mirrored in Hosea's love for Gomer. God described his love for Israel in Hosea 11:8-9,

37

How can I give you up Ephraim? How can I hand you over, Israel? How can I treat you like Admah? How can I make you like Zeboiim? My heart is changed within me; all my compassion is aroused. I will not carry out my fierce anger, nor devastate Ephraim again. For I am God, and not man – The Holy One among you. I will not come in wrath.

Have you ever known a father with a rebellious child? I mean the kind of child that's in constant trouble, maybe even in trouble with the law. And the father keeps going down and bailing the child out of jail, keeps trying to help, keeps showing kindness and gets no appreciation in return. From your position on the outside you can just see that father setting himself up to get hurt. You shake your head and say, "Why does he keep doing it?" You don't understand because you're not the father. Why did God keep blessing Israel even after they rebelled many times? Because he was Israel's Father. According to Isaiah 49:15, his love for his children even exceeded that of a mother's love for her baby. We need to be cautious in criticizing what appears to us to be an over generous expression of parental love for their children, lest we also find ourselves in the unenviable position of criticizing the love of God.

THE FATHERHOOD OF GOD IN THE NEW TESTAMENT

While there is no difference between the God of the Old Testament and the God of the New Testament, there is a difference in emphasis. The holiness of God is emphasized throughout the Old Testament. J. I. Packer observed,

The whole spirit of Old Testament religion was determined by God's holiness. The constant emphasis was that man, because of his weakness as a creature and his defilement as a sinful creature, must learn to humble himself and be reverent before God. Religion was the "fear of the Lord" – a matter of knowing your own littleness, of confessing your faults and abasing yourself in God's presence, of sheltering thankfully under His promises of mercy and of taking care above all things to avoid presumptuous sins. Again and again it was stressed that man must keep his place, and his distance in the presence of a holy God. This emphasis overshadowed everything else.[5]

There's a shift of emphasis in the New Testament and with this shift in emphasis, more attention is given to the fatherhood of God. Matthew's gospel describes God as Father 44 times. In the writings of John, the fatherhood of God is referred to more than 100 times. Paul makes liberal use of the term. If the holiness of God demands a posture of distance in the Old Testament, the fatherhood of God invites closeness in the New Testament. Paul wrote in Romans 8:15, "For you did not receive a spirit that makes you a slave again to fear, but you received the Spirit of sonship. And by him we cry 'Abba' Father."

A new factor has come in. New Testament believers deal with God as their Father. "Father" is the name by which they call Him. "Father" has now become His covenant name – for the covenant which binds Him to His people now stands revealed as a family covenant. Christians are His children, His own sons and heirs. And the stress of the New Testament is not on the difficulty and danger of drawing near to the holy God, but on the boldness and confidence with which believers may approach Him: a boldness that springs directly from faith in Christ, and from the knowledge of his saving work.[6]

Jesus, the Unique Son
The New Testament reader is made aware of the fact that

God has a unique Father relationship with Jesus Christ as his son. Jesus was virgin born, conceived by a special act of the Holy Spirit (Luke 1:35). At his baptism, the Father opened the channels of audible communication and declared, "This is my Son, whom I love, with him I am well pleased" (Matt. 3:17). A similar procedure took place on the mount of transfiguration (Matt. 17:5). Throughout his personal ministry Jesus expressed a consciousness of his unity with the Father. In John 5:19 he said, "I tell you the truth, the Son can do nothing by himself; he can only do what he sees his Father doing, because whatever the Father does the Son also does." When Philip asked Jesus to show them the Father, he responded, "Anyone who has seen me has seen the Father" (John 14:9). In the prayer of John 17 he affirmed his oneness with the Father. He prayed that his disciples might be ". . . one, Father, just as you are in me and I in you . . ." (John 17:21).

Jesus did not come to this earth for the purpose of asserting his unique identification with the Father. There was no need to. From the beginning he enjoyed the position of glorified sonship. In the John 17 prayer he asked, "And now Father glorify me in your presence with the glory I had with you before the world began" (John. 17:5). In order to make his appearance on the earth, Jesus voluntarily relinquished his heavenly privileges. Paul said that even though he was God in his very nature, he "made himself nothing, taking the very nature of a servant, being made in human likeness" (Phil. 2:7).

Christians – God's Children

In the prologue of John's gospel, the writer emphasized the capacity of people to enter into God's family.

Yet to all who received him, to those who believed in his

name, he gave the right to become the children of God – children born not of natural descent, nor human decision or a husband's will, but born of God (John 1:12-13).

Christ's earthly ministry was begun for the purpose of enabling the people of the earth to enjoy a child – Father relationship with the God of heaven. There is a sense in which every person on the earth can claim God as Father. In the sermon on Mars Hill, Paul said, "For in him we live and move and have our very being. As some of your own poets have said, 'We are his offspring" (Acts 17:28). However, it cannot be said that every person in the world is a child of God in the spiritual sense. Pratney observed,

> God does sustain a fatherly relationship to all men because of his creatorship. "He maketh his sun to rise on the evil and on the good and sendeth rain on the just and the unjust" (Matt. 5:45). But to sin is to abandon our true Father's house and to lose ourselves in a foreign land. What we lose in relationship with our Creator can only be restored in redemption by the Savior. Jesus said of the Pharisees, "You are of your father the devil" (John 8:44) and that no man could come to the Father but by him (John 14:6).[7]

The New Testament uses two important metaphors to describe the beginning of our family relationship with God. In one sense of the term we are born into God's family. In John 3:5, Jesus said to Nicodemus, "I tell you the truth, unless a man is born of the water and the Spirit, he cannot enter the kingdom of God."

In Paul's letter to Titus, he employed the birth metaphor. "He saved us through the washing of rebirth and by renewal of the Holy Spirit" (Titus 3:5). Peter wrote, "For you have been born again, not of perishable seed, but of imperishable, through the living and enduring word of God" (I Pet. 1:23).

The new birth experience takes place when the penitent believer is baptized into Christ. Paul identified it as the beginning point of the new life when he wrote, "Or don't you know that all of us who were baptized into Christ Jesus were baptized into his death? We were therefore buried with him through baptism into death in order that, just as Christ was raised from the dead through the glory of the Father, we too may live a new life" (Rom. 6:3-4).

The other figure of speech is the adoption metaphor. In Ephesians 1:5, Paul wrote, ". . . he predestined us to be adopted as his sons through Christ Jesus in accordance with his pleasure and will." As God's adopted children, we are entitled to the same kind of inheritance that natural children receive. Paul claimed that we have the "full rights of sons" (Gal. 4:5).

WHAT IT MEANS TO HAVE GOD AS FATHER

1. Closeness. Some people have difficulty identifying with God as father because they have negative memories of their earthly Father. Many fathers fail to perform as they should. Some are violent and abusive. Others mistreat their families as the result of chemical dependency. Some fathers are too wrapped up in their careers to provide any kind of meaningful role model for their children. In today's society many fathers are on the road a great deal of the time and serve as father in absentia. It's understandable that people who have grown up with those kinds of negative role models might have difficulty understanding what God has communicated to us by telling us that he is our Father.

On the other hand, even the best father has feet of clay.

Perhaps it would help to clarify the picture if we could develop a mental picture of what our fathers might have been like had they been the kind of men they should have been. Actually God is not telling us that he is like any earthly father. He is the ideal Father.[8]

To be able to relate to God as Father means that we are privileged to enjoy closeness with him. The Hebrew writer captured the essence of this blessing when he wrote, "Let us then approach the throne of grace with confidence, so that we may receive mercy and find grace to help us in time of need" (Heb. 4:16). The Aramaic name "Abba" also suggests closeness. In Gal. 4:6, Paul wrote, "Because you are sons, God sent the Spirit of his Son into our hearts, the Spirit who calls out 'Abba' Father." The proof that we are sons comes from the instinctive cry of the heart. In his deepest need, man looks up and cries, "Abba! Father!"

At one time all four of my children lived a great distance from me, but all of them knew that if they had a serious problem they could pick up the phone and call me. In fact it's not even necessary to have a serious problem. Sometimes they call just to share good news. They also know that if they had a real need that required my presence, I would find a way to be on a plane within twenty-four hours to respond to their need. That's the kind of closeness a father has with children. God is willing to respond to us in the same way. He's always right there to hear our prayers and to give us what we need. God may not always give us what we ask. My children have sometimes asked for things I didn't grant, because I thought what they asked wasn't good for them. God does the same thing. He never withholds what we truly need.

To be adopted in the family of God means that we are given the privileges of childhood status without consideration of any merit on our part. We have an adopted son. He has all the same rights and privileges as our natural children. In fact there have been times that the bond has been so close that we had to stop and think about it when somebody asked which one is adopted. We knew that we were going to get Jim before he was born. There are always questions that come up. Some people asked us, "What are you going to do if this child is born with a physical deformity? What are you going to do if he's born with Down's Syndrome?" Our answer was always the same. "We're going to do what we would do if one of our natural children had been born that way." We've made a commitment to that child. He did not have to qualify himself for entrance into the family. As a matter of fact I remember a time when one of our children became angry with Jim over some little disagreement and he said, "You're not really part of our family." My wife, Ann, said, "Oh, yes he is. In fact, he was chosen to be a member of our family. We had to take what we got when you were born." That was the last time we heard that complaint.

The Bible says that "God so loved the world that he gave his one and only Son that whoever believes in him shall not perish but have eternal life." The passage doesn't say that God loved the beautiful people in the world. It doesn't say that God loved the talented people in the world or those with great potential. God loved the world without qualification. He loved us so much that he was willing to adopt us into his family regardless of our background, regardless of the sinfulness of our past and regardless of our abilities and skills.

Let me tell you about a friend, whom I shall call Clarence. Clarence was born with certain mental deficiencies. He has never been able to comprehend an in depth Bible discussion and I would suspect that most sermons probably go right over his head. But Clarence loves the Lord. Many years ago, he surrendered to Jesus, confessed his faith and was baptized for the remission of sins. His devotion to the Lord is apparent to all. I can recall a time when the person who unlocked the church building was always the second person to arrive. Clarence got there first. If Clarence didn't get there first, you could be absolutely certain that something was wrong. Clarence always read his Sunday School lesson, read the Bible every day and led simple prayers. Many times he has passed the Lord's Supper to me. Clarence is getting old and is now spending out his last years in a public care institution. The people who care for his needs just see a mentally deficient old man, but God sees a child whom he adopted into his family and soon He will bring Clarence home to enjoy his fellowship. And the good part is the fact that Clarence will no longer feel disadvantaged by his intellectual shortcomings.

The Father relationship means that God continues to love us even when we've disappointed him as children. Remember what he said to Israel in Hosea 11. "My heart is changed within me. All my compassion is aroused" (v. 8). The compassion that God has for his wayward children is communicated to us most graphically in the parable of the prodigal son in Luke 15. Think of the extremity of love that's displayed in this passionate story. The boy does everything but throw mud in his father's face. He's self-centered, demanding and immoral. He has treated the values of his home with disrespect. But the father never loses his love for the son. He's just waiting for the day when he can see that familiar figure top the horizon. And when the day comes, he doesn't say, "Son, go take a shower and we'll talk." He doesn't say "You're not going to live under my roof unless you meet my conditions." He really didn't need to. The son had already imposed far more severe conditions upon himself than the father would ever impose. The father said, "Get the barbecue pit ready. We're going to have a party."

Our picture of the fatherhood of God is not complete until we recognize that a father has to discipline his children. Remember that God is holy and so are his children. These children are not true to their holy nature unless they are living in holiness. Because we all live in the flesh, discipline is necessary. The Hebrew writer said,

> My son, do not make light of the Lord's discipline, And do not lose heart when he rebukes you, because the Lord disciplines those he loves, and he punishes everyone he accepts as a son (Heb. 12:5)

Discipline is one of the toughest jobs that a parent has to perform. It's difficult to know when you're holding the reins too lightly and when you're cutting a child too much slack, but every responsible child knows that discipline is essential. When my oldest son was two years old, we were living in Houston, Texas. One day he walked to the edge of North Shepherd Drive, one of the busiest streets in that city. When I caught up with him he was not a foot from the cars that were speeding down the street. My disciplinary action was swift and painful. I didn't dust his britches because I had some kind of violent desire to vent my anger on my child. I spanked him so he would associate pain with the experience of walking into traffic. My love for my son dictated disciplinary action. He doesn't hate his father because I gave him a spanking. Now he has children of his own and on occasion he has to assume the same role I did out on North Shepherd Drive that day. God has not abandoned us when he disciplines us through circumstances, through firm people, or perhaps even through our enemies. He's shaping us and making us more responsible members of his family.

CONCLUSION

We still don't know what God looks like. I can't send you to the chalkboard and say, "Now, draw a picture of God." But we do know a great deal more about what our Holy Father is like. He's not just the God who is out there beyond all the boundaries of human experience. As our heavenly father, God is always available to us. Paul said on Mars Hill we can "reach out and find him, though he is not far from each one of us" (Acts 17:27).

Endnotes

1. Many of the names of God are in the form of metaphor and analogy. A metaphor is a figure of speech, which suggests likeness. When the Bible describes God as a "Rock," a metaphor is being used. A metaphor is different from the object to which it is being compared. An analogy, on the other hand bears similarity. Thomas Aquinas once suggested that the nearest we can come to comprehending God is through analogy. Analogy is in the realm of similarity. There is a partial resemblance between the objects being compared. "Father" is an analogy. For an excellent discussion of the use of metaphors, analogies, and symbols in describing God, see Donald G. Bloesch, *The Battle for the Trinity* (Ann Arbor, Michigan: Servant Publication, 1985). Of special interest is his chapter, "The Enigma of God-Language" pp. 13-27. Bloesch responds to the efforts of extreme feminists to change the names by which we recognize God. He contends that metaphors may be changed, but not analogies. He points out, "It is important to understand that it is not we who name God, but it is God who names himself by showing us who he is" (p. 25).

2. George Morrison, "Transcendence and Immanence of God." *Pulpit Helps* (February, 1990), pp. 1, 4.

3. Arthur Wainwright, *The Trinity in the New Testament* (London: SPCK, 1961), p. 43. quoted by W.A. Pratney, *The Nature and Character of*

God. (Minneapolis: Bethany House Publisher, 1988).

3. R.L. Saucy, "God, Doctrine of." *Evangelical Dictionary of Theology.* (Grand Rapids, Michigan: Baker Book House, 1984), p. 461.

4. J.I. Packer, *Knowing God.* (Downers Grove, Illinois: InterVarsity Press, 1973), p. 183.

5. Ibid., pp. 183-184.

6. Pratney, *The Nature and Character of God.* pp. 332-333.

7. William Barclay, *The Daily Study Bible. The Letters to the Galatians and Ephesians.* (Edinburgh: The Saint Andrew Press, 1954, reprint 1965) p. 38.

Jesus Christ

Johnny Pressley

It is generally acknowledged among educated persons of all religious and philosophical persuasions that Jesus Christ was a real historical character. But a great controversy erupts when you consider the question of who was this man and what good did he accomplish. It is on this issue of the person and work of Christ that many people take exception to the traditional view of the church. The Apostle Paul summarizes the New Testament teaching regarding the person and work of Jesus in Philippians 2:6-11.

Paul speaks of him as a divine being who chose to come to earth in human nature in order that he might die for the sake of mankind and then be resurrected as the ruler of creation.

This picture of Jesus is entirely rejected by the various religions of the world, grossly distorted by the many cults associated with Christianity, and greatly modified by a so-called modern theology in which Biblical history and doctrine are explained without reference to supernatural or miraculous elements. But the resulting views of Jesus are vastly inferior to the majestic image revealed within Scripture.

If we as Christians are going to wear the name of Christ, then it seems essential that we have a clear understanding of who Christ is and what he accomplished in our behalf.

THE ETERNAL DEITY

". . . although He existed in the form of God, [He] did not regard equality with God a thing to be grasped . . . "(Phil. 2:6).

Jesus Christ did not look like God as he walked upon this earth in human flesh. And yet he clearly identified himself as deity.

Jesus often claimed to possess powers that belong exclusively to God. One of those divine powers is control over the eternal destiny of mankind. According to Jesus, it will be his voice that calls forth all who have died and summons them to the Judgment (John 5:28; 11:25). Jesus declared that he would be the judge of creation, determining who would receive life or damnation (Matt. 7:21-23; John 5:26-29). In anticipation of his exercising this authority, Jesus sometimes announced that he already had forgiven a person's sins (Mark 2:5; Luke 7:48).

Jesus acknowledged that by making these claims he was in effect claiming equality with God. He declared, "For not even the Father judges any one, but He has given all judgment to the Son, in order that all may honor the Son, even as they honor the Father" (John 5:22-23).

This claim of equality with God was expressed by Jesus in various ways. On the one hand, he might challenge the thinking of his disciple Philip by suggesting that anyone who had seen him had in some sense seen God the Father (John 14:8-11). On the other hand, he would stun his Jewish audience by stark statements such as "I and the Father are one" (John 10:30).

Now some suggest that we in the twentieth century have misunderstood what Jesus said. It is argued that Jesus' words would not imply deity if we could understand them from a first century Jewish context. But the Gospels prove that this is not the case.

Jesus' Jewish audience clearly understood that Jesus was claiming equality with God the Father, and they reacted with hostility. And whereas this presented Jesus the opportunity to correct any wrong impression, his response was to reinforce what he had just said.

When Jesus declared that a paralytic man was forgiven, the Jews reasoned in their hearts that "He is blaspheming; who can forgive sins but God alone" (Mark 2:5-8). Jesus responded with proof that "the Son of Man has authority on earth to forgive sins" (i.e., that he has this power of God) by healing the paralytic (Mark 2:9-11).

In John's account of the confrontations between Jesus and the Jewish leaders, the charge of blasphemy (i.e., trying to put a man on God's level) is highlighted. "For this cause therefore the Jews were seeking all the more to kill Him, because He not only was breaking the Sabbath, but also was calling God His own Father, making Himself equal with God" (John 5:18). "The Jews answered Him, 'For a good work we do not stone You, but for blasphemy; and because You, being a man, make Yourself out to be God" (John 10:33). Though several false charges were considered at Jesus' trials, the charge for which he was crucified was blasphemy (Matt. 26:65-66; John 19:7-8).

Of course Jesus was not actually guilty of blasphemy, for it is not blasphemy to claim to be equal to God if you are in fact deity. The significance of noting this consistent charge is that it demonstrates that Jesus' contemporary audience clearly understood him to be claiming deity. And they were not reading into Jesus' words what they wanted to hear (as some suggest that we Christians do today), for this was not what they wanted to hear.

The testimony of Jesus' apostles regarding the deity of Christ is instructive because they, like the Jewish leaders, were resistant to this idea. They abandoned their faith in Christ when he died, despite the testimony of others who said they had seen him resurrected (Mark 16:11, 13, 14). As long as he lay dead in the tomb, they were not of a mind to create the story that Jesus was the divine Son of God (as some suggest they did). It was not until the resurrected Jesus displayed his crucifixion scars to each one of the apostles (not just Thomas) that they finally understood that Jesus was more than just a man (John 20:20, 25, 27). As Thomas declared upon his inspection of the wounds, Jesus is "my Lord and my God" (John 20:28).

Perhaps no attribute of God is more characteristic of deity than the quality of existing eternally. Thus a key testimony in the New Testament for the deity of Christ is the emphasis upon Jesus' pre-existence in eternity past.

Jesus publicly declared that "before Abraham was born, I AM" (John 8:58). By this phrase he not only claimed the special ability to have existed hundreds of years into the past, but he appropriated God's most special name ("I AM"), the name God told Moses to use to identify which deity was speaking to Pharaoh (Exod. 3:14). This statement was clearly understood by the Jewish leaders, enough so that they gathered up stones in an effort to kill Jesus for blasphemy (John 8:59).

The apostle John himself emphasized the pre-existence of Jesus by declaring that "in the beginning was the Word, and the Word was with God, and the Word was God" (John 1:1). It is evident within chapter one that John is referring to Jesus when he speaks of the "Word." John says that the Word became flesh and was spoken of by John the Baptist through the riddle "He who comes after me has a higher rank than I, for He existed before me" (John 1:14-15). Later John the Baptist identified Jesus as the person of whom he had spoken the riddle (John 1:29-30), thus equating Jesus with the Word who was with God in the beginning and who in fact "was God."

The apostle Paul refers to Jesus' pre-existence in heaven in Philippians 2:6. At that time, Paul maintains, Jesus "existed in the form of God." The Greek word *morphe* (form) conveys the idea of possessing all the attributes that belong to the subject being discussed. Thus in this phrase, Jesus is said to have possessed all of the attributes of God. Furthermore, Jesus possessed "equality with God." Some have mistakenly interpreted this verse to mean that Jesus did not in fact possess equality with God, and humbly chose not to reach for it ("he did not regard equality with God a thing to be grasped"). But the Greek word *harpagmon* (grasped) means to cling to something that is already in your possession. Paul is declaring that Jesus already possessed equality with God, but for the sake of man's salvation he humbly released his hold upon his divine position in heaven and came to earth to live on human terms (as will be explained in the next section).

Thus the testimony of both Jesus and the New Testament is clear that Jesus Christ was more than just the man he appeared to be. As Paul succinctly declares, "in Him all the fullness of Deity dwells in bodily form" (Col. 2:9).

THE INCARNATE SON

". . . but emptied Himself, taking the form of a bond-servant, and being made in the likeness of men . . ." (Phil. 2:7).

One of the more impressive terms in Christology is the word Incarnation. It is taken from the Latin term *incarnare*, which refers to taking something that does not naturally exist in a physical form and making it "fleshly." This is certainly the case with Jesus Christ. Prior to his coming to earth, he would have existed in heaven in a spiritual state rather than in a physical body, for deity is by nature an invisible spirit (John 4:24; I Tim. 6:15-16). But a radical change occurred for the Son of God when "the Word became flesh and dwelt among us" (John 1:14).

Christ chose to live for a period of time in a human body. But this was more than just another theophany (a brief appearance by a spiritual being in a bodily form), as was common in the Old Testament. Christ lived on this earth in a manner consistent with normal human existence.

Consider how he arrived on earth through the natural process of child birth. It is true that there were extraordinary aspects of Christ's birth. The manner of his conception was miraculous (i.e., the virgin birth idea of Matt. 1:20-23 and

Luke 1:34), and the circumstances of his birth were unusual (such as the use of a manger in a stable for a crib or the announcement of his birth by angels and a star). But nevertheless, it appears that he experienced a normal delivery following a normal term of pregnancy.

According to Luke, Jesus grew and developed in a manner typical of human beings (Luke 2:40, 52). His body grew in size and strength ("he kept increasing in stature"). He learned the things a child would be taught in his culture ("increasing in wisdom"). He was taught how to relate socially to other persons and how to fit in with his society ("increasing in favor with men"). And we would assume that as a boy he was instructed in the Old Testament Scriptures and the mechanics of prayer and praise ("increasing in favor with God").

In his day to day existence, Jesus behaved in a manner with which all humans can identify. For example, He would become hungry and thirsty (Matt. 4:2; 21:18; John 19:28), as well as tired and sleepy (Matt. 8:24; John 4:6). Judging by some of his statements in the Gospels, such as his reference to trying to force a camel through the eye of a needle (Matt. 19:24), he apparently enjoyed a healthy sense of humor. Likewise, Jesus could be moved to tears of sorrow on sad occasions (Luke 19:41; John 11:35). And, of course, a major indication of just how human the Son of God had become was his experience of death (Luke 23:46), something we would expect of him if he were truly human.

Even in spiritual matters Christ lived like us. He regularly prayed to the Father in heaven (Matt. 26:39-44; Luke 6:12-13). He had to deal with a variety of temptations (Matt. 4:1-22; Heb. 4:14). And as he served the Father through his teaching and healing ministry, he was assisted by the Holy Spirit (Luke 4:1; Acts 10:38). Of course we would expect some qualitative differences between Christ's spiritual experiences and our own because of his unique position as the divine messiah. But even so, there is a basic similarity that testifies to the reality of Christ's humanity.

Beyond the human experiences of Jesus specifically mentioned in Scripture are a host of possibilities we often wonder about. For example, what kind of schools did Jesus attend? Did he ever participate in games and athletic competition? Did he have any hobbies, or play a musical instrument? Did he ever get sick? The best we can do with such questions is suggest what we think could have been possible for him, and then acknowledge that we are simply guessing.

Such questions may seem pointless, since they do not lead to any certain answers. And yet they can serve a purpose in that they expand our thinking and help us to picture Jesus as a real human person. It is important to the writer of Hebrews that we recognize Jesus to have been as fully human as we are. For the death of Christ to save us, he will argue, Christ "had to be made like his brethren in all things" (Heb. 2:17).

It may seem at this point that we are presented with a contradiction. How can Scripture present Jesus as being fully divine and at the same time fully human?

The answer is not to accept one teaching and disregard the other. Nor is it correct to suggest that Christ changed from being a divine person to being a human only. This is the approach made popular by modern theology in this century as it dealt with Philippians 2:7. When Paul says that the Son of God "emptied Himself" in the Incarnation, many have interpreted this to mean that he relinquished his divine nature. Thus he was no longer deity.

In contrast to this view, the apostle Paul presents Christ as possessing a dual nature in which he is both divine and human. For example, both natures are represented in Colossians 2:9 when Paul declares that there was no aspect of deity lacking in Jesus during the Incarnation. "In Him all the fullness of Deity dwells in bodily form."

A better understanding of Philippians 2 is the idea that Christ chose not to use the privileges of his divine nature nor to live like deity during his Incarnation. This would be consistent with the context, in which Paul urges his readers to imitate the attitude of Jesus (vs. 5) and humbly put the needs of others ahead of their own needs and rights (vs. 3-4). In saying this, Paul is not arguing that Christians relinquish their human nature and become something non-human (if such were even possible). Rather, he is asking them to set aside things they have the right and power to do in order to serve the needs of others.

Thus we should not assume that Christ gave up being deity (which sounds no more possible than that we could choose to give up being human). Christ "emptied Himself" by voluntarily choosing not to use the powers and privileges of deity that remained his throughout the Incarnation.

For example, Christ subdued the radiant glory of deity and took on "appearance as a man" (Phil. 2:8). He demonstrated on the mount of transfiguration that he still possessed this quality (Matt. 17:2), and on the eve of his crucifixion he expressed his anticipation of renewing that glory again (John 17:5). But during the Incarnation, Christ's natural glory was veiled.

As an eternal being, Christ was exempt from ever having to experience death. And yet for our sake he freely chose not to exercise this power at Calvary. Prior to his Incarnation, Christ had the ability to be present in all places at the same time (omnipresence), as is natural to deity (Psa. 139:7-10; Jer.

23:23-24). Yet this ability was restricted when Christ focused his presence into a physical body.

The ability to know all things (omniscience) is a characteristic of deity (Psa. 147:5; Isa. 41:22-23). And yet during the Incarnation Christ apparently chose not to take advantage of all of this knowledge available to him. Instead, he "increased in wisdom" (Luke 2:40, 52) as a boy and even acknowledged during his ministry that he did not know the date God had set for the second coming (Matt. 24:36). Likewise, we associate with deity the ability to do anything that can possibly be done (omnipotence; Psa. 135:5-6; Rom. 1:20). And yet Christ did not exercise any supernatural powers until his first miracle in Cana at age 30 (John 2:11).

Another restriction of divine privilege is evidenced in the way Christ gave up the status he enjoyed on the throne in heaven, where angels continuously worshipped and served him. Rather than being worshipped during the Incarnation, he was subject to the ridicule and abuse of men. Rather than being served by his creatures, he "learned" (experienced) obedience to others, such as his parents, his teachers, the religious and political leaders, and to God the Father (Heb. 5:8). As Philippians 2:7 says, he took on "the form of a bond-servant."

It is with observations such as these that we can get some idea of how Jesus could appear human and act very human and yet claim to be fully equal with God. Within that human body dwelt "all the fullness of Deity" (Col. 2:9), and yet the divine nature was not used to circumvent the natural experiences of being human. It is indeed fitting that Isaiah dubbed the coming messiah "Immanuel" (Isa. 7:14), for as Matthew 1:23 explains regarding the Incarnation, Christ was literally "God with us."

THE CRUCIFIED SAVIOR

". . . and being found in appearance as a man, He humbled
Himself by becoming obedient to the point of death, even
death on a cross . . ." (Phil. 2:8).

The ministry of Jesus on this earth was multi-faceted.
When considering the question of what good did Christ
accomplish during his ministry, you could emphasize his roles
as a master teacher, a miracle-worker and healer, and a moral
example for men to imitate. But the greatest work Christ
accomplished was when he offered his life at Calvary in order
to obtain our salvation. This was the primary purpose for
which he came (Mark 10:45; I John 3:5).

It is the common belief among Christians that Christ's
death on the cross is a key concept within Christianity (as
illustrated by our use of the cross as the predominant symbol
of our religion). But the purpose of Christ's death is often
misunderstood. Some have taken the view that Christ's death
was nothing more than an object lesson in which God was
trying to motivate sinners to repent by showing them either
how much he loves us or how much he hates sin. Some have
even ventured the idea that the crucifixion was an unfortunate
mistake, the untimely death of a great teacher.

The true meaning of the cross, however, is found in the
phrase substitutionary atonement. The idea of atonement is to
pay God whatever penalty you deserve because of your sin. In
theory, once you have satisfied your debt to God's justice,
you would once again resume good terms with God. The
practical problem for sinners is that it requires an eternity of
suffering in hell in order to satisfy our debt to God for our
sins. Thus it is possible for you to make your own atonement
with God (as many, in fact, will do), but there will be no time

left over for you to enjoy a peaceful relationship with God.

God's extraordinary solution to this problem was to arrange for a substitute to make atonement in our place. The beauty of this plan is that we are able to avoid experiencing the suffering of hell and the practical impossibility of ever being at peace with God again, while at the same time God's justice is fully satisfied in that someone is suffering the full force of his wrath as he promised. The great truth of Scripture is that the death of Jesus Christ is the substitutionary atonement that provides sinners the opportunity to avoid the penalty of hell.

It is in this light that we should remember that the suffering Christ experienced at Calvary was God's wrath against sinners. In prophecy Isaiah described the messiah as being "stricken," "pierced," "crushed," "chastened," and "scourged" (Isa. 53:4-5). The source of this punishment was God himself, for as Isaiah explains, the messiah would be "smitten of God and afflicted" (Isa. 53:4). This affliction was the act of a righteous judge distributing justice to one who presented himself as ready to accept the punishment for man's iniquities and transgressions. It is in this context that "the LORD was pleased to crush Him, putting Him to grief" (Isa. 53:10).

This idea of using a substitute was not something man devised and then persuaded God to accept. Both the plan and the execution of the plan were wholly derived from the grace of God. And this scheme was not without certain carefully considered rules designed to insure that this action appeared fair and above board. It is apparent from Scripture that God had in mind certain conditions that Jesus would have to meet in order for his death to be acceptable as a substitutionary atonement.

For example, God apparently required that the substitute

for humanity be of a comparable nature, that is, that he be another human being. It is clear that nothing less than human would suffice, for it was impossible for animal sacrifices to take away sins (Heb. 10:1-4). And it would seem that deity alone would not be an acceptable substitute. The writer of Hebrews argues that the savior took on "flesh and blood" because that was the nature of the people he came to save (Heb. 2:14). The necessity of the Incarnation involving a full humanity (and not just a theophany) is evidenced in the statement "He had to be made like His brethren in all things . . . to make propitiation for the sins of the people" (Heb. 2:17).

We would expect God to require the substitute to be sinless. Otherwise, the substitute would first need to arrange an atonement for his own sins before he could consider helping others. This requirement was symbolized in the Old Testament period by the rule that an animal sacrifice must be unblemished. So it is that Christ is referred to as an unblemished lamb (I Pet. 1:19) because he was a completely sinless savior (Heb. 7:26-28).

It would also appear that Jesus could not provide a substitutionary atonement for all of mankind unless he was also deity. Hebrews argues that the eternal nature of Christ is significant for our atonement in that it guarantees that our salvation will last for ever (Heb. 7:14-16, 23-28). The idea seems to be that there will be no possibility of our forgiveness ever being rescinded as long as Christ remains present to defend what he accomplished at Calvary.

It also seems reasonable to assume that the deity of Christ was necessary for his death to count for all of humanity. We would expect the rules of substitution to be that one human could substitute for only one other person. But if the substitute has a value beyond that of a single human being, as an eternal deity should, then we could see how he could rightly substitute for more than one person.

Perhaps the most significant reason why the substitute must be deity is that it is the divine nature of Christ that accounts for his relatively brief period of suffering being comparable to our eternal suffering in hell. As horrible a death as crucifixion is, it is not in and of itself equal to the suffering of a day in hell, let alone an eternity in hell. What puts Christ's crucifixion on a level with hell is the nature of the person who suffered. The intensity of the suffering at Calvary was immeasurably amplified for Christ because he was experiencing things that radically contradicted his nature as God.

For example, as an eternal being, Christ should never have had to experience pain, suffering, or death. As a perfectly holy being, he should never have had to experience the humiliation of dying the death of a criminal while bearing a load of sins. As the exalted creator of heaven and earth, he should never have had to experience the humiliation of the abuse and mocking he received during his trials and execution. And perhaps the greatest suffering of all derived from his position as the beloved Son of God, for which he should never have had to experience the hostility and wrath of God the Father. Their perfect unity from eternity past was broken on this occasion when Christ the sin-bearer was "smitten by God and afflicted" (Isa. 53:4), so that Christ expressed his extreme agony through the words "my God, my God, why have you forsaken me" (Matt. 27:46).

God's scheme for a substitutionary atonement was not focused upon the location of hell nor did it require an eternal duration. The key to the substitution was that the intensity of suffering be comparable, as it apparently was. Truly it can be said that Christ in a sense suffered hell for us.

The Scriptures are rich in its use of analogies to illustrate the meaning of Christ's death. Four examples are particularly worth noting.

The New Testament often refers to Christ's death as a sacrifice for sins (Eph. 5:2; Heb. 10:10-12). This would be imagery with which every Jew could identify, for God had established within Judaism the practice of killing certain animals as a sacrifice for sins. The symbolism of substitution was conveyed each time an animal was slain with a knife and the sinner returned home unharmed by the knife. Thus John the Baptist could introduce Jesus as "the Lamb of God who takes away the sin of the world" (John 1:29) and a Jewish audience could later understand the significance when Jesus died as our sacrificial lamb and we remain unharmed by the "knife (wrath) of God."

Another good analogy of Christ's death is the Old Testament practice of redemption. The basic idea was that a piece of family property that had been sold off in the past or a member of the family who had sold himself into slavery could be bought back (redeemed) by a family member who was willing to pay the price set by the current owner. Thus we speak of Christ as our redeemer because he paid the price we owed to God's law (the suffering of hell) in order that we could be released from our bondage (Gal. 3:13; Eph. 1:7).

The New Testament writers not only borrowed analogies from their Jewish background, but they also used imagery that would have been familiar to a Gentile audience as well. For example, the death of Christ was described as a reconciliation (Rom. 5:8-11; II Cor. 5:18-20). This referred to a common practice within both Jewish and Gentile society in which two parties in a dispute used the services of a mediator to help them resolve their differences. The mediator would listen to both sides, determine where any fault lies on either side (or both sides), and then establish what conditions for settlement should be met by either side (or both sides). When the imagery is applied to Jesus, he becomes the mediator who determines that man as sinner is at fault in the disruption of the relationship with God and that man is obligated to satisfy the punitive demands of God's law. Where Christ goes beyond the typical role of a mediator is his offer to fulfill the condition for settlement in behalf of man so that peace with God can be resumed.

Perhaps the imagery most unfamiliar to modern readers is that of Christ's death as a propitiation (Rom. 3:25; I John 2:2; 4:10). This analogy appears to have been drawn from the old pagan practice of Gentiles in which they offered gifts to angry gods (such as tossing a person into a volcano) in hopes that the gods would consume the gift with their anger and then be content to leave the people alone. We should not expect all aspects of this pagan analogy to have relevance to Christ's death (just as we would not assume that Jesus' parable of the unjust judge in Luke 18:2-8 implies that God is sometimes unjust). The value of this illustration for a Gentile audience is that it would say that Jesus' death on the cross was a propitiation gift that satisfied God's anger enough that he does not desire to express his wrath against those who lay claim to that gift.

However one describes or illustrates Calvary, the important thing to remember is that Christ's death was a substitution for the atonement each one of us was indebted to pay to God.

THE RISEN LORD

. . . therefore also God highly exalted Him, and bestowed on

Him the name which is above every name, that at the name of
Jesus every knee should bow . . . and that every tongue should
confess that Jesus Christ is Lord . . . (Phil. 2:9-11).

Much of modern theology has found it difficult to believe
that Jesus' body and spirit were literally resurrected from the
dead on Easter Sunday. Many speak of Christ's resurrection,
but with the idea that Christ is alive in the sense that his
example lives on in our hearts and directs our lives. Some
would allow for a spiritual resurrection in which the spirit of
Christ proceeded to wherever spirits go, while the body of
Christ remained in the tomb to decay.

But such ideas are not consistent with the testimony of the
New Testament. We are told that Jesus' body was not found
in his tomb (John 20:1-13) because, as the angels announced,
he had returned to life (Matt. 28:5-7; Luke 24:4-7). Jesus
appeared to his disciples several times in a body that could be
touched (Luke 24:39-40; John 20:17) and could eat food
(Luke 24:41-43). It was apparently the same body that had
been nailed to the cross and then buried in the tomb, for it
bore the scars of the crucifixion (Luke 24:39; John 20:27).
But it was not a wounded body at this point, for it had been
renewed to life and vitality.

A belief in the bodily resurrection of Christ is essential for
our Christian faith because it is the basis for believing everything else the Scriptures teach regarding the person and work
of Christ. During his ministry Jesus staked all of his claims
regarding his deity and his mission upon one key miracle: that
he would be raised to life on the third day after his death
(Matt. 12:38-40). It would not be enough that there be a spiritual resurrection, for he specifically claimed that his body
would be resurrected (John 2:19-22). And having declared
that the event would occur on the third day, a resurrection on

any other day would not be enough to substantiate the credibility of Christ.

It is in this context that Paul says that if Christ has not been raised from the dead, then "our preaching is vain" and "your faith is worthless; you are still in your sins" (I Cor. 15:14, 17). But indeed "Christ has been raised from the dead" (I Cor. 15:20) and his resurrection now serves as God's verification that Christ is all that he claimed to be (Acts 17:31; Rom. 1:4).

The resurrection was not only a vindication of Christ's word, but also a symbol of triumph over the forces of Satan. On the evening of his betrayal Jesus indicated that he was soon to engage Satan in a confrontation (John 12:31; 14:30). We assume that the conflict took place during the three days Jesus was within the realm of death, but we have no clear description of what actually happened. It is possible that the conflict focused around the body of Jesus lying in the tomb. Satan's strategy may have been to use all of his demonic forces to guard that body and hold it in the tomb until at least the fourth day (at which point a resurrection would be useless for Christ's purposes).

But whatever occurred during those three days, Jesus emerged from the grave proclaiming that he had broken through the power of death (Rom. 6:9; II Tim. 1:10) and that he now possessed "the keys of death and of Hades" (Rev. 1:17-18). In some sense, he had "rendered powerless him who had the power of death, that is, the devil" (Heb. 2:14) and, in fulfillment of the first messianic prophecy, had "crushed the head" of the serpent who had "bruised his heal" at Calvary (Gen. 3:15). For Satan it was a humiliating defeat that not only demonstrates to the world that they no longer need to fear him (Heb. 2:15), but also foreshadowed his ultimate destruction when Christ returns (Rev. 20:10).

As a result of his successful completion of his mission at Calvary and his convincing triumph over the forces of Satan in the resurrection, Christ earned for himself the position of Lord of all creation. During his resurrection appearances he announced that he was now entitled to exercise "all authority . . . in heaven and on earth" (Matt. 28:18). The official coronation occurred forty days after his resurrection when he ascended in the clouds to heaven (Mark 16:19; Acts 1:3, 9). Christ was seated upon the throne of God (Heb. 1:3) and instructed by the Father to begin exercising his authority (Dan. 7:13-14; I Pet. 3:21-22). As prophesied in Psalm 110:1-3, the reign of Christ began with those who would "volunteer freely in the day of Thy power" while he waits for the appropriate time when God will "make Thine enemies a footstool for Thy feet." Thus the focus of Christ's rule today is the church (Eph. 1:20-23), but at the second coming he will forcefully establish his rule over all creation. Those who are sent to hell will recognize throughout eternity that Christ is actually in charge of their lives.

It is on the basis of his resurrection that Christ now wears "the name which is above every name" (Phil. 2:9). Though some might imagine that this is a reference to the name "Jesus" ("God saves") or one of his many titles, Paul is referring in Philippians to the title Lord. As he goes on to say, "every tongue should confess that Jesus Christ is Lord, to the glory of God the Father" (Phil. 2:11). Thus it became the great confession of the early church to proclaim that "Jesus is Lord" (I Cor. 12:3; I Pet. 3:15), the "King of Kings and Lord of Lords" (Rev. 19:16).

And this is still the confession we are called upon to make today. The Gospel message challenges us to believe that all of the facts that Scripture presents regarding Christ are true. We are expected to acknowledge that Jesus Christ was fully divine and fully human, and that his death on the cross provided a substitutionary atonement for our sins. But in addition to this, we are required to commit our lives to the lordship of the resurrected Christ. "If you confess with your mouth Jesus as Lord, and believe in your heart that God raised Him from the dead, you shall be saved" (Rom. 10:9).

Doctrine of the Holy Spirit

John D. Castelein

CHRIST'S SPIRIT RETURNS GOD'S CHILDREN HOME!

John's gospel preserves for us a strange saying of our Lord Jesus Christ that he spoke on the occasion of the Last Supper. It surely ranks as one of the most puzzling statements he ever made to his disciples: "But I tell you the truth, it is to your advantage that I go away; for if I do not go away, the Helper shall not come to you; but if I go, I will send Him to you" (John 16:7). The disciples must have been astounded. Was he saying that his absence would be to their *advantage*? How can anything be better than having the Master physically present in all his wisdom and power? In this chapter we will try to solve this riddle and, in doing so, we will come a long way in understanding what is central and essential to the nature

69

and work of the person we know as the Holy Spirit.

Home

One good place to start a study of who the Holy Spirit is, and what he does, is to go back to Eden when God's children were still at home with the Father. "Home" does not refer to a location as much as to a condition in which God and humans dwell together in peace, joy, and love: the children's hearts are not restless (as Augustine says human hearts are now) and the Father's heart is not searching. "Home" is where God is lovingly called "Abba," and His children gladly honor His name, freely welcome His kingdom authority, and always want His will to be done (Matt. 6:9-10).

God's Spirit helped create our original Home. In the Old Testament God's Spirit is often referred to as the wind or breath of God (in Hebrew *ruach*). And so we read that this Spirit fluttered, hovered or brooded over the chaos of Genesis 1. Somehow, God's breath joined with God's word in creating a world fit for mankind (Gen. 2:7; Psa. 33:6). Now, the Greek word for world is *cosmos*. This word indicates order and beauty (it is related to our English word cosmetics). How then does God's *Ruach* create a Home for us? By transforming that which is *chaos*—dark, empty, formless, and void—into that which is *cosmos*—light, full, orderly, and beautiful.

But what is the exact nature of this transforming "breath" of God? In the Old Testament *ruach* is also often used of humans. It refers to that which is energetically alive in the human being: the vital life force of the self asserting itself in the human mind, heart, will, moral disposition, temperament, attitudes, motives, and strong emotions (both good and bad). When used of God in the Old Testament, *ruach* points to a

manifestation of God's glorious presence, loving face, inter-
vening hand, eternal wisdom, awesome holiness, and overwhelming power. So the Spirit of God refers to God's innermost Self in all His creative and redemptive power on behalf
of His people (compare, for instance, I Cor. 2:11). Therefore,
when we speak of the Spirit we are referring to God as the
One who makes us feel at Home.

Obviously, then, the Ruach of God refers to something
divine, but it is not clear from the Old Testament that the
Spirit of God refers to a distinct person within the Trinity
(three persons in one divine Being). Genesis regularly uses
plural expressions to refer to God (1:26-27; 3:22), and Isaiah
hints at the more distinct and personal nature of the Spirit
(48:16; 63:10-14), but the Christian understanding of the
nature of God is much more dependent on the evidence found
in the New Testament.

Homeless

Genesis 3 records the tragic story of how one of God's
highest creatures, Lucifer, invades Adam and Eve's home and
seduces them into joining in his rebellion against the Father.
As in Matthew 4 ("if you are the Son of God"), Satan in Genesis 3:1-5 focuses his attack on the relationship between the
divine parent and the human child. He first questions the fact
of the Father's command (v. 1), its scope (v. 1), and its truth
(v. 4). Then he questions the Father's motives, goodness, and
unique privileges as Father (v. 5). Thus Adam and Eve begin
their running away from Home in sin: seeing, desiring, eating,
knowing, hiding, blaming, wandering restlessly without peace
or joy.

Why does the Father have to evict His children from

Home? The answer may well be: because rebellious children cannot stay at home without wrecking the peace, joy, and love of the Father's Home. They have become "by nature children of wrath" (Eph. 2:3).

To understand what is needed for sinners to return Home to the Father we must understand our fallen condition. That condition is movingly described in the Parable of the Prodigal Son (Luke 15). The Father is waiting and watching for His children while we squander all that is good for us, and in us, in the Pig Pen of sin, far from our true Home. In sin every aspect of our being is deeply affected: our eyes, our mind, our heart, our desires, our body (Rom. 1:18-32; 3:9-18; II Cor. 4:3-4; Eph. 2:1-3; 4:17-19; I John 2:16).

The New Testament refers to this fallen condition as "the Flesh." In the Flesh of sin we disown God as our Father and renounce our sonship. The Flesh is that condition in which humans reject and resist the Father's love (Rom. 8:5-8). The Flesh itself is part of "this age" or "the World," Satan's greater cosmic system of rebellion against the Father (Matt. 13:22; II Cor. 4:3-4; James 4:4). Although the Bible teaches us that the Father loves the world (John 3:16), Christians are urged not to love the world (I John 2:15) because as a spiritual environment it is not the world God intended. Satan uses the Flesh and the World to keep us willing hostages in the Pig Pen (Eph. 2:1-3). And, tragically, evidence that we are living in the Pig Pen can be seen daily in the events of the evening news.

Homesick

The Bible indicates that knowledge of the Father is deeply ingrained in every human heart, but the sinner suppresses this truth and runs away from Home (Ps. 14:1-3; Acts 14:16-17; Rom. 1:18-20). Modern man has been described by some careful observers of modern life as being "homeless." Now that does not mean that humans have completely forgotten about Home (as many myths and utopias can testify). It just means humans are haunted by Eden. Christian writers like Augustine, Pascal, G. K. Chesterton, Peter Kreeft, and C. S. Lewis have written about this innermost longing in the human soul, calling it mankind's deepest and truest Joy.

But besides the natural reminders of Home, in creation around us and in human conscience within us, the Spirit Himself reminds us of Home by supernaturally inspiring divine revelation. As the Spirit of "wisdom and understanding, of counsel and strength, of knowledge and fear of the LORD" (Isa. 11:2), He acts as the Spirit of truth to show us the Way Home (John 14:17; 15:26; 16:13).

Throughout the Bible we are told that it is the Spirit who inspires humans so that they can understand and express truth about God and the world (Zech. 7:12; I Cor. 2:10-16; I Pet. 1:10-11; II Pet. 1:20-21). In fact "all Scripture is inspired" (II Tim. 3:16), or as the NIV translates it even more literally: "all Scripture is God-breathed" (in Greek, *theopneustos*). Furthermore, the Spirit also illuminates our darkened minds so we can see God's work clearly and interpret it rightly (Psa. 143:10; John 14:26; 16:12-15; Eph. 1:15-21; I John 2:18-28).

But reminders of Home are not enough. The nation of Israel learned a very important lesson about returning Home to the Father: the external Law is not enough to make us loving, obedient children! With the giving of His Law at Sinai, God posted His house rules at the center of Israel's national life. Many divine institutions served to remind Israel of the holiness and love required to live at Home with the Father:

sabbath, circumcision, purifications, tithes, sacrifices, festivals, kosher food laws, jubilees, and rules of dress, of sexual behavior, and of conduct toward animals, slaves, and enemies.

However, though the life of each and every Jew in the Old Testament was surrounded with all kinds of reminders of the Father's will, yet the nation did not return to God. Furthermore, her Spirit-empowered leaders failed Israel: the judges became tyrants, the prophets prophesied lies, the priests extorted the people, the craftsmen constructed idols, and the kings erected altars to Baal. The temple was the closest thing to God's Home among His people, but He eventually departed from it and wrote "Ichabod" over it.

What went wrong? Stephen pinpoints the problem in Israel's failure to return Home: "You men who are stiff-necked and uncircumcised in heart and ears are always resisting the Holy Spirit" (Acts 7:51). The Law can not overcome the Flesh because the Flesh with its hardened heart always subverts the good intentions of the Law and produces more sin in us and, therefore, more wrath from the Father (Rom. 4:14-15; 5:13; 7:5-13). For all practical purposes, God's good Law actually serves as the trigger and power of sin (Rom. 3:20; 6:20; I Cor. 15:56; Gal. 3:9-19).

This is indeed a strange development, and Paul thinks it very important that Christians understand this situation fully. Though good, the Law at best can only serve as *paidagogos*, the slave who brings the master's children to the school house (inappropriately translated "tutor" in Gal. 3:23-25 in the NASV). This is our great disadvantage. What God's wayward children need is to be taught in the inner man by God Himself (Isa. 54:13; Jer. 31:33-34; Phil. 3:15; I Thess. 4:9; I John 2:20,27). As Jesus Himself explains: "No one can come to

Me, unless the Father who sent Me draws him; and I will raise him up on the last day. It is written in the prophets, 'And they shall all be taught of God.' Every one who has heard and learned from the Father comes to Me" (John 6:44-45). This wonderful solution is at the heart of the Christian religion in contrast to all other world religions.

This is foundational to a proper understanding of the Spirit's work: God has promised that He would initiate a "new covenant of the Spirit" (II Cor. 3:6) whereby His children would indeed have the means to overcome the flesh (Isa. 44:3-5; 59:21; Jer. 31:31-34; Ezek. 36:26-27; Joel 2:28-29). The Old Testament prophets came to understand that all flesh is in need of a circumcision of the heart and ears—from sinful rebellion to loving obedience—before we can truly be God's children (Jer. 4:4; 6:10 (margin); 9:26; 31:33; Ezek. 36:25-26). And it is only God's Spirit who can perform this indispensable circumcision of the heart (Rom. 2:28-29), bringing about the true circumcision (Phil. 3:2-3) when the scalpel of God's living Word (Heb. 4:12) cuts us off from the World (Gal. 6:12-16). Physical descent is not enough to be restored as a child of God (Luke 3:8; John 1:12-13; Rom. 9:6-7). Children of wrath must become children of the promise (Rom. 9:8; Gal. 4:28), as evidenced by the growing fruit of Christlike character (Rom. 7:4-6; Gal. 5:22-23; 6:7-8).

Throughout the New Testament, then, the *promise of God* refers to a new covenant relationship: He will pour out His Spirit on a whole new people (the Church) in order to transform us, from the inside out, so that the righteousness of Christ, which He has imparted to us, may grow as a living reality in us. This promise is what Christianity—in any age— is really about (Luke 24:49; Acts 1:4-5; 2:33,38-39; Gal. 3:13-14; 4:28-29; Eph. 1:13-14).

And since flesh and blood cannot inherit what the Father has in store for His children in Heaven (John 3:6; I Cor. 6:9-10; 15:50), the Holy Spirit not only fulfills God's past promises to us, but is also a pledge or first installment to us of even better things to come in the future (Rom. 8:23; II Cor. 1:22; 5:5; Eph. 1:13-14; 4:30).

Homesteader

If we are going learn more about what is central to the Spirit's work on our behalf, we must now focus on Jesus Christ, the Bearer of the Spirit. If only God could find one man who would be born in the Pig Pen, yet not allow the Pig Pen to be born in him, that man would have the moral right, the legal authority, and the spiritual power to overthrow the master of the Pig Pen. Our good news is precisely that God's Son left His heavenly Home to become that man on our behalf (Phil. 2:5-11). The Bible teaches that Jesus' conception was directly dependent on the Holy Spirit's overshadowing of creation—once again—in the person of the virgin Mary (Luke 1:35; Matt. 1:18-20). In fact, Luke 1:35 may mean that the reason Jesus will be called "holy" and "the Son of God" is precisely because His incarnation is the product of the Holy Spirit's activity.

"Homesteader" is an interesting word. It refers to someone who pioneers a home by claiming a territory that no one else has yet made a rightful claim on, and then lives on it, cultivates it, and settles it for future inhabitation by his descendants. Jesus Christ is our Pioneer, our Homesteader (John 14:1-6; I Cor. 15:20-24; Heb. 6:19-20), who is preparing our Home for us, first in the Church while we are yet on earth, and later eternally in heaven.

How did Jesus open the way back to the Father for us? He began by subjecting Himself to John the Baptist's baptism of repentance for sin. Though entirely sinless, he shared in this penitent baptism because He wanted to be completely obedient to the Father and completely identified with God's fallen children. In response, the Father strongly confirmed Jesus' sonship by pouring out His Spirit on Jesus (Mark 1:10 says "into" Him), thus anointing Him to fulfill the role of the long-awaited Messiah. At this time the Father joyfully told the world: "This is My beloved Son in whom I am well-pleased" (Psa. 2:1-7; Isa. 42:1; 61:1-3; Matt. 3:16-17; Luke 4:16-21).

Jesus laid the foundation for our sonship when in Him the Spirit found an unrestricted and abiding Home (John 1:32-33; 3:34). Though tempted by Satan to reject the Father, Jesus never wavered in disbelief, mistrust, or disobedience.

Laying aside all divine privileges inherent in being God's Word (Phil. 2:7), Jesus learned to obey God as a *human* son (Heb. 2:14-18; 4:15; 5:7-9) ministering through the power of the Holy Spirit within Him (Matt. 12:15-21,28-29; Luke 4:1,14-19; John 3:34; Acts 1:2; 10:37-38; Heb. 9:13-14). By living and dying as a loving and obedient child of His heavenly Father, Jesus has opened *the Way within Himself* for all of us to become God's loving and obedient children. Jesus' character is the Way—our itinerary Home (John 14:1-6; Heb. 10:19-22).

The decisive battle, however, that broke the walls of the Pig Pen, and opened the way Home again, took place on the cross of Jesus Christ. Here Jesus freely took upon Himself the full penalty of that terrible Homelessness that the Pig Pen ultimately leads to: "My God, my God, why hast Thou forsaken me?" (Matt. 28:46). But the Father with the power of the Holy Spirit resurrected Him from the dead (Rom. 1:4;

8:11), and turned apparent defeat into glorious victory over Satan (John 12:31-33; 16:8-11; Col. 2:15; I John 3:8), over the just but unattainable demands of the Law (Rom. 7:4-6; Gal. 2:19-21; 3:13; 4:4-5; Eph. 2:15; Col. 2:14), and over death itself (Eph. 4:8-10; I Cor. 15:23-26, 54-57; Heb. 2:14-15).

On the cross Jesus completely rested His rightful claims to the world on the Father's love and promises. Jesus' faith was vindicated as the Father resurrected Him (Acts 2:22-24; 3:15; 4:10; 5:30; I Tim. 3:16) and gave Him all Kingdom authority in heaven and on earth (Matt. 28:18; Phil. 2:9-11; Eph. 1:18-22). Thus Home rule was once again established on earth in the midst of enemy territory.

As we have seen, Jesus was conceived by the Spirit, anointed with the Spirit, and ministered through the power of the Spirit. The cooperation between the incarnated Son and the descended Spirit was extremely close during Jesus' three year ministry. It should not come as a surprise, then, that Jesus indicates that the Spirit will succeed Him and will very much continue Jesus' own presence and mission (John 7:37-39; 14:16-26; 15:26; 16:13-15). In fact, Jesus explains that the coming of the Spirit means that He is not leaving His disciples as orphans (John 14:16-18), but that He Himself in the person of the Spirit is returning to them forever (that is, for the entire age).

In telling of the coming Holy Spirit, Jesus goes well beyond the Old Testament descriptions of the Spirit. Jesus uses highly personal language in speaking of the Holy Spirit: He will be "another" comforter (in contrast to *heteros*, the Greek word *allos* means another of identical nature). Jesus also at times (John 14:26; 15:26; 16:8, 13-14) uses the masculine personal pronoun ("he") of the Spirit though the Greek word for spirit (*pneuma*) calls for a neuter pronoun ("it").

Paul also refers to the Spirit's continuation of Jesus' presence and ministry when he speaks of "Christ in you, the hope of glory" (Col. 1:27; see also Gal. 2:20; 4:19). He is most likely not thinking of the presence of the Son, who is now located at the right hand of the Father in heaven, but of the presence of His Spirit living within Christians (Rom. 5:5; 8:9-11; Gal. 4:6; Eph. 3:16-17; I John 3:24; 4:13). No wonder the New Testament occasionally calls the Spirit the "Spirit of Jesus" (Acts 16:7; Rom. 8:11; Phil. 1:19; I Pet. 1:11; see also II Cor. 3:17-18 and I Cor. 15:45).

Now we are finally ready to try to answer the question we started this study with. Why is it to the disciples' advantage that Jesus be absent from them? The answer is because our transformation into loving obedient children of God can only be initiated from within the human heart, from the inside out, not as the Law attempts from the outside in. Only when we have Jesus' Spirit of sonship poured into our hearts do we begin once again to love the Father (Rom. 5:5) and to become ready to be adopted as His children. In fact, it is through the Spirit that the Father and the Son make their home with us (John 14:16-17, 20, 23, NIV). In other words, once we receive Jesus' Spirit of sonship within us, He functions as our Spirit of adoption (Rom. 8:14-23; Gal. 4:4-7; Eph. 1:5).

It is painfully self-defeating to attempt to live the Christian life without the Spirit's power or guidance. Such a person seeks to establish his or her own righteousness, thus earning God's favor by religious activities (Rom. 10:3-4). But merely being religious has never returned anyone Home because the flesh exploits the commands of the Law in order to create more sins (Rom. 7:5-13). Even Christianity, if lived as a religion of works and achievements, will produce an inner civil war between the converted mind and the persistent flesh (Rom. 7:14-24). Unfortunately, when it comes to this wonderful advantage that Jesus gives us through His Spirit, some Christians today are no better off than the twelve disciples in Ephesus who admitted to Paul: "We have not even heard whether there is a Holy Spirit" (Acts 19:2). Jesus has given us this astounding promise: "I will not leave you as orphans; I will come to you" (John 14:18)—would we rather live in the orphanage than follow His Spirit back Home?

The apostle Paul tells us, as it were, that through His Spirit freely given to us we have a real "Home advantage":

> There is therefore now no condemnation for those who are in Christ Jesus. For the law of the Spirit of life in Christ Jesus has set you free from the law of sin and of death. For what the Law could not do, weak as it was through the flesh, God did: sending His own Son in the likeness of sinful flesh and as an offering for sin, He condemned sin in the flesh, in order that the requirements of the Law might be fulfilled in us, who do not walk according to the flesh but according to the Spirit (Rom. 8:1-4).

Great! But how does all of this work exactly?

How do we receive this Spirit which we need so desperately to become God's loving children once again? The uniform testimony of the New Testament is that Jesus is the Baptizer in (or "with") the Holy Spirit. As John's ministry was characterized by immersion with water unto repentance in order to be ready for the Messiah, so Jesus' ministry is to be characterized by an additional and distinct immersion in (or with) the Spirit unto new life (Matt. 3:11; Mark 1:8; Luke 3:16; John 1:33; Acts 1:5; 11:16; I Cor. 12:13). It is not that immersion in the Spirit of Jesus replaces water baptism for the

Christian but that it fulfills water baptism's deepest meanings of death and rebirth (John 3:5; 7:37-39; Acts 2:38; 10:47; Rom. 6:3-4).

But when exactly do we receive this promised Spirit? In trying to determine whether some disciples in Ephesus had received the Spirit, Paul asked: "Did you receive the Holy Spirit *when you believed*?" Next he questioned them about their baptism (Acts 19:1-3). Apparently, receiving the Spirit occurs somewhere at the time of conversion. The book of Acts, however, does not present a uniform sequence of receiving the baptism with the Holy Spirit: some received the Spirit at the time of baptism (Acts 2:38-39), some at the time of faith (Acts 10:44-48), and some a little later (Acts 8:14-17).

In Ephesians Paul makes reference to the *one* baptism all Christians share in (4:5). This one baptism apparently has a visible aspect (when a convert is immersed in water), and an invisible aspect (when the Lord immerses a convert in His Spirit). Ideally, then, a person who clearly understands the gospel, truly believes it, fully repents, freely confesses Christ's Lordship, and is immersed in water, at that time receives the immersion in the Spirit. This is the only basis upon which *we* as Christians are at liberty to preach God's promises of forgiveness of sins and of the gift of the Spirit (Acts 2:38). But God in His grace can blow His Wind freely in people's lives (John 3:8), as He so often also graces even our own lives with His Spirit when we least deserve it because of our incomplete obedience or faithfulness.

If being baptized in the Holy Spirit is part of every Christian's birthright, two misunderstandings need to be cleared up. First, an artificial and confusing distinction needs to be eliminated which restricts "being baptized in the Holy Spirit" to only two occurrences in the New Testament (Acts 2 and 10), and receiving "the gift of the Spirit" is made into a separate experience for Christians today. As we have seen, Christ's ongoing implanting of the promised Holy Spirit in every new generation of God's people is indispensable to the very nature of the new covenant promised in the Old Testament.

Secondly, some insist it was only the Twelve who received the promised Spirit ("they" in Acts 2:1 is the apostles in Acts 1:26). Luke's account is not really clear, but it seems more probable that all 120 followers would have been united in the temple area at 9 a.m. when the ceremonies of Pentecost would have started. The Apostles could indeed initiate and enhance the giving of the Spirit (Acts 8:14-19; 19:6; Rom. 1:11), but it is only Jesus who is the ongoing Baptizer in the Holy Spirit (See Stott in the bibliography on I Cor. 12:13).

Each Christian has the Spirit or he or she is not Christian at all (Rom. 8:9). All Christians wear the name of "Christ" (the Anointed One) because they have been anointed with His Spirit (II Cor. 1:21-22). All Christians belong to the one Body of Christ because they have been immersed in the one Spirit of Christ (I Cor. 12:12-13). The "Baptism in the Holy Spirit" (a term not used in the New Testament) is best understood as the initial and universal experience of all Christians, not a "second work of grace subsequent to salvation" that only some persistent Christians are granted. What Christians regularly experience as further workings of the Spirit, subsequent to their conversion, is best called "fillings with the Spirit" (Acts 2:4; 4:8, 31; 7:55; Eph. 5:18).

Homework

Chapters 13 through 17 in John's gospel preserve for us

Jesus' master plan of how the Spirit will complete the Son's pedagogical work in us. In that final great discourse on the night of His betrayal, Jesus repeatedly calls the Spirit our "Paraclete." The Greek word *paraclete* refers to a helper, a person called to one's side (as a counselor or attorney in a court of law), a strengthener (the original meaning of "comforter" in early English). Our pedagogical theme suggests the metaphor of a "tutor": the specialized helper who drives home the lessons of the teacher in daily, personalized, and intensive follow-up with the student.

As Christians we have one, and only one, Teacher, the Lord Jesus Christ, God's final and fully authorized Word to the world (John 1:1; Heb. 1:1-2; Matt. 28:18-20). But it is our great advantage to have Christ's Spirit as our constant inner Tutor: explaining, correcting, drilling, encouraging, reminding, disciplining, and challenging us in our apprenticeship to become sons and daughters of God in Christ's likeness.

The Tutor comes in Jesus' name (John 14:26) to bear witness to Jesus (John 15:26) and to glorify Him (John 16:14). He has no separate agenda apart from the Teacher (John 16:13), but seeks to remind us of Jesus' curriculum in our discipleship (John 14:26) and to teach us the further implications and applications of Jesus' message (John 16:12-15; see also I John 2:20,27). Pentecost announced the official opening of Christ's school.

Our homework in becoming loving children of God is both of a private inner nature and of a public corporate nature. We return Home to the Father as individual disciples but also as a family. The inner work of the Spirit is often referred to as the Spirit's work of sanctification. Individually we are tutored to become extensions of Christ's incarnation in the world as the Spirit pours out love between God and child into each disciple's heart (Rom. 5:5). There is therefore only *one* fruit of the Spirit, and that is Christlikeness, as proven in our love, joy, peace, patience, kindness, goodness, faithfulness, gentleness, and self-control (Gal. 5:22-23).

Where once it was only sin that indwelt each of us (Rom. 7:17, 20), the Tutor now also indwells each Christian (Rom. 8:9-11). Therefore, the New Testament urges us to "keep on letting ourselves be filled with (or by) the Spirit" (a literal translation of Eph. 5:18b), as Jesus kept on letting himself be filled with wisdom (see the margin of Luke 2:40). This schooling in Christlikeness involves our consciously obeying many commands concerning the putting to death of our flesh-nature and the putting on of our Christ-nature (Rom. 12-15; I Cor. 6:9-20; Eph. 4:17-6:20; Phil. 3:15-19; Col. 3:1-4:6; I Thess. 5; Heb. 12:12-13:19; I Pet. 2:11-5:11).

Our individual homework involves "sowing to the Spirit" (Gal. 6:8), that is, carefully investing our attention and energies in the Tutor's instructions, so each of us can continue to march in step with the Spirit (the literal meaning of Gal. 5:25). We should, therefore, not resist the Tutor (Acts 7:51), lie to Him (Acts 5:3), insult Him (Heb. 10:29), or quench Him (I Thess. 5:19), lest we end up blaspheming His person and work (Matt. 12:31-32).

A good indicator of how well the sanctification process is working is the individual's conscience. "The goal of our instruction is love from a pure heart and a good conscience and a sincere faith" (I Tim. 1:5; see also I Tim. 3:9; Heb. 10:22; 13:18; I Pet. 3:16). But by resisting the Tutor's work in our lives we defile our conscience (Titus 1:15), sear it as with a branding iron (I Tim. 4:2) and may eventually suffer a complete shipwreck of our faith (I Tim. 1:19).

Now there is also outward and corporate homework to be

done by the Church and all its members so that a new spiritual Israel may return Home to the Father. If the inward work involving the fruit of the Spirit is called *sanctification*, the outward work is called *edification* and involves the charismatic gifts of the Spirit.

The Church is the one Body of Christ because it is quickened by the one Spirit of Christ. The Spirit of Christ gives the Body of Christ the mind of Christ (I Cor. 2:16; Phil. 2:5). The Spirit also gives the Body its kinship, unity and fellowship and keeps the Body healthy and growing (Acts 15:28; I Cor. 6:15-17; 12:4-27; II Cor. 13:14; Eph. 2:14-18; 4:3-16; Phil. 2:1).

The Spirit is the one common source of a great variety of grace-gifts (Rom. 12:3-21; I Cor. 12:4-11, 28-30; Eph. 4:11-16; I Pet. 4:7-11). In I Cor. 12:1-4, Paul prefers speaking of *charismata* (in Greek this term refers to things that result from God's *charis* or grace) rather than about *pneumatika* (spiritual things). For Paul all expressions of God's presence and power among His people are linked to God's grace. These grace-gifts may involve the enhancement of natural abilities or the giving of supernatural abilities not previously possessed. Either way, it is God who distributes the gifts as He chooses according to His will (Rom. 12:3; I Cor. 12:6-28; Eph. 4:7; Heb 2:3-4). And He does this for the building up (edification) and common good of the Body (I Cor. 12:7; 14:3-5,12-31; Eph. 4:12), so it can carry on the mission of Jesus Christ.

God wants us to grow as His children—individually and corporately—into the maturity (perfection or completion, as indicated by the Greek word *teleios*) of the fullness of Jesus Christ (Heb. 5:9; Eph. 4:11-16). Until this state of perfection occurs (probably at the second coming of Jesus Christ), the

Spirit will continue to build up the Church by equipping it with a variety of grace-gifts as He chooses to allocate them. Fewer and fewer interpreters are willing to see the completion of the Biblical canon as being the "perfect" (I Cor. 13:10), which will end the functioning of the charismatic gifts. There-fore,many Christians trust the Holy Spirit to give whatever grace-gifts He deems necessary for the church to do God's work in the world today.

However, in wanting to be open to the reality and variety of the Spirit's working in the Churches today, several cautions should be heeded. First, since we all interpret the world around us through worldview perspectives which are given to us by our history and culture, we need to remain humble and seek to learn from each other, wherever truth may be found. We all need to quit insisting that other Christians must have the exact same experiences with God that we have been granted. None of us can prevent *or* force the genuine blowing of the Spirit where He wills, when He wills, as He wills.

Second, Christians should not outright forbid speaking in tongues (I Cor. 14:39), quench the Spirit or despise prophecy (I Thess. 5:19-21) as some were already doing in the first century. Third, all things claiming to be of the Spirit should be examined carefully according to the *measure* of God's will as revealed in Jesus Christ and in the Scriptures (John 8:31; 15:7-10; Rom. 12:3; I Cor. 14:29; Eph. 4:7, 11-16; II Thess. 2:1-2, 8-12; I John 3:21-24). It is very dangerous to go beyond the measure of God's revealed truth (I Cor. 4:6; II Cor. 10:12-15; II John 8-10). As we have said before, the Spirit is our Tutor not a second Teacher. Fourth, the Spirit will not lead in anything, be it tongues or prophecy, that will contradict or undermine the authority of God's once-and-for-all revelation in His Son Jesus Christ (John 1:1; Heb. 1:1;

I Cor. 12:3; II Thess. 2:2; I John 4:1-3; Jude 3).

Individually and corporately the Paraclete is tutoring us to continue the presence and mission of Jesus Christ in the world. This homework can be summed up in the concept of *parakalein* (a Greek word meaning to comfort). *Parakalein*, a verb related to John's title of "Paraclete" for the Spirit, is used in the Greek Old Testament (LXX) to speak of the Messiah's mission of bringing comfort to God's homeless children in a miserable world (Isa. 40:1; 49:13; 51:3,12; 52:9; 61:2; 66:13). The Messiah did this by becoming so identified with God's wayward children that He took the sufferings and punishments of their sins upon Himself in complete redemptive suffering (Mark 10:45; Isa. 52-53; II Cor. 5:21). This is also the Church's mission as the Church is commissioned to continue the work of Christ in the power and wisdom that the Spirit of Christ supplies (Matt. 28:18-20; John 17:18; 20:21; Acts 1:8; 9:31; II Cor. 1:3-7; 5:14-21; Phil. 3:10; Col. 1:24).

Homecoming

Heaven means that the Father and His children are once again reunited in a loving, peaceful, joyful Home (Rev. 21:1-6). "He who overcomes shall inherit these things and I will be His God and he will be My son" (Rev. 21:7). How creation awaits this final glorification of God's sons and daughters (Rom. 8:18-23,29-30) as they share in Christ's glory (John 17:5,22-24) in God's ultimate Temple (Rev. 21:21)! The Pig Pen and its cruel masters are to be burned (II Pet. 3:10; Rev. 19:20; 20:10,14). Those who resist being transformed into loving children cannot return Home (Rev. 19:21; 20:9, 15; 21:8).

But until then, the Spirit of Christ and the Body of Christ

together continue to invite us: "come!" (Rev. 22:17). "Come"—to all those in need of a Home. "Come" to Him who is preparing our Home. Our Home-preparer has answered the Spirit's call: "Yes, I am coming quickly" (Rev. 22:20). Have you accepted the Spirit's call to come Home? Are you daily letting the Spirit guide you in the Way Home?

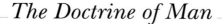

The Doctrine of Man

Tony Newby

INTRODUCTION

Curiosity does not belong only to cats. More than any other creature man has a craving for knowledge. This insatiable hunger and thirst to learn drives him to examine any piece of data that might offer a clue to the explanation of his origin and the reason for his existence. Man does not need to apologize for this condition, for he has been created in the image of the one and only God, who Himself is the all-knowing One. Part of man's image bearing is to be understood in the fact that he is the superior piece of creation. His being in God's likeness involves among other things the ability to reason.

Indeed, man is the original question machine. He wants to know this and that about that and this. But one of the most important questions that he could ever ask was asked by the psalmist David about three thousand years ago: "What is man, that Thou dost take thought of him?" (Psa. 8:4). It is almost with a touch of irony that David reveals that man is positioned between two seemingly incongruous thoughts: (1) God is majestic and His works of creation bear the marks of His splendor. (2) Man is dwarfed and seemingly insignificant in the presence of the rest of God's creation. However, the incompatibility is resolved when man admits that he is the crowning point of creation and that his majesty reflects the majesty of God. In the most human way the quest at this point becomes the philosophical/religious searching for man's true identity and reason for being. It is not to mimic the ancient Greeks who thought that man was a microcosm. Neither was Alexander Pope correct that "the proper study of mankind is man." It is to agree with Berkouwer that "Today, more than at any time, the question, 'What is man?' is at the center of theological and philosophical concern."[1]

The oldest series of questions known to man permeates the entire race: "Who am I?" "Where did I come from?" "Why am I here?" "Where am I going?" The problem with this line of questioning is that it flows as a divergent stream into two basins. The first of these can be summarized in the statement attributed to Protagoras, "Man is the measure of all things." This view has its advocates in the secular humanism of this age. This view believes that man came on the scene accidentally, i.e., by determinism, but that his progress is ever upward, i.e., by self-determinism. The second line of reasoning that man may take is the biblical or Christian view. This position holds that man has his origin and destiny wrapped and revealed in the truth of the Bible that man was created in God's image to serve and enjoy Him forever.

But what went wrong? SIN entered the human race. The parents in Eden had a choice: Obey God or die. The Bible explains only how sin entered into the race of man and gives no clear-cut account of its activity prior to this. There was no need to, for the Scriptures' main objective is to explain how this act of rebellion affected the relationship between God and man and what steps God took in response. This is not to imply that God was in a quandary over the situation, because His response was decided before man's rebellion (Matt. 13:35; I Pet. 1:20; Matt. 25:34). Not until man admits culpability in the whole of the situation will he find his real purpose for being.

Any attempt to explain man's nature, activities, rewards, etc., on any basis other than the absolute standards of the Scriptures is a mistake with grave consequences. Man's reluctance and refusal to admit guilt began in the Garden of Eden. The traditional "passing of the buck" was practiced by Eve and Adam alike. Each subsequent generation, down to modern man, has tried to shift the blame for its failures on someone else: (1) "I'm a victim of my environment." (2) "I'm just doing what comes naturally." (3) "Man just needs a better education." Ironically, much of the rebellion and anarchy that exists in societies ferments and foments on the university campuses where the intelligentsia exist to espouse their atheistic and humanistic views. President Lyndon Johnson held that better education was the bench mark of a civilized society. His failure was to specify how one was to be better educated. Today, mankind has greater and freer opportunities for a college education than ever before, but men's morals and ethics are at an all-time low. The job markets are glutted with those holding Ph.D's and Masters degrees, but for all this, crimes of violence and deception are at an all-time high. Man cannot make himself better alone. He is absolutely helpless in solving his problems by himself. Environment, education, economics, evolution—none of these solves man's dilemma: He lives in a world demanding law and order; he lives a life violating this demand.

The study of man is not something that one can isolate from all other categories. It is, as George Carey argues, to see man as he relates to all the rest of creation, but especially to his Creator:

> You reject God and claim to have no need of him in order to run your lives, and yet you value man and seek to find a true definition of him. Until God is brought back into the picture your whole idea of man is found to be faulty and incomplete.[2]

Jürgen Moltmann and Philip E. Hughes heartily concur with Carey: "Accordingly a book about 'Man' will inevitably slip into being a book about God."[3] And, "Speak about God, indeed, we must, for we cannot begin to speak truly about man unless we speak of him in relation to God his Maker."[4]

The objective of this study is to appreciate man, in spite of his failures, as the image of God and to understand the value that God places on him by His scheme of redemption. It should be noted that the word *man* is used in its generic sense and includes *woman* as God's image, as well. The plan and approach for this study is to isolate man as the epitome of creation and to examine his legitimacy by using three corollaries: I. MAN: CREATED IN THE IMAGE OF GOD; II. MAN: CORRUPTING THE IMAGE OF GOD; and III. MAN: COMPLETED IN THE IMAGE OF GOD THROUGH JESUS CHRIST THE SON OF GOD/SON OF MAN.

This effort goes out with the prayer that the dignity that is due both God and man will be apparent and that the strength of the statements will be in accordance with the Word of God.

I. MAN: CREATED IN THE IMAGE OF GOD

Man as a created being is described as having a unique relationship with the Creator. All other things, animate and inanimate, were created without God's special conferring with Himself, "Let us make man in our image" (Gen. 1:26). This verse undeniably signifies that the Godhead is plural. The so-called "Plural of Majesty" is not a viable solution for the plurality of the Godhead. The idea that God was conferring with angels does not fit the idea either, for nowhere does God conclude that angels are in His image and that man subsequently was made in the image of angels. The creation of man account in Genesis does not explain it, but the New Testament revelation of the Father, the Son, and the Holy Spirit is appropriate for understanding this concept. It brings an accord between statements such as those in Genesis 1; 2; 3:22; 11:7; and Isaiah 6:8 with those made in John 1:1-3, 14; Colossians 1:15-17; and Hebrews 1:2. Man does enjoy a special relationship with God which has special privileges and responsibilities. None of the rest of creation has a mandate from the Sovereign God that it should rule over the earth. As viceregent man is a "dominion-haver," to use the expression of Leonard Verduin. Moses and David agree. Notice the similarities between Genesis 1:26 and Psalm 8:4-8.

> Let us make man in our image, after our likeness, and let them have dominion over the fish of the sea, and over the birds of the air, and over every creeping thing that creeps upon the earth (Gen. 1:26).

What is man, that Thou dost take thought of him? And the son
of man, that Thou dost care for him? Yet Thou hast made him
a little lower than God, and dost crown him with glory and
majesty! Thou dost make him to rule over the works of Thy
hands; Thou hast put all things under his feet, all sheep and
oxen, and also the beasts of the field, the birds of the heavens,
and the fish of the sea, whatsoever passes through the paths of
the seas (Psa. 8:4-8).

Indeed, man has domesticated and trained nearly every
kind of animal. At least three basic reasons can be seen for
this dominion that man has over the animal kingdom: (1)
Some of them he has trained for labor. Examples: oxen, horses, camels, elephants. (2) Some of them he has domesticated
for food. That is to say, the animals either produce the food,
e.g., milk, cheese, butter, eggs; or, the animals themselves
become the food, e.g., fried chicken, pot roast, leg of lamb.
(3) Some animals are trained for man's sheer companionship
and enjoyment, e.g., dogs and cats for house pets and dogs
and horses for sporting events. Man is not viewed as a bizarre
anomaly if he rides a horse to market in order to purchase a
thick steak and a dozen eggs, so that he may prepare a meal to
be enjoyed on a bearskin rug before a glowing fire in the
presence of his drowsy German Shepherd. Although these
three basic reasons intrude their way into a proper application
of man's dominion over the rest of creation, there is a more
basic and essential reason for man's control over the natural
order of creation. Man is the manifest revelation of the God
of creation. This is not to say that man is a theophany, or that
man is a deity. It is, simply put, that man is the epitome, the
very apex of creation. He is God's highest work. And how is
it that man has this delineation? It is because he is in the
image and likeness of God.

Although attempts have been made to show basic differences in meaning between the words *image* and *likeness*, it is apparent that the words are used in a rather synonymous fashion. Unquestionably, the clearest proofs of this usage appear in Genesis 1:26; 5:3; and in Genesis 1:27; 5:1. Three observations are readily made: (1) In Genesis 1:26 the words are used together and seem to be synonymous. (2) In Genesis 1:27 and 5:1 the words are used separately and are obviously synonymous. (3) In Genesis 5:3 the prepositions and nouns are in the reverse order of Genesis 1:26 and appear to be synonymous, even though the subjects of the two verses are different, viz., God and Adam.

Perhaps the earliest Christian attempt at explaining the creation event comes from the pen of Irenaeus (c. 130-202). He tried to understand what it meant for man to be *created* in God's *image* and *made* in God's *likeness*. In a sense, he became the predecessor for those who eisegete the Scriptures (read a meaning into) instead of those who exegete the Scriptures (draw the meaning out of). Sometimes dichotomies are drawn, polarizations are made, and contrasts and comparisons are seen in particular word studies and their true meanings are often sacrificed for the sake of a conclusion that has been drawn without warrant. For example, Irenaeus devised an interpretation of Genesis 1:26 where *image* of God had more of a reference to man's physical side and *likeness* was more of his spiritual nature. On the other hand, certain of the Christian scholars, coming from more of a philosophic position, which had been influenced somewhat by Philo and his adaptation of Platonic philosophy, adopted the view that inherent in man's nature were his mental and moral assets which corresponded to the *image* of God, while his growth toward perfection, which came through all of life's complex struggles, worked out his being in God's *likeness*.

Thomas Aquinas (1225?-1274) thought by many to be the greatest thinker of the age of Scholasticism (10th-15th centuries), assiduously applied the conclusions of Plato and Aristotle to the theology of his day. The appeal to reason, i.e., that form of reason which depended on the postulations of such philosophers as Plato and Aristotle, was actually taking man farther from the statement in Genesis 1:26 which says that man was created in the image and likeness of God. The desire of Scholasticism to wed philosophy with its dialectic to the Scriptures resulted in a paying of too serious attention to the conclusions of the philosophers and a reconciling of the Scriptures to those conclusions. Had the reverse order of this procedure taken place the authority of the Word of God would have held precedence and the oft-disputed meanings of such words as *image* and *likeness* would not have occurred. The Christian faith is not threatened by philosophy, however, as John and David Noss have found:

> Philosophy begins with the world of sense experience and by the exercise of scientific reflection (reason) ascends to God. Theology begins with the revealed truths that are from God and descends to man and the world. Both supplement and need each other.[5]

God does not require a sacrificing of reason on the altar of revelation. On the contrary, the two elements are always compatible in the area of truth. The problem arises when one accepts human and arcane explanations for the divine mystery instead of the Bible's clear and obvious meaning.

Ray S. Anderson summarizes the teaching of Thomas Aquinas on the subject of the creation of man in God's image: "There is an image of creation, an image of re-creation, and an image of likeness."⁶ Aquinas apparently was not content to accept the synonymous usage of *image* and *likeness* and opted for more of a Platonic approach. However, no adequate explanation for the phraseology *image of likeness* was offered. Emil Brunner has a similar arrangement, but he is explicit in warning that no mysterious interpretation of the creation account can explain what one can find only in Jesus, the Word of God. He says,

> Hence the Christian doctrine of man is threefold: the doctrine of man's origin, the doctrine of the contradiction, and the doctrine of the actual state of man as life in conflict between his origin and the contradiction.⁷

Brunner argues that the Christian takes Colossians 3:10 seriously when it says that he "is being renewed to a true knowledge according to the image of the One who created him."

Although Brunner is correct in drawing one's attention to the importance of man's re-creation in Christ, he makes a serious mistake in his rejection of the Old Testament historical account of creation. He offers as an unembarrassing solution (unembarrassing, that is, to modern man, who in his unregenerate state offers existential and humanistic explanations for discoveries in science; although Brunner does maintain, tongue in cheek, that it is not for the sake of science but for the sake of keeping Christian doctrine pure) the thesis that the historicity of man's creation in Genesis is of inconsequential value.

> Above all, by this new formulation it will become clear that when we talk about the origin of man we are not speaking of a certain man called Adam, who lived so many thousand years ago, but of myself, and of yourself, and of everyone else in

the world. Only in this way will the Christian doctrine cease to be bad metaphysics; for in its old historical form, without intending it, it was a metaphysic of history, and thus bad theology.[8]

Brunner is the one who has bad theology when he refuses to let the narrative of the creation of man be seen as an historical event. The Apostle Paul saw it as a real episode in man's history (I Tim. 2:13,14; I Cor. 11:8-12), as well as did Jesus (Matt. 19:4,5). Moreover, Brunner's concept of the "contradiction" would have greater meaning if it were seen within the framework of the historical Fall. But even Brunner is forced to give credence to the significance of this 'unhistorically' created man. He admits that man, even man who denies that he has been created as a higher being, refuses to be treated with anything less than respect. He quips, "No man is a cynic where his own claim to be considered is concerned."[9]

Interpreting the meanings of *image* and *likeness* has not been the only difficulty for scholars and commentators down through the centuries. A bigger Gordian knot has been the problem of explaining what man lost as a result of the Fall. Was it the whole image? Was it universal? Was it only something spiritual? Was it only something physical? Was it temporary? Was it irretrievable? Certain aspects of these questions will be considered in the following section.

II. MAN: CORRUPTING THE IMAGE OF GOD

The loss of the image of God in man was not a total loss. That is to say, there is still the value of God's image in man. This fact is seen in the Scriptures of both the Old and New Testaments (Gen. 9:6; I Cor. 11:7; James 3:9). After the devastating incident in Eden's garden and the pervasive wickedness of antediluvian man, God declares in Genesis 9:6 that if a man is killed then his blood is to be avenged, because he was made in God's image. Some have argued that since the verb is in the past tense that this only means that God originally created man in His image but that he no longer has this distinction. But this approach hardly explains the premium that God has placed on the image-bearer by the stringent penalty He exacts of the one who shed the blood, whether beast or man. Moreover, since God is declaring this value subsequent to the Fall and the Flood, He intensifies it by referring to the Creation as the prior event, thereby using the past tense for emphasis. The Apostle Paul places the fact of man's being in God's image in the present tense in I Corinthians 11:7. Man not only *was* made in God's image, "He *is* the image and glory of God." Clearly Paul means that man continues to manifest the reality of his likeness to the Creator. Strangely enough, the ones who argue that the past tense of Genesis 9:6 is not to be understood in the present tense also argue that the present tense of I Corinthians 11:7 is to be understood in the past tense. James 3:9 may offer the most help in this matter. James inveighs against the absurdity of attempting to practice propriety of thought and conduct by using the same tongue to bless God and curse man. To James cursing man is tantamount to cursing God, because it is men "who have been made in the likeness of God." It is significant that James uses the perfect participle to illustrate this. It is obvious that he intends by this grammatical device to show that the past activity of God's having created man in His image has a present, continuing effect.

Much of the above point is denied by several of the confessions of Reformed theology, e,g,. Westminster, Scottish, Gallic, Later Helvetic, etc., which have as the conclusion that man is wholly corrupt and possesses only enough light to do things wrong. According to the Reformed position, man is totally depraved. His will is bound and God alone, arbitrarily, and by sovereign grace, converts him by giving him faith. For centuries the Augustine vs. Pelagius/Calvin vs. Arminius debate has centered in the extent of the effects of the Fall on Adam and his descendants. In reality, the argument has been an academic one, for the whole problem has been resolved in the atonement of Jesus. Romans 5 has as its clear message that whatever effect Adam's sin had on the human race, the second Adam, Jesus Christ, nullified it and "much more." This is not to say that man is now as free to enjoy Paradise as he was before the Fall, for it is evident that mankind is still plagued by disease and death. It is to admit, however, that in the ultimate sense death will be destroyed at Jesus' second coming. Neither does this teach that because Jesus won back what Adam lost that the descendants of Adam are free from personal responsibilities and the judgment of God against dis- obedience. This is where the "much more" expressions in Romans 5 have meaning for all men since Adam.

In what ways does man in his present world corrupt the image of God? Essentially, he corrupts it in the same way that Adam did, i.e., through asserting his autonomy. This failure to submit to God results in a plethora of problems for man which affect every stratum of his existence: sociological, psy- chological, economic, physical, and spiritual. Man out of sync with God is man out of sync with man and all the rest of cre- ation. His relationships with people become strained and sick. His mind becomes deluded and his judgment is dulled. His greed consumes him and he lives in the wasteland of want. His energy diminishes and his activities wear him down. His soul languishes and repines over his dreadful condition. Yet, he is unwilling to submit to God and this stubbornness keeps him in the bondage of his self-will. This bondage has also affected the rest of creation, as man's raping and ravaging of the earth has so painfully demonstrated.

Man moving into the 21st century will have to provide a better accountability for his stewardship of the earth. If the problem of his pillaging of the earth exists on the one hand, surely the problem of his neglecting it exists on the other hand. A large segment of Evangelical Christianity has relegated the earth virtually to the realm of non-important things, all the while believing that a secret rapture will snatch them up and away to a place where they will remain forever as spirit beings. Man in his triumph will be in a glorified body. He is not destined to become an ethereal spirit or an angel. He is destined to reign with Christ in a glorified body on a glorified earth (Matt. 5:5; 19:28; Rev. 3:21; Heb. 2:5; II Pet. 3:6-13; Isa. 65:17; 66:22). Paul did not argue in I Corinthians 15:37-54 that man in his glory would be bodiless. On the contrary, he argued that the body would be a spiritual, heavenly, imperishable, incorruptible one, but a *body*, nonetheless.

Alongside this depreciated view of the body has existed a depreciated view of the earth. But the Bible teaches that man's stewardship of the earth is part of his having been created in the image of God (Gen. 1:26-30). Leonard Verduin suggests that

> We must stop apologizing for the fact that to an unprecedented extent we have succeeded in subduing the earth, have found ways and means to make the earth serve man in ways heretofore undreamed of. We must stop apologizing for the fact that we are no longer a society of gatherers, that we have become first a farming civilization, and then an industrial one.

> There are those . . . who try to tell us that the subduing man is an evil man. There are those who seem to think that if we were to return to the "gathering" stage we would be moving in the right direction, with everybody stripping edibles from a supposedly ever-abundant vine! No, we must continue to produce; and continue not only, but produce as never before, produce "like mad."[10]

Man's production must not mean Earth's reduction. Proper utilization of the earth's resources augments man's freedom. But man's freedom also means creation's freedom (Rom. 8:19-22). Ultimately, this freedom is available only through the One who came as the absolute and perfect Image of God. In Jesus Christ man finds his own image restored and completed.

III. MAN: COMPLETED IN THE IMAGE OF GOD THROUGH JESUS CHRIST THE SON OF GOD/SON OF MAN

The Incarnation is important because it profoundly brings together the heart of theology and anthropology. In this single event God and man were drawn together in an unparalleled, unprecedented relationship. God in His mercy and grace effected the plan that would restore to man His image which man had corrupted. He did this through the sending of His own Son in the likeness of human flesh. Galatians 4:4,5 states, "But when the fulness of time came, God sent forth His Son, born of a woman, born under the Law, in order that He might redeem those who were under the Law, that we might receive the adoption as sons." John in the Prologue of his Gospel states, "In the beginning was the Word, and the

Word was with God, and the Word was God" (John 1:1). In verse 14 of the same chapter John writes, "And the Word became flesh, and dwelt among us, and we beheld His glory, glory as of the only begotten from the Father, full of grace and truth."

The identity of Jesus by the designation *Son* has two aspects: Son of God and Son of Man. He fills both of these titles completely. Philip E. Hughes in *The True Image* shows how these descriptions of Jesus may be used in the same breath without any suspicion of contradictions in the Incarnation. (1) At Caesarea Philippi Jesus asked Peter who men said that He the *Son* of *Man* was. Peter recited a few of their answers and then gave his own, "Thou art the Christ, the *Son* of the living *God*" (Matt. 16:13-16). (2) In describing His power over death (both physical and spiritual), Jesus said, "The dead shall hear the voice of the *Son* of *God*, and those who hear shall live." He then concluded that God had granted Him authority for judgment, "because He is the *Son* of *Man*" (John 5:25-27). (3) When Jesus testified before the Sanhedrin that the *Son* of *Man* would be seated at God's right hand, they asked Him if He was the *Son* of *God* (Luke 22:69,70). Thus, the titles *Son of God* and *Son of Man* signify two elements of the Incarnation: (1) the identity that Jesus has with God, and (2) the identity that Jesus has with man.

In the relationship that Jesus has with God He is identified as the absolute representative of the invisible God. He images God as no other being is capable of doing. Colossians 1:15 calls Him "the image of the invisible God." Hebrews 1:3 says that as the image of God Jesus is "the exact representation of His nature." John 1:18 declares, "No man has seen God at any time; the only begotten God, who is in the bosom of the Father, He has explained Him." In His last public discourse,

Jesus announced, "And he who beholds Me beholds the One who sent me" (John 12:45). In the final hours of His earthly existence Jesus tried to communicate encouragement to His disciples. "Philip said to Him, 'Lord, show us the Father, and it is enough for us.'" To which Jesus replied, "Have I been so long with you, and yet you have not come to know me, Philip? He who has seen Me has seen the Father; how do you say, 'Show us the Father?'" (John 14:8,9). Paul says in II Corinthians 4:4 that Christ "is the image of God." Philippians 2:6-8 explains the Incarnation in terms that show at least three unique experiences of Jesus: (1) His laying aside of His privileges of deity which belonged to Him in His pre-incarnate existence; (2) His taking the form of a bondservant; and (3) His becoming in the likeness and appearance of man. Colossians 1:19 and 2:9 state that in Jesus all the fullness of the Godhead dwelt in bodily form.

In relationship to man the Incarnation means that Jesus came to identify, indemnify, and intensify. His very name *Immanuel* means "God with us." He identifies with mankind in every respect except sinning and He becomes for man the perfect high priest who intercedes and delivers from death's power (Heb. 2:14-18; 4:15). He is the only mediator between God and man (I Tim. 2:5), a point of truth with which Job could have found great delight (Job 9:32-35). He indemnifies man by reimbursing him, as it were, for the loss in Eden. In addition, His indemnification exempts and protects against future loss (Heb. 2:14,15; Gal. 3:13; and Col. 2:14). He intensifies right relationships between men through His perfect example of service (Phil. 2:1-5; Matt. 20:25-28; and John 13:13-17).

The telos or goal for all mankind is that they become "partakers of the divine nature" (II Pet. 1:4). This promise for

God's creation, according to Hebrews 12:10, is "that we share His holiness." In no way does this mean that man becomes in the ontological sense God, but only that he receives the glory of God's highest reward for him, namely, sharing His presence forever. The view that man is to be deified was held by several church fathers in the early centuries. But it must be reiterated that the deification was seen in a relational sense and not an ontological one. Athanasius (c. A.D. 296-323) was a classic example of this position and Hughes points out that his concept of deification presents a problem only in a semantical sense.

> When Athanasius said that the Word of God became incarnate in order that we might be deified he was speaking of the redemptive purpose of the Son's coming, which was not only to set us free from the guilt and power of sin and to reconcile us to the Father but also to exalt us in himself to the glorious perfection of God's everlasting kingdom and to that imperishable life that swallows up our mortality.[11]

SUMMARY

Man was created in the image of God that he might live out before all of creation that special relationship that he had with his Creator. He was not like the rest of creation; he was like God. But his freedom of will was exercised for the wrong purpose and he distorted both his reason for being and his relationship with his Maker. God did not reject him completely, however, and offered him in Christ an escape from his predicament. Along with the escape, God has also provided an entrance into His heavenly kingdom through the obedience of His one and only Son, Jesus Christ. It is through this God/man that all of the rest of mankind finds both full restoration and perfection of the image of God that was lost in Adam and his descendants.

ENDNOTES

1. G.C. Berkouwer, *Man: The Image of God* (Grand Rapids: Wm. B. Eerdmans, 1962), 9.

2. George Carey, *I Believe in Man* (Grand Rapids: Wm. B. Eerdmans, 1977), 26.

3. Jürgen Moltmann, *Man: Christian Anthropology in the Conflicts of the Present* (Philadelphia: Fortress Press, 1974), Preface, x.

4. Philip Edgcumbe Hughes, *The True Image* (Grand Rapids: Wm. B. Eerdmans, 1989), 149.

5. John Noss and David Noss, *Man's Religions* (New York: Macmillan Pub. Co., 1984), 465, 466.

6. Ray S. Anderson, *On Being Human* (Grand Rapids: Wm. B. Eerdmans Pub. Co., 1982), 218.

7. Emil Brunner, *Man in Revolt* (Philadelphia: The Westminster Press, 1939), 83.

8. Ibid., 88.

9. Ibid., 82.

10. Leonard Verduin, *Somewhat Less Than God: The Biblical View of Man* (Grand Rapids: Wm. B. Eerdmans, 1970), 39.

11. Hughes, 286.

Doctrine of the Church

Marshall J. Leggett

THE CHURCH CHRIST CAME TO BUILD

Jesus said, "I will build my church." The foundation upon which His church would rest was the faith that prompted the Apostle Peter to pronounce the "Good Confession," "Thou art the Christ, the Son of the living God" (Matt. 16:16).

Surely Jesus envisioned what the church would be. But where can that Church be found? Certainly not in any era of church history, or any existing denomination. The early leaders of the Restoration movement believed that the church Jesus came to build could be found in the church that was *given*—given to the Apostles. They felt that its essential marks could be found in the New Testament church as it was shaped and guided by the Apostles. The restoration of the essence of that church would bring into existence the church Jesus envisioned.

Alexander Campbell was the most eloquent champion of this ideal. Robert Richardson wrote his impression of Campbell's work in *The Memoirs of Alexander Campbell*. He said,

> Here was an effort not so much for the reformation of the church, as was that of Luther and Calvin, and to a certain extent that of the Haldanes, but its complete *restoration* at once to its pristine purity and perfection. By coming at once to its primitive model and rejecting all human imitations; by submitting implicitly to the Divine authority as plainly expressed in the Scriptures, and disregarding all assumptions and dictations of fallible man, it was proposed to form a union upon a basis to which no valid objection could possibly be offered.[1]

This effort led the early leaders of the Restoration movement to some great *principles* which contemporary Christian Churches/Churches of Christ use in *practical* ways.

THE PRINCIPLES

The Centrality of Christ. Walter Scott discovered in 1821 what he called "The Golden Oracle." It was that Good Confession of the Apostle Peter in Matthew 16. Scott believed that this truth—Jesus is the Christ—is the heart of the Christian faith, the foundation upon which Jesus would build His church. He said, "'Jesus is the Christ' is the sun to which all other Christian truths are planets in a Christian solar system."[2] This insight helped the Restoration movement become a Christ-centered people.

It is interesting, and significant, that I hear one hymn sung more often than any other at morning worship services in Christian Churches as I travel from church-to church-to church-to church as a college president. It is neither "The Old Rugged Cross" nor "How Great Thou Art." The hymn I hear sung most often at morning services is, "All Hail the Power of Jesus' Name," which may well be the theme song of the Restoration movement.

Over the New Year's holiday of 1832, the Christians in the West who followed the leadership of Barton Warren Stone, and the Reformers in the East, led by Thomas and Alexander Campbell, met in Lexington, Kentucky. It was a unity meeting at which Raccoon John Smith spoke. He said, "Let us, then, my brethren, be no longer Campbellites or Stoneites, New Lights or Old Lights, or any other kind of *lights*, but let us come to the Bible, and the Bible alone, as the only book in the world that can give us all the light we need."[3]

As Smith finished his address, the group gathered there began to sing spontaneously:

> All hail the power of Jesus' name!
> Let angels prostrate fall;
> Bring forth the royal diadem,
> And crown him Lord of all.

There is one Scripture I hear read more often than any other at morning worship services. It is an obvious one when you stop to think about it: *I Corinthians 11:17-30.* It describes the meaning of the Lord's Supper, which is the center of the Lord's day experience in the Christian Churches/Churches of Christ; not the preaching or singing, but the Communion which reminds the participants of the central fact of the Gospel message—"Christ died for our sins."

When someone comes down the aisle at a Christian Church service and says, "I want to become a Christian," what is he asked? "Do you subscribe to the thirteen propositions in the *Declaration and Address*?" or "Do you accept the principles in the *Last Will and Testament of the Springfield Presbytery*?" No, of course not. Instead he is asked one Christo-centric question, "Do you believe that Jesus is the Christ, the Son of the living God?"

The Christian Churches/Churches of Christ are composed of a Christ-centric people.

Christians Only. Because the Restoration movement centers in the right Creed, its constituency wears the best name. They are *Christians*, a beautiful name and a meaningful one. It is a combination of the Greek and the Latin, "Christianos," which represents those who have given themselves to Christ and belong to Him. It is the most honorable name a person can wear. Peter said, "If any man suffer as a Christian, let him not be ashamed: but let him glorify God in this name" (I Peter 4:16 ASV).

Barton W. Stone believed that the name had been both prophesied and oracularly given. He believed Isaiah referred to it when He said that God's people would be called by "a new name, which the mouth of the Lord shall name—a name better than sons and daughters—an everlasting name that shall never be cut off" (Isa. 62:2 and 56:5). Therefore, Stone said that when the disciples were first called Christians in Antioch in Acts 11, it was no coincidence or nickname. Instead, they were *oracularly* called Christians by God Himself.

Stone said in his *Discourse on Christian Union*, "To be united we must receive the one name given by divine appointment, which is the name Christian. Let all others be cast away and forgotten."

A People of the Book. Some historians point to a meeting at the home of Abraham Altars near Washington, Pennsylvania, in the early summer of 1809, as the beginning of the Restoration movement. There Thomas Campbell arose, believing the Bible to be the only rule of faith and practice for Christians, and said, "WHERE THE SCRIPTURES SPEAK, WE SPEAK: AND WHERE THE SCRIPTURES ARE SILENT, WE ARE SILENT."

From that point the Christian Churches/Churches of Christ became known as a "people of the Book". They look upon the Scriptures as the inspired, authoritative, written Word of God; the only authoritative Word man has from Him. The whole Book is about Christ and there is not one authoritative truth known about Him that was not learned from this Book. It is the spiritual milk, bread, meat, and honey that nourishes the soul, the water of life that slakes spiritual thirst.

Most members of the Christian Churches would agree with the old mountain evangelist near Milligan College. He said, "I believe the Bible is inspired from kivver to kivver. I ain't got much edication, but I can preach sermons all the way from *Generations* to *Revolutions*, including the *Book of Palms*." They accept the Bible as inspired from cover to cover, including the *Book of Palms*.

An Undenominational Stance. Many in the religious world find it difficult to understand this position. They think in terms of interdenominational which represents an amalgamation of denominations. Some liberals sarcastically refer to the Restoration movement as "the undenomination." The difficulty necessitates that Christian Churches/Churches of Christ work hard and continually to clarify the attempt to be undenominational.

The key to understanding an undenominational stance lies in the term *restoration*. If a church models after the church that was given to and guided by the Apostles in the New Testament, it cannot be denominational. It must seek to be undenominational, because that was a characteristic of the church after which it models.

The Last Will and Testament of the Springfield Presbytery expresses this idea beautifully. It says, "We will, that this body die, and sink into union with the body of Christ at large; there is but one body, and one spirit, even as we are called in one hope of our calling." The writers of this document saw themselves as striving to be undenominational as they modeled after the church that was given.

The Plan of Salvation. Walter Scott is given much credit for popularizing the Restoration ideal espoused by Thomas and Alexander Campbell. He was in his early years of ministry an evangelist who sought to make the steps one takes to become a Christian both rational and understandable for the common person. The elder Campbell traveled with Scott on an evangelistic tour and wrote a note to Alexander concerning his observation:

> We have spoken and published many things correctly concerning the ancient gospel, its simplicity and perfect adaptation to the present state of mankind—but I must confess that, in respect of the direct exhibition and application of it for the blessed purpose, I am at present, for the first time, upon the ground where the thing has appeared to be practically exhibited to the proper purpose.[4]

Scott and the Campbells rejected the Calvinistic doctrine that man was totally depraved and that God must act upon him personally and directly in order for him to be saved. This "act" was called the "act of irresistible grace." Those upon whom God chose to give His act of irresistible grace, according to Calvin, were saved, and those upon whom He elected not to act were the lost.

The Campbells and Scott disagreed with Calvin. They felt that every person was capable of responding to the Gospel message. Faith was the positive response to the teaching and preaching of God's Word. People had the free will to accept or reject Christ.

Scott outlined what he called "the Gospel restored." It begins when one realizes that he is a sinner and must have God's forgiveness, for the wages of sin is death, which is separation from everything good, godly, holy, and happy for eternity. The *Gospel* says, "Christ died for our sins." This means that He who knew no sin, but who was prepared from the foundation of the world to be the Lamb of God to take away the sin of the world, went to the cross and paid the penalty for man's sins there. *Faith* means to trust in Christ alone to save, not one's virtue, or righteousness, or good works, for by *grace* he is saved. The picture is that, in the occasion of judgement, all will stand before God guilty because "all have sinned." But Christ will say, "I paid the penalty for that Christian's sins on the cross," and with the penalty paid, God will treat him just as if he had not sinned.

When one realizes that he is a sinner and wants Jesus to be his Savior, he must decide to become a Christian. The Bible calls this *repentance*. It means to turn from sin to walk in righteousness; to give himself to Christ so that he will belong to Him.

So, when one realizes he is a sinner, wants Christ to be his Savior, and desires to become a Christian, Jesus tells him to take two steps. First, he must *confess* his faith before men,

"Thou are the Christ, the Son of the living God." At this point, *Christian baptism* becomes the mark, seal, sign, climax, and culmination of one's acceptance of Christ in faith. It marks his becoming a Christian. And with that faith and obedience come four blessings: the remission of sins, the gift of the Holy Spirit, the promise of heaven, and adoption into the family of God, the church.

Scott called this explanation of the plan of salvation, "the Gospel restored." It was a simple, rational statement of the steps one takes in order to become a Christian. Whole congregations would respond to this explanation. Scott is credited with baptizing 35,000 persons into Christ during his ministry that was truncated by a break in his health. One historian said, "The Ohio River became a veritable Jordan," so many were baptized.

The Noble Plea. Alexander Campbell looked upon his work as a *movement* of free Christians within the church. He abhorred the possibility of starting a denomination. He wrote, "I have no idea of adding to the catalog of new sects. I labor to see sectarianism abolished and all Christians of every name united upon the one foundation upon which the apostolic church was founded." He did not view those who participated in this movement as being the *only* Christians, but as those who sought to be Christians only.

The Restoration ideal was looked upon as a means to bring about the unity of all believers in Christ for which He prayed in His "high priestly prayer" in John 17. Thomas Campbell wrote eloquently about this plea in this quotation of Scripture at the conclusion of his *Declaration and Address*:

—and "this is my commandment that ye love one another as I have loved you; that ye also love one another." And

114

again, "Holy Father, keep through thine own name, those whom thou hast given me that they may be one as we are," even "All that shall believe in me—that all may be one; as thou Father are in me and I in thee, that they also may be one in us; that the world may believe that thou hast sent me. And the glory which thou gavest me, I have given them, that they may be one, even as we are: I in them and thou in me, that they may be perfect in me; and that the world may know that thou hast sent me and hast loved them as thou hast loved me". May the Lord hasten it in His time. Farewell.

Peace be with all of them that love our Lord Jesus Christ in sincerity. Amen.

THOMAS CAMPBELL, Secretary
THOMAS ACHESON, Treasurer[5]

This was the noble plea of the Restoration movement in its early days: the unity of all believers on the basis of the Bible.

The leaders of the Restoration movement in its formative years gave the Christian Churches/Churches of Christ some great principles that have served them well. Their ideal was to restore the essence of the New Testament church to its pristine purity as a means to Christian unity that would enable all men to believe.

Almost two hundred years have passed since the Restoration movement began. Each following generation has had to take these principles and apply them to its challenges in the attempt to be the church Jesus envisioned. The principles must be applied by each local congregation in a practical way. Let us now turn to the practical.

THE PRACTICAL

Years ago, while a student at Milligan College, I preached

a meeting at the Upper Shell Creek Church of Christ, in upper Carter County, in Upper East Tennessee. After one of the evangelistic services I had a certain denominationalist cornered in the back of the church building and, like the proverbial bulldog on the calf's hind leg, I was determined to devour him. Then when I paused, ready to unleash my climactic argument that would have thoroughly vanquished the man, he just turned and walked out the door.

Standing nearby was one much older than I in the faith. He had been standing there, arms folded, listening in amusement as I had lost my prospect. Then he came up to me, put a fatherly arm about my shoulders, and said, "Young man, you don't argue religion, you witness for it."

So it is with the Christian Churches/Churches of Christ. The time was when they could make an impact upon the religious world by the force of their debate and the logic of their argument. But time has now decreed that they must not only talk about the church Christ came to build, but they must begin to be that kind of church—the dynamic body of Christ on earth, going, glowing, and growing! Our congregations must compose the body Jesus envisioned when He said, "I will build my church."

If I remember my freshman biology class correctly, there are four tests that scientists give to determine if something is alive or dead, animate or inaminate. These four tests are: ASSIMILATION, SENSITIVITY, MOBILITY, and REPRODUCTION. Anything alive can assimilate; it possesses sensitivity, mobility, and can reproduce its own kind. Let's apply these four scientific tests to the congregations of which we are a part to determine if they are the alive, dynamic bodies of Christ on earth, or whether they are just dead cadavers. The principles of the Restoration ideal should produce live bodies.

116

I. ASSIMILATION. Assimilation is something easy to define but difficult to illustrate. Assimilation means the ability to consume something and make it a part of yourself.

Let's see if we can illustrate that. Ministers are away from home a lot of the time, aren't they? At least two parties in Lexington, Kentucky, thought I was out of town too often: my wife and the elders of the Broadway Christian Church. So, sometimes when I was out of town, I would stop and pick up a great big box of chocolate candy—not for the elders, but for my wife. It would help placate my conscience.

However, my wife says that she is not built for chocolates. She says every time she eats a piece of chocolate, she performs a miracle. She says she can eat half an ounce of chocolate and gain five pounds. That is a miracle, is it not?

That illustrates "assimilation": the ability to consume something and make it a part of yourself.

If the congregation of which you are a part is the church Jesus envisioned, it is busy consuming the Word and assimilating it into the body until every member is filled with the Spirit of Christ.

Ministers sit around and talk about what makes a great church. And I suppose that is a good exercise just as long as they do not sit around too long and talk about it. But let me tell you what does not make a great church. A large crowd does not make a great church. For if you get me a good talker, a good singer, and a good promoter, I will get you a large crowd. But that crowd may not have any of the Spirit of Christ within it at all. A beautiful church building does not make a great church. For some of the most beautiful church edifices in America are whited sepulchers. The reason? They are filled with dead men's bones.

Let me define for you how to measure the greatness of a

church. It may be two or three thousand persons or it may be only two or three persons. But you measure the greatness of a church by the extent to which the members allow the Spirit of Christ to live within them. This is what the Scripture means when it says, "filled with the Spirit," which is always in the present tense, which means "to be filled over and over again, repeatedly." Jesus intended for His church to be His body on earth, the continuing incarnation, which means that it must embody His Spirit and manifest the fruit of that Spirit, "love, joy, peace, patience, goodness, gentleness, kindness, and self-control." Someone has said that a Christian should be so filled with the Spirit of Christ, that if a mosquito bit him on the arm, he would fly away singing, "There is power in the blood."

The church Jesus envisioned is one that consumes His Word, assimilates it into the body until every member is filled with His spirit.

II. SENSITIVITY. Anything alive is aware of its environs; responds to stimuli. Prick it and it will pull back; nudge it and it will move. If the church of which we are a part is the alive, dynamic body of Christ on earth, it, too, will be aware of its environs.

Bob Schuller says, "If you want to succeed, find human need. Fill that need and you will succeed."

Back in 1978 I taught a course in Practical Ministries at the Cincinnati Bible Seminary. I asked the students on the first night of the class to go back to the churches where they ministered and identify minority groups that need especial ministry. I did not mean ethnic or racial minorities. I meant minorities in every congregation, some of which are so obvious that we look right over them. Let me identify some of these.

What about our SENIOR CITIZENS? These are people who have been the pillars of the church for a generation or two, then they get some years on them, and we put them on the shelf. Sometimes they testify that they do not even feel that they are a part of the church anymore.

The Broadway Church, to which I ministered, called the first minister to senior adults of any congregation of our movement to my knowledge. When he arrived for the interview with the Pulpit Committee, I took one look at him and said to the chairman, "He's the guy we have to have." He was sixty-two, looked forty-two, and tried to act like he was twenty-two. One morning while we were sitting on the platform waiting for the service to begin, I looked and he was coming down the aisle limping. I turned to one of the younger associates and said sarcastically, "The old rumatiz and arthuritis have got him." But there was no rumatiz or arthuritis. The day before he had hurt himself waterskiing.

When Joe Dampier, Vice President of Emmanuel School of Religion, heard that we had called a minister to senior adults, he telephoned me. He said, "That's the way we have to go. We have reached zero population increase. There will be fewer and fewer young people in our churches, but there will be more senior adults. They will live longer, retire earlier, and have good health. They will be a viable resource within the church."

Let me ask you: What are you doing for those senior saints who need an especial ministry?

Then consider the DIVORCEES. I am not talking about the theology of divorce. I am not sure I have any definitive answers on that subject. I go to many men's retreats, and the first question that is asked is, "What about divorce and remarriage?" I am not talking about the theology. I mean the Christian who is dragged through a divorce and emerges on the other side feeling unloved, unwanted, and unworthy.

We had a lovely lady who was a little older than her husband. He took up with a younger woman at work, started living with her, divorced his wife, and procured a transfer to another state. Their only child, a teenage son, opted to go with his father to California. That left this lovely Christian lady on the edge of Lexington feeling lonely, unloved, unwanted, and she testified that she felt unworthy. She would get to church just after services began and leave immediately before the benediction, because she did not feel worthy to be with the Lord's people.

The church must stand for the permanence of marriage and family. But it also must be sensitive to the needs of those who are dragged through a divorce and need an especial ministry. Jerry Falwell says, "Sometimes we Christians shoot our wounded."

Also, there are the SINGLES. These are not married, they will never marry, and if you ask them, they don't want to marry. Much of my ministry has been aimed at young married couples—triple the size of the nursery, get those germicidal lamps on in the nursery, because the future of the church is with young couples with families. Then one Mother's Day I stood up to preach my annual Mother's Day sermon, looked out over the congregation, and for the first time, realized that that sermon was not appropriate for about two thirds of those gathered. Then I began to investigate and discovered that some of our finest Christians and best workers were singles. Sometimes they felt like fifth wheels because of the emphasis on family. They are a minority group in every church that needs an especial ministry.

There are also EXCEPTIONAL PEOPLE. These are those

"angels unawares," some of the happiest people in the church. There was one of them in a congregation to which I ministered who would go all the way around the auditorium to go out my door, but could not pronounce my name. She would say "Hi, Bror Leg." We investigated and found that she was over thirty years of age and had been left in the eighth grade girls' class. How insensitive can you get?

Let me give you Bob Schuller's definition of the church and see if you agree with it. He says, "The church is a fellowship of happy, Holy Spirit-filled Christians—." Aren't you glad he included the adjective "happy"? I have met some Christians who you would vow had just sucked sour pickles and had been baptized in vinegar. One's faith in Christ and His providential plan should give one a smile on his lips and a light in his face. "A fellowship of happy, Holy Spirit-filled Christians," he says, "the Body of Christ on earth, helping hurting people in the community." I do not know if that is a very good theological definition of the church, but is a good practical definition. "Happy Holy Spirit-filled Christians—the Body of Christ—helping hurting people in the community."

In the early days of my ministry, I emphasized two necessities for the church to be the body of Christ: *evangelism* and *discipleship*. However, I now believe that there is a third necessity: *ministry,* helping hurting people.

The church Jesus envisioned is a body filled with His Spirit that is sensitive to the needs of people and reaches out to meet those needs.

III. MOBILITY. Anything alive is able to propel itself: able to move on its own volition.

I do not have to remind New Testament Christians of the necessity of the church having mobility. All they have to do is look at the Great Commission. It says, "Go—Teach—Baptize—teach all things whatsoever I have commanded you." It is the Lord's imperative: "*You* go—*you* teach—*you* baptize—*you* teach whatsoever I have commanded you." A church that does not have a world-wide vision of evangelism is a church that dies.

But there is another sense in which the church must possess mobility. It must have the kind of mobility to move into the new era and accept its opportunities and challenges. This does not mean the Gospel changes. Jesus is the same yesterday, today, and forever. The authority of the Bible does not change. Jesus said that heaven and earth should pass away, but His Word will never pass away. The Restoration ideal is as relevant today as it has ever been. But times change; situations come and go; and new opportunities present themselves. The church must have the kind of mobility to accept these opportunities and challenges of the new era.

Do you know what I would hate to hear worse at a Board meeting than anything else? Now, I am not too high on Board meetings. I agree with a friend of mine who says, "If I die and wake up at a Board meeting, I will know that I have gone to the wrong place." Another friend says, "Hell will be one eternal Board meeting." However, I do not know how the church can have oversight without committees and boards. But do you know what I hate to hear worse at a Board meeting than anything else? It is, "I've been a member here forty years."

Do you know why I hate to hear that worse than anything else? It is because I know what comes next, "We ain't never done it that way before." Then you know what comes next, "It won't work nohow." But a church that tries to operate the way it did forty years ago is a church that will die. We ministers and elders oftentimes wring our hands in frustration and wonder why the church will not grow. Sometimes it is because we will not *let* it grow.

The Broadway Church, to which I ministered, had Medford Jones come for a church growth seminar. It was some of the best money we spent. I told Medford that he was insultingly honest with his frankness. For example, he said that the church worked under the assumption that the auditorium would hold eleven hundred people. At the concluding session he said, "I took my tape measure, measured the pews, and the auditorium will only hold nine hundred and seventy-five if everybody were eighteen inches across when he sits down. I watched you leave last night, and it is obvious that it will not hold over eight hundred and fifty of you." He also told us that you can get only so many pickles in a jar. I asked, "Medford, why did you have to compare us to pickles? Why not marachino cherries or something like that?" But Medford is right: when the building is full, it is full, and you can't make it any fuller.

Winston Churchill said, "We shape our buildings and then our buildings shape us." This is true of churches. They reach saturation point in their facilities and must move into the new era and provide larger facilities, start new congregations, and/or go into multiple services. This is a challenge to every congregation that wants to stay alive. One demographic expert says, "Nine out of ten churches in America need to relocate." They cannot provide the facilities and reach the people where they are.

The congregation to stay alive must also consider its ministerial staff. I have always been too stingy in this area. I did my apprenticeship under P. H. Welshimer at First Christian Church, Canton, Ohio. I was his only associate, was only twenty-two years of age, and the church ran over twenty-five hundred per Sunday. Brother Welshimer did not believe in a large staff. He would say, "The most efficient form of government is autocratic, if you have a good autocrat." He considered himself a good autocrat.

However, I believe even Brother Welshimer would agree that in this age of specialties, the church must have a multiple staff. You cannot expect the preacher to deliver "fresh bread" consistently if he has to be concerned about counseling, youth programs, the ladies' group, and on and on. Good stewards in the church will provide adequate vocational leadership. This is an increasing challenge for the church as it moves into the new era.

Parking presents a challenge. They say the average American has three problems: what to do with leisure, how to lose weight, and where to park his automobile. This is never more nearly accurate than at eleven o'clock on Sunday morning. People do not walk to church anymore. They drive their automobiles. If the church does not provide shopping center-like parking, people will go somewhere else to church or not go at all.

Some of our people at Broadway would say, "I have no trouble finding a parking place on Sunday morning. I go up Broadway, to 2nd Street, to Jefferson Avenue, turn left, and I am right there at St. Mark's Catholic Church parking lot, and I can always find a place to park at St. Mark's Church." But these people have been members of the church forty years. The congregation must provide parking for that young mother, with an infant and a three-year-old, who wants to attend the church on a rainy Sunday morning and her husband does not come with her.

Advertising presents the church of the new era with opportunity. This is an area in which the Christian Churches have not been either active or effective. We now have the means for every ear to hear, so that every knee can bow and every tongue confess that Jesus is Christ. Home Shopping Network, for example, reaches into sixty-six million American homes. Ziden Nutt, of Good News International, says they can produce a program in their studios in Joplin, beam it to the satellite, and it can be seen by one third of the world.

It is true that a couple of televangelists have messed up morally. They have crucified Christ anew and held him to an open shame. However, this must not blind Christians to this opportunity they have to reach people with the good news of God's love. It is an area into which they must have the mobility to move for the new era.

The church Jesus envisioned is a body filled with His Spirit, sensitive to the needs of people, that moves into the new era and accepts its opportunities and challenge.

IV. REPRODUCTION. Anything alive is able to reproduce its own kind.

One of the hardest years of my ministry was when we built a family life center. It was during an era of spiraling inflation in the construction business. The architect told us in April that the building would cost $498,000. In July he said that inflation had caught up with us and it would cost $600,000. Then in August we opened the bids and the lowest bid was $1,059,000. It more than doubled in five months. You can imagine the questions that would provoke in a congregation! "What dummy made that kind of mistake?" You can guess the dummy that many of them decided on—the little dummy up in the big office! If it had not been for strong leadership in the church, it could have been an even deeper source of division.

However, there was an antidote even to that kind of year. It was two hundred and fifteen additions the next year. It was like new life, new vitality, as if the body had received a blood transfusion. That kind of year would not be possible in a small congregation. But there is no substitute for reproducing one's own kind in any church. The alive body has the ability to reach out, find those who are lost, and bring them into the fellowship as newborn babes in Christ.

CONCLUSION

There is a legend which comes out of antiquity which says that, when Jesus ascended back to Heaven after the resurrection, He was approached by the archangel, Michael, commander-in-chief of the angelic army. Michael said to him, "Jesus, you went down to earth to accomplish the redemption of mankind. There they despitefully used you. They cursed you, blasphemed against you, spat upon you, beat you with rods, and at last they crucified you. Now you have come back to Heaven and have left the task to redeem man in the hands of eleven disciples—eleven disciples who have not always proven faithful. One denied you, another doubted you, and a third of like kind betrayed you. Now, Jesus, what plan do you have to redeem man if those eleven men fail you?"

Jesus replied, "If those eleven men fail me, I have no other plan."

So it is with the church as far as Scripture reveals. It has been called into existence to be the Body of Christ on earth. It is to consume the Word of God, assimilate it into the Body, until every member is filled with the Spirit of Christ; sensitive to the needs of people, and reaching out to meet those needs; moving into the new era to accept its opportunities and challenges; reproducing its own kind. This is the church Jesus envisioned when He said, "I will build my church," and the one He gave to the Apostles for them to shape.

ENDNOTES

1. Richardson, Robert. *Memoirs of Alexander Campbell* (Cincinnati: Standard Publishing, 1897), vol. 1, pp. 257-258.
2. Murch, James DeForest. *Christians Only* (Cincinnati: Standard Publishing, 1962), p. 99.
3. Garrett, Leroy, *The Stone-Campbell Movement* (Joplin, Mo: College Press, 1981), p. 270.
4. Richardson, Robert, *op. cit.* Vol. 2, pp. 219-220.
5. Campbell, Thomas. *Declaration and Address of the Christian Association of Washington* (Washington, PA: Brown & Sample, 1909, 1990), p. 23.

Baptism

Jack Cottrell

A comprehensive explanation of baptism must answer three main questions. First, what is the purpose of baptism? Second, who should be baptized? And third, how should baptism be performed? These are the questions of the *meaning*, the *subjects*, and the *mode* of baptism. This chapter will attempt to answer them in this order.

I. THE MEANING OF BAPTISM

Most important is the *meaning* of baptism, since the answer to this question helps us to determine the answers to the other two. It is important also because it has been a source of serious controversy ever since the Reformation of the sixteenth century, and likewise because it is an issue that distinguishes the conservative churches of the Restoration Movement from almost all other Protestants.

The heart of the issue is whether baptism has a crucial role in the reception of salvation. More specifically, is baptism something a sinner does in order to receive salvation and *become* a Christian, or is it simply a good work (an act of obedience) done for some other purpose by someone who is *already* a Christian?

The Bible is very clear about this. In every New Testament passage that says anything at all about the meaning of baptism, the only purpose with which it is connected is the salvation of sinners. The various aspects of salvation are described as being bestowed upon the believing, repentant sinner in and through the act of baptism. This is the consistent and exclusive New Testament witness; no other purpose for baptism is mentioned or even hinted at.

A. Salvation as a Double Cure

To see the connection of baptism with salvation, we must first of all understand the nature of the sinful predicament from which we need saving, and also the nature of the salvation that delivers us from it. We may speak of these as the "double trouble" and the "double cure."

The idea of double trouble means that sin has two distinct effects on a person. First, it makes him *guilty*. Guilt is a legal problem; it comes from the fact that sin is the transgression of God's laws (I John 3:4). To be guilty means that the sinner is required to pay the penalty attached to the law, which in this case is eternity in hell. Second, sin makes a person *sinful*. That is, it affects the person's very nature; it makes him depraved, spiritually sick (Jer. 17:9), even spiritually dead

(Eph. 2:1, 5). These two problems are quite different. Whereas guilt is external to the individual, the spiritual sickness corrupts the sinner's inner being, saps his spiritual strength, and traps him in the grip of sin.

God's gracious salvation addresses both sides of this predicament. As a familiar hymn says, "Be of sin the double cure: cleanse me from its guilt and power." God's solution to guilt is the redeeming blood of Christ, by which he paid the penalty deserved by those who have broken God's divine law. When the blood of Christ is applied to the penitent sinner, his guilt and condemnation are washed completely away. In Biblical terminology this is called justification; it is also called the forgiveness or remission of sins.

On the other side, God's cure for the sinner's depraved nature is the gift of the Holy Spirit, whose life-giving presence renews and regenerates the sin-sick heart and breaks the death-grip of sin upon the soul. Biblical terms for this work of the Holy Spirit include new birth, new creation, being made alive, resurrection, regeneration, renewal, and circumcision without hands. Following this initial act of spiritual resurrection, the Holy Spirit dwells within the saved person as a source of spiritual strength and continuing sanctification.

In summary, in the "double cure" of salvation God takes away the sinner's guilt through the blood of Christ and renews his heart through the life-giving power of the Holy Spirit.

B. Baptism and the Double Cure

As stated above, the Bible consistently relates baptism to the salvation of sinners. Almost everyone would agree that this is true in some sense. All would acknowledge, for example, that baptism and salvation are connected at least *symbolically*. i.e., the act of baptism is a physical symbol of the reality of spiritual salvation. It is "an outward sign of an inward grace"; the application of water to the body depicts the cleansing of the soul.

Some would go further and discern a *psychological* connection between baptism and salvation; i.e., they see the act of baptism as affecting the mental state of the person being baptized, as confirming or sealing upon his heart a deeper assurance of the salvation that God has already bestowed upon him. The baptized person can say to himself, "Just as surely as I am experiencing the baptismal water upon my body, I can be sure that God has applied his grace to my soul."

Some have gone to the extreme of affirming a *causal* connection between baptism and salvation. They have attributed to the baptismal water itself, or at least to the act of baptism, the power to cleanse the soul from sin. Thus anyone who submits to the physical act of baptism will surely be saved, even in the absence of a proper knowledge of Christ and a positive faith in him. This is the doctrine of "baptismal regeneration," and is usually held in connection with certain forms of infant baptism.

How shall we evaluate these views in the light of Scripture? Actually, none of them adequately expresses the New Testament's teaching about the relation between baptism and salvation. The causal view described in the previous paragraph must be rejected altogether. There is no basis for ascribing any saving power to the baptismal water or to the act of baptism itself. God's power and God's action alone can save; the sinner is saved when God applies the blood of Christ to his heart and gives him the gift of the Holy Spirit.

Also, the symbolical and psychological views must be rejected, not because they are completely wrong, but because in themselves they do not go far enough. That is, they do not give us the whole picture of the relation between baptism and salvation. It is true that water baptism symbolizes the reality of inward salvation, and that it strengthens faith in Christ and increases assurance of salvation. The problem is that those who emphasize these points often limit the meaning of baptism to these ideas while denying that it is the *specific time* when God bestows his gifts of salvation. They claim that as a rule a person is already saved before he is baptized. Baptism is a *subsequent* outward sign of a *previously-given* inward grace; it strengthens one's faith in a salvation already possessed. Such a view, however, is much too weak. It simply does not do justice to the New Testament's teaching about what really happens during baptism.

We may summarize as follows. First, we reject any causal relation between baptism and salvation. Second, we agree that baptism is symbolically and psychologically related to salvation; but such is not actually stated in Scripture and is only inferred from what *is* taught therein. Third, the clear and specific teaching of the New Testament is that baptism is the *time during which* God graciously bestows upon the sinner the double cure of salvation. As such it is a divinely-appointed condition for salvation during this New Covenant era.

Our purpose now is to set forth the Biblical evidence for this temporal relation between baptism and salvation. First, we will look at the passages which connect both aspects of the double cure with baptism, especially Acts 2:38 and Colossians 2:12.

We begin with Acts 2:38: "And Peter said to them, 'Repent, and let each of you be baptized in the name of Jesus

Christ for the forgiveness of your sins; and you shall receive the gift of the Holy Spirit.'" This is Peter's response to an audience of Jews whose rejection of their Messiah had put them into a lost state and who thus needed salvation. Their question to Peter (v. 37) was, "What shall we do?" I.e., what shall we do to be saved? Peter names two things they must do: repent, and be baptized. He also names two things they would receive as a result: forgiveness of sins, and the gift of the Holy Spirit—the double cure.

This verse specifically says that baptism is "for the forgiveness of sins." Forgiveness (or remission) is equivalent to justification; it is the cancellation of all guilt by the power of the blood of Christ. This is the first part of the double cure. A key word in this statement is the word *for*, which translates the Greek preposition *eis* (pronounced "ice"). Physically this term represents motion toward something; conceptually it signifies purpose or intention or result; i.e., Peter says to be baptized *for the purpose of bringing about* the forgiveness of sins. It is used in exactly the same way in Matthew 26:28, where Jesus spoke of his blood as being "poured out for many for [*eis*] forgiveness of sins," i.e., for the purpose of bringing about the forgiveness of sins. The original NIV translated the sense of Acts 2:38 quite accurately: "Repent and be baptized . . . so that your sins may be forgiven."

This verse also says that those who are baptized "shall receive the gift of the Holy Spirit." This refers to the indwelling presence of the Spirit as promised by Jesus in John 7:37-39; the specific immediate result of this indwelling is the new birth promised in John 3:3-5. The Spirit's presence raises the spiritually dead sinner to a state of spiritual life, which is the second aspect of the double cure. This is specifically stated to be a consequence or result of baptism.

Thus Acts 2:38 makes the meaning of baptism clear. It is the time God has appointed for removing the sinner's guilt and for bestowing upon him the regenerating presence of the Holy Spirit.

Another passage that expressly states that baptism is the time when God works the double cure is Colossians 2:12. It speaks of being "buried with Him in baptism, in which you were also raised up with Him through faith in the working of God." Here two things are said to happen in baptism. First, we are "buried with Him," i.e., with Christ. According to Romans 6:3-4 this means we are buried into the death of Christ. To be buried with Christ into his death means to receive all the saving benefits of his atoning death; it means to come into contact with his justifying blood and thus to receive the forgiveness of sins.

The second thing that happens in baptism is that we are "raised up with Him." This refers to the initial act of the indwelling Holy Spirit. I.e., as soon as God gives us the Holy Spirit (as promised in Acts 2:38), the Spirit infuses new life into our dead souls. Our spirits are raised from the dead by the same life-giving Spirit that raised Jesus' body from the tomb (Rom. 8:10-11). See Colossians 2:13.

What is so significant about Colossians 2:12 is that it clearly and expressly says that these things happen "in baptism." This does not means before baptism, nor does it mean after baptism. It means exactly what it says: *in* baptism, in the act of baptism, at the time of baptism. We could not ask God to be more specific than this. *In baptism* God works the two-fold work of salvation upon our hearts.

Without going into detail we may point out that the same relation between baptism and salvation is specified in Romans 6:3-5. It is the act that unites us with the death and resurrection of Christ.

Other New Testament passages relate baptism to the two aspects of the double cure individually. For example, Acts 22:16 connects it with the washing away of sins, which is equivalent to forgiveness. Thus when Ananias said to Saul, "Arise, and be baptized, and wash away your sins, calling on His name," he was saying exactly what Peter said in Acts 2:38: "Be baptized, for the purpose of bringing about the forgiveness of your sins." The fact that baptism is the time of salvation is seen in the addition of the phrase, "calling on His name." According to Joel 2:32 and Acts 2:21, the purpose of calling on His name is to be saved.

Passages which individually relate baptism to the second part of the double cure are John 3:5 and Titus 3:5. In John 3:5 Jesus says, "Unless one is born of water and the Spirit, he cannot enter into the kingdom of God." This is a reference to being "born again" (John 3:3), which is the same as the spiritual resurrection that Colossians 2:12 says takes place in baptism. That this new birth is somehow the result of both water and the Spirit brings to mind Acts 2:38, which connects water baptism with the gift of the Spirit. For this and other reasons we may rightly conclude that Jesus' reference to water in John 3:5 speaks of baptism and makes it a condition for being born again.

Titus 3:5 in a similar way refers to baptism ("the washing") as the time when the Holy Spirit regenerates and renews us. It says that God "saved us . . . by the washing of regeneration and renewing," which are accomplished in that moment "by the Holy Spirit."

The passages discussed above clearly set forth the meaning of baptism as the time when God bestows salvation's double cure. Other New Testament passages relate baptism to salvation in the same way, only in more general terms. For example, Matthew 28:18-20 says we are baptized into union with the Trinity; Galatians 3:27 says we are baptized into union with Christ; and I Corinthians 12:13 says we are baptized into the body of Christ. Two other verses state simply that the result of baptism is salvation: "He who has believed and has been baptized shall be saved" (Mark 16:16); and, "Baptism now saves you" (I Pet. 3:21).

C. Why "Baptism Now Saves"

Many do not understand why God would add a new condition for salvation not required in Old Testament times. If faith in God's gracious promises and a repentant heart were sufficient for salvation then, why not now? In reply we can identify at least two good reasons why God has connected salvation with baptism.

First, this new condition has been added because the salvation process under the New Covenant includes new elements not present under the Old Covenant. Baptism brings these new elements into focus and assures that the sinner is coming to God in full cognizance of them and not in terms of a framework that is obsolete and no longer adequate.

What are these new elements that raise New Covenant salvation to a higher level? First, there is a more complete revelation of the nature of God and thus an advanced understanding of the very object of our faith. We now know unequivocally that God's nature is triune, i.e., that the Lord God of the Old Testament is a Trinity of Father, Son, and Holy Spirit. Baptism was established to ensure that this new understanding of God would not be lost. This is why Jesus commanded that baptism be "in the name of the Father and the Son and the Holy Spirit" (Matt. 28:19).

Another new element in New Covenant salvation is the living presence and historical reality of the Redeemer himself, Jesus of Nazareth. The fact that Jesus is the incarnation of God the Son gives concrete reality to the doctrine of the Trinity. His death on the cross and his resurrection from the dead—prophesied in the Old Testament but for all practical purposes unknown in that era—are the literal source of our salvation. Baptism was established to ensure that we would never separate our salvation from the divine Redeemer Jesus nor from his saving death and resurrection. Thus baptism is not just in the name of "the Son" (Matt. 28:19) but "in the name of Jesus Christ" (Acts 2:38), who we must never forget *is* God the Son. Also, baptism is intended to draw our attention unmistakably to his death and resurrection as the works that bring us salvation (Rom. 6:3-11; Col. 2:12).

Still another new element is the specific saving work of the third person of the Trinity, the Holy Spirit. In Old Testament times the Spirit worked to empower some of God's people for roles of service, but he did not enter a sinner's heart to work salvation therein. The latter was something God reserved for his New Covenant saints, as promised by Jesus (John 7:37-39) and as begun on the day of Pentecost (Acts 2:38-39). Baptism was established as the time when the penitent sinner receives this gift of the Spirit, thus highlighting the newness and uniqueness of this blessing for this Messianic age.

All of these new elements in the New Covenant salvation process necessarily lead to one more, namely, a newness of the very faith that is required for salvation. Though not different in form, the faith that is necessary for salvation in this age is very different in content from that of the Old Covenant. A general faith in the general promises of the general God of

Israel no longer qualifies a person to receive salvation. When confronted with the new revelation of God as Trinity and especially with the identification of Jesus as the divine savior, even Jews who once enjoyed a saving relationship with the God of Israel had to adjust their faith accordingly or be lost (Rom. 11:17-23). To accept baptism as the concrete embodiment of all this new faith-content is a humble confession that one does indeed believe these things; thus in a real sense baptism is a kind of extension of faith itself.[1]

This is one reason why "baptism now saves," namely, because the newness of salvation in this age requires a new and distinguishing element in the process of receiving it.

The second reason why God has connected salvation with baptism in the New Testament age has to do with our need for a personal assurance that God has indeed saved us. There are times when it is easy to be plagued by doubts and uncertainties as to whether we have truly met the God of our salvation and have truly received his gifts of saving grace. We know what God has promised, but has it really happened to *us*?

As a concession to our human frailty in this respect, God has tied his promises to baptism as a concrete, objective event that will always stand out in our memories. It is an unforgettable reference point to which we can always return when we begin to doubt that we have received God's grace. It is the "stake" that God himself has provided for our comfort and assurance. We do not have to torture ourselves, wondering at what point our faith was strong enough or our repentance sincere enough to be saved. The sufficiency for our salvation lies in the power of God and the truth of his promises. He has promised to save us in baptism. Just as surely as we can remember our baptism, so can we be sure that God has kept his promises to us.

This is the sense in which there is a psychological connection between baptism and salvation. Knowing that we have been baptized has a definite effect on our state of mind, in the sense that it undergirds our assurance of salvation. This psychological effect is possible, though, only because baptism is in itself the *time* when salvation is given.

II. THE SUBJECTS OF BAPTISM

Who should be baptized? Everyone agrees that adults and young people who have reached the age of accountability are proper subjects for baptism. The main issue here is whether infants and young children ought to be baptized.

Today many denominations practice infant baptism. Some, such as Roman Catholics and Lutherans, baptize babies for salvation. They do this because they believe that babies in a sense "inherit" the double trouble of sinfulness and guilt from Adam and Eve, and because they rightly understand the New Testament's teaching that baptism is the time when God gives sinners the double cure of forgiveness and new birth. Thus infants are baptized so that they may be saved.

Others, such as Presbyterians and Methodists, baptize babies because they believe that the children of Christian parents are automatically members of the covenant community (the church), and because they equate baptism with Old Testament circumcision and take it to be an outward sign that such infants do indeed belong to the church. They assume a continuity of the covenants and thus of the covenant people and the covenant signs. Since babies were members of the covenant people by physical birth under the first covenant, so are they today. And since the sign of membership, i.e., circumcision, was applied to (male) babies then, so should baptism be applied to babies today as the sign of their membership in the church.

Some of us, however, believe that there are several good and decisive reasons why infants should *not* be baptized. First and foremost, the very meaning of baptism rules out infants as proper subjects of baptism. Baptism is indeed for salvation; therefore it is meaningful and necessary only for those who are lost sinners. Babies, however, are not in this category. They should not be regarded as sinners in need of salvation. Whatever sin and condemnation all children may have potentially inherited from Adam has already been nullified and canceled for every member of the human race by the atoning work of Christ (Rom. 5:12-19). As a result babies are *not* born guilty or sinful; thus they do not need baptism. Only when children become old enough to understand the meaning of God's law and the significance of breaking that law are they considered accountable for it and thus in need of baptism (Rom. 4:15).

Another reason why infants should not be baptized is that Christians are under a *New* Covenant, which does *not* imitate the conditions for membership which existed under the Old Covenant. The Old Covenant, even the provisions that began as far back as Abraham, was completely fulfilled in the first coming of Jesus (cf. Acts 13:32-33). Jeremiah 31:31-34 prophesies the coming of a new and different covenant, and Jesus declared that this New Covenant was established with his own blood (Luke 22:20). Therefore it could not have been in existence prior to his death (Heb. 9:17).

One of the main differences between the covenants is the basis or means of membership. A baby born to Jewish parents was a member of the Old Covenant community simply by means of physical birth. As the child grew, he had to be taught to know the Lord, even though he was already under the covenant. But it is quite different today. One becomes a member of the New Covenant community not by physical birth but by the new birth or spiritual birth, which is possible only for those who are old enough to make a conscious decision for God and "believe in His name" (John 1:12-13). We are children of God "through faith in Christ Jesus" (Gal. 3:26). For this reason a distinctive characteristic of the New Covenant is that those who are under it do not have to be taught again to know the Lord, "'for they shall all know Me, from the least of them to the greatest of them,' declares the LORD" (Jer. 31:34).

Male children born under the Old Covenant indeed were circumcised as infants, but this has no parallel whatsoever under the New Covenant and is not in any sense a pattern for the practice of baptism today. Nowhere in the New Testament is baptism described or depicted as a sign of belonging to the church. The only connection the New Testament makes between circumcision and baptism is in Colossians 2:11-12, and the relationship given there is not substantive but figurative; i.e., the physical removal of a bit of skin by human hands is a figure or a type of the spiritual removal of the old sinful nature "without hands," which is equivalent to the regeneration or spiritual resurrection that takes place during baptism. Imposing the meaning and use of circumcision upon Christian baptism is completely without Biblical warrant, and it leads ultimately to a denial of everything the New Testament does teach about the meaning and subjects of baptism.

A third reason why infants should not be baptized is that there is absolutely *no mention* of infant baptism anywhere in the New Testament. Some maintain that infants must have been baptized because the New Testament refers several times to the baptism of households (Acts 11:14; 16:15, 33; 18:8; I Cor. 1:16), and it is assumed that such households would have included infants. This is only an inference, however, and an unwarranted one at that. Such references most likely included only those old enough to make a conscious response to the gospel. This seems obvious from the fact that the members of these households are also said to have *feared God* (Acts 10:2), *heard* (Acts 10:44; 16:32), *believed* (Acts 16:34; 18:8), and *rejoiced* (Acts 16:34). Thus the New Testament's silence concerning infant baptism remains complete.

A final reason why infants should not be baptized is that in the New Testament baptism is preceded by other actions which by their very nature can be performed only by those old enough to have a conscious understanding of what is taking place. Before being baptized a person should be able to hear the gospel (Acts 18:8), believe its promises (Mark 16:16; Acts 2:41; 8:12-13; 16:14, 31, 34; 18:8; Col. 2:12), repent of his sins (Acts 2:38), and call upon the Lord (Acts 22:16). Since infants cannot do such things, baptism has no relevance for them.

Because of these reasons we must conclude that infants need not be baptized, nor should they be baptized, indeed they *cannot* be baptized. They can of course be dipped in water, but such a dipping would have no spiritual significance. Infants cannot be baptized any more than they can vote or get married. It is simply not something that applies to them. Baptism applies only to adults and to young people who are old enough to know what they are doing.

III. THE MODE OF BAPTISM

The last main question in reference to baptism is its mode:

how is it applied to the penitent, believing sinner? The specific issue here is whether immersion in water is the only valid way to baptize. While accepting immersion as true baptism, many in Christendom believe it is proper to apply the baptismal water in other ways also, especially by daubing it or sprinkling it or pouring a small amount of it on the head. Others believe that immersion is the only valid form of baptism. The latter view is the one presented and defended here.

We may state unequivocally that, in its physical form, baptism is by definition the momentary immersion of the body into a pool of water.[2] Nothing else really counts as baptism. To say that one can *baptize* in some way other than immersion is like saying one can *drink* from the cup of the Lord's Supper (Matt. 26:27) in some way other than swallowing, e.g., by pouring the juice out on the floor, or rubbing a bit of it on one's forehead. Such actions as sprinkling and pouring have no more relation to baptizing than these actions do to drinking.

In defense of this view we will briefly set forth the two main arguments Martin Luther cited for it when he said, "I would have those who are to be baptized completely immersed in the water, as the word says and as the mystery indicates."[3] I.e., the Greek words for baptism *mean* immersion, and the symbolism of the act requires it.

First, the word *baptize* in the Greek language literally means "to dip, to immerse." As Luther says, the act of baptism "is that immersion in water from which it derives its name, for the Greek *baptizo* means 'I immerse,' and *baptisma* means, 'immersion'" (p. 186). In explaining the meaning of these words, Greek lexicons consistently use such terms as *dip, plunge, immerse, submerge, sink, go under,* and *drown.* When the emphasis is on the result of the action rather than the action itself, other terms may be used, e.g., *dye, drench, soak,* and *overwhelm.* In any case the only action inherent in baptism is immersion.

Second, the symbolism of baptism requires immersion. Early in this chapter we pointed out that some people see only a symbolic relation between baptism and salvation. While this is completely inadequate as the *sole* meaning of baptism, it is certainly true as far as it goes. The action of immersion in water is by design intended to symbolize the saving events of death, burial, and resurrection, as Romans 6:3-11 and Colossians 2:12 clearly show. This is true in two ways. On the one hand, immersion symbolizes the death, burial, and resurrection of Jesus; on the other hand, it symbolizes the sinner's own spiritual death, burial, and resurrection that are taking place simultaneously with the act of baptism itself.

Romans 6:4 says that "we have been buried with Him through baptism into death, in order that as Christ was raised from the dead through the glory of the Father, so we too might walk in newness of life." Colossians 2:12 says we were "buried with Him in baptism," in which we were also "raised up with Him." Can anyone honestly say that sprinkling or pouring a small amount of water on a person in any way even comes close to the events that are supposed to be symbolized in baptism? This is why Luther says that nothing except immersion can "bring out the full significance of baptism," because it is "a symbol of death and resurrection" (p. 191).

Thus we conclude that the literal meaning of the word and the figurative significance of the act both require that baptism always be done by immersion.

IV. CONCLUDING QUESTIONS

The preceding discussion has raised several questions that

must now be briefly discussed. First, how can baptism be for salvation, if we are saved by grace through faith, and not by works (Eph. 2:8-9)? After all, isn't baptism a work? The reply to this question is simple: no, baptism is *not* a work. At least, it is not a *human* work, in the sense in which Paul uses the term. If anything, it is a *divine* work, a "working of God" (Col. 2:12). In baptism God works his gracious double cure upon the sinner. He applies the blood of Christ to cover the sinner's guilt, and he raises him up to new spiritual life. The sinner himself is doing only two things: praying (Acts 22:16) and believing (Col. 2:12). Such actions are in no sense inconsistent with being saved by grace. There is absolutely no conflict between baptism for salvation and salvation by grace.

Second, how is it possible for anyone to deny the clear teaching of baptism for salvation in passages such as Romans 6:3-5, Galatians 3:27, and Colossians 2:12? The fact is that ever since the reformer Huldreich Zwingli changed the doctrine of baptism in 1523-1524, most Protestants have denied that baptism is the time of salvation—the view that had prevailed almost unanimously for 1500 years. But how do they get around the clear Biblical teaching? The main answer is that they have divided the "one baptism" (Eph. 4:5) into two separate events. They say that a sinner receives *spiritual* baptism from the Holy Spirit, which is the baptism that actually saves; then usually at some later time he is baptized *in water* as a kind of witness to the salvation already received. Then, arbitrarily, they declare that any passage connecting baptism with salvation must be talking about spiritual baptism, not water baptism. As one of my Calvinistic seminary teachers declared, "There's not a drop of water in Romans 6!"

In response to this idea we need only go back to Ephesians 4:5, which affirms that just as there is "one Lord" and "one faith," so there is but "one baptism." A sinner is baptized once, period. This one event has an external side, which is immersion in water; it also has an internal side, which is the saving work of God. We may call the latter "spiritual baptism," but it is not separated in time from the former. Thus unless we want to deny this cardinal truth of Scripture—that there is but one baptism—we must understand the New Testament passages about baptism and salvation as referring to our baptism in water.

Finally, what is the spiritual status of the millions of people who have mistakenly followed the false views of baptism, whether in regard to meaning, subjects, or mode? This is a very difficult question and cannot be thoroughly answered in the brief space available here. In general, though, we may answer it in two steps.

First, in view of the clear teaching of Scripture on the subject, we must say that only those who have consciously received immersion as a saving work of God can be confident of their *present* status as Christians and as members of the body of Christ. It is, of course, possible that in some cases God has made exceptions and has acted outside his stated plan of bestowing salvation upon believers in immersion, but we have no right to presume upon God in this respect. If someone who has not been Biblically baptized is nevertheless convinced that God has saved him, we may follow this procedure. One, while granting that God may have made an exception, we must insist that no one can know this for sure. Experience can be deceiving (Matt. 7:21-23). Two, we must make sure that the Biblical teaching on baptism is clearly understood and accepted. Three, we must invite the person of unsure status to receive baptism properly, while calling upon God to work upon this person whatever works of salvation he has not already worked. Only then can a person be sure of his present status before God.

Second, with regard to the *future*, in the final judgment we can expect God to judge all persons who have received baptism improperly in the same way that he will judge everyone else, namely, in accordance with their *conscientious response to available light*. No one will be condemned for failing to meet some particular requirement as long as he is conscientiously responding to whatever light is available to him (see Romans 4:15). It is obvious that human traditions have seriously distorted and limited the light of Scripture concerning baptism, but many sincere people have responded in good conscience to what light they have. For this reason we can expect to see such people in heaven.

This last point does not permit us to give anyone false assurances about his present state of salvation, however; nor does it give us the right to change the clear teaching of Scripture on believers' immersion for salvation. The "available light" principle applies only to future judgment, and it can be applied only by the omniscient God. For us today, as individuals and as the church of Jesus Christ, we must continue to believe and proclaim the clear Biblical teaching about baptism without cowardice and without compromise.

ENDNOTES

1. At this point it should be clear that we are talking about *Christian* baptism only, and not John's baptism. Some have wrongly equated the latter with the former and have assumed that the two have the same meaning. It is obvious, though, that John's baptism could have no relation to any of the new elements of salvation (trinitarian knowledge, death and resurrection of Christ, the gift of the Spirit), since they were not yet known or had not yet happened when John began baptizing. Baptism for salvation began only on the Day of Pentecost.

2. The nature or location of the pool is irrelevant as long as it provides a quantity of water sufficient for the act of immersion. Anything from the ocean to a bathtub may suffice.

3. The quotes from Luther are from his treatise, "The Babylonian Captivity of the Church," printed in *Three Treatises* (Philadelphia: Fortress Press, 1960), pp. 123-260. This is from p. 191.

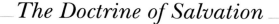
The Doctrine of Salvation

Robert C. Kurka

During the waning days of 1991, the world witnessed the final dissolution of the mighty Soviet Union—a phenomenon that few, if any, considered imaginable in this lifetime. Collapsing in a heap of economic, political, and social ruin, the Evil Empire of communism gave way to that godsend of all cultures, the great and glorious free-market system. With their new "Western" eco-political system, Soviet citizens (now known to the world as the populace of the Commonwealth of Independent States [CIS]) would experience the exhilarating freedom and democracy enjoyed by such nations as the U.S., Great Britain, Germany, and a whole host of others. After all, what could be finer than life in a free (market) society?

And so it came about. The twentieth-century's greatest experiment in repressive systems of government found an emancipator. The free-market had arrived! The proletariat had finally come to taste the first-fruits of economic salvation.

Yet the free-market capitalism and the democratic reforms begun by Boris Yeltsin are proving to be no more liberating than the lies and harsh realities the Soviets experienced under Marxism. Their "free society" is no more than a kaleidoscope of chaos. Left to the whims and desires of entrepreneurial individuals, the CIS political and economic climate is no better (and in many ways, far worse) than the noxious aroma exuded by Soviet collectivism. As 1991 drew to a close, newspaper reports spoke of 300 percent inflation, unmanned emergency phone lines, bloody civil wars (Georgia), closed schools, and, just like the good ol' U.S., urban crime and vandalism. The freedom of conforming to the West is proving itself a poor liberator. No doubt the "slavery" experienced during the pre-Gorbachevian days appears to many Soviets as a far better life than their current economic uncertainty.

What has gone wrong?

This new, democratically orientated, free-market CIS should demonstrate, once and for all, the inherent superiority of the Western credo and way of life, should it not?

Then why is a freed U.S.S.R. no better than a tyrannical old one?

An unknowing prophet residing in Moscow may have muttered the most profound words of all, when, to a L.A. Times reporter, he commented, "Before, we were afraid — not of God, but of power. . . . Now, we're afraid neither of God nor of power."[1]

His statement correctly identified the source of the new capitalism's failure, as well as why the old system self-destructed: a lack of fear for God.

Certainly, one reading a book on Christian doctrine would

almost expect to find the above thesis offered in an analysis of contemporary societal chaos. After all, more than a few evangelical authors have applied this same absence of divine fear to the moral demise of Western cultures. One expects "religious-types" to provide "spiritual" explanations for "real-world" occurrences. Yet a spiritually oriented diagnosis may not be as trite or far-fetched as many would expect, especially when more commonly accepted social science analyses have been tried and found wanting.

Marxism has long contended that human beings are determined by their relationship to material possessions. When a person, or more correctly, a society of people, becomes disenchanted with their lack of economic power, a revolution ensues in order to redistribute the wealth more equitably. Marxist historians read the spectrum of history through this "class struggle" framework, forecasting the time when these struggles will finally give way to the perfect, classless society. The former U.S.S.R. was the most intentional application of Marxist "communal salvation" and it paradoxically produced one of the greatest populations of "have nots" in human history. Not only that, their empire was a short-lived one, collapsing after only 74 years.

On the other hand, Western economic salvation (i.e. the free-enterprise system) has indeed produced nations more prosperous, productive, and human rights affirming. Yet even these bastions of freedom have begun to show the signs of age and decline. For all of their affluence, they are lands devastated by immorality, illiteracy, greed, chemical dependence, and political apathy. Economic betterment, no matter how "this-worldly" and "practical," has not brought peace and stability.

In short, the old Soviet Union has merely exchanged one

false economic savior for another, albeit in democratic clothes. The glistening hope of experiencing the golden "California dream" has been dashed upon the rocks of reality (as if it were really working in California anyway). After all, the West is undergoing the various stages of life-support itself. Once again the question arises: Is true human liberation to be found solely in the rescue of the physical person?

Our twentieth-century world is full of "pseudo-saviors," (e.g. education, science, technology, militarism, etc.), yet suffice it to say, all have proven themselves bankrupt. The U.S., having adopted many of these secular structures as the cure-all of its ailments, has witnessed its own ironic decline in these very virtues.[2] Could it be that the aforementioned "religious diagnosis" of society's ills, coupled with the prescription for spiritual salvation, may be the only satisfactory solution to lasting health? Certainly a figure as Mother Teresa of Calcutta would contend as much, for although living in the most squalid of conditions, she readily reaffirms that she lives a liberated life. Certainly thousands, if not millions, of Eastern European Christians would claim that they found true, personal liberation BEFORE their communistic government collapsed. And all that prior to (or perhaps, in spite of) the results of their democratic reform. Unfortunately, many so-called "spiritual solutions" have arisen, other than Christianity, to redeem the world. Witness the explosion of cults and New Age/occult movements offering remedies during this freedom trek.[3] Yet all of these spiritual analysts have one understanding in common. All realize that there is a fundamental void in man's relationship to himself and his universe which cannot be filled by mere physical objects or experiences. The human being cannot be reduced into neatly quantifiable parts. Rather, there is a person within who seeks more than purely secular satisfaction from life.

Yet while there may be this fundamental assumption within all spheres of religion, it is here Christianity parts company as to the solution. Christianity has no association with New Age spiritualism, for Christianity alone locates man's alienation and subsequent redemption within the context of a relationship with the Creator and living God. This God has clearly announced the human predicament in the Christian Scriptures, the Bible.

As we survey the biblical presentation of salvation, we should not lose sight of the contemporary setting which we have set in these introductory remarks. The doctrine of salvation cannot truly be appreciated in our day without first addressing the avowedly more "practical," secular substitutes —and their failure. Augustine recognized the dilemma of today's humanity when he wrote 1500 years ago, "Lonely is the human heart until it finds itself in thee." Yet it has taken modern man the majority of this century to realize this truth.

Only in this admittance can we meaningfully explore what the Bible teaches about human salvation. Human theories of salvation, as current as today's newspaper, must be scrutinized, lest we read the Bible in some dichotomous fashion, rendering Scripture as religious truth, yet regarding it in practicality as irrelevant. We have seen the practical irrelevance of the secular saviors of our century. Now let us accept the real-world truths of the Bible. Let us examine with open hearts the only viable answer to our search for salvation.

SALVATION: A WORKING DEFINITION

"Salvation is the application of the work of Christ to the life of the individual," writes Millard Erickson in his massive book of systematic theology. This concise definition may appear, at first glance, too simple. Yet its constituent elements suggest the rich and complex realities of the Biblical portrait of salvation.

"Salvation is the application of THE WORK OF CHRIST to the life of the individual."

First, Erickson's definition implies that salvation is a Christocentric act. It is based primarily in the sacrificial death of Jesus Christ upon the cross, followed by his burial, resurrection, and ascension into Heaven. Indeed, the Apostle Paul called this death/resurrection event a matter of "first importance," and the message of which was paramount to his preaching (I Cor. 15:1-5; 2:1-2). This observation grounds salvation solely into a divine activity, separating it from human initiative or achievement. This, therefore, breeds a second implication: salvation presupposes a certain defectiveness in humanity (sin). This defective quality renders humanity incapable of achieving salvation through works or virtues. Therefore, our definition assumes that this human condition is universal, without regard to race, gender, or culture (cf. Rom. 3:23).

Furthermore, this definition suggests that the fundamental nature of man's problems, as well as his subsequent deliverance, rests at a spiritual level. More specifically, because of a broken vertical relationship with God, humanity's ills cannot be fully dealt with until this relationship is restored. Mankind's quest for perfect solutions to his problems and the problems of society can never be completely fulfilled so long as these solutions are anchored in the works of imperfect people.

"Salvation is the APPLICATION of the work of Christ TO THE LIFE OF THE INDIVIDUAL."

Also carried within this definition are the undertones of human responsibility. The terms "application" and "individual" denote a personal appropriation of Christ's saving work. This differs from some mystical "universal" bestowal of deliverance to society. In Christ, salvation directly benefits the individual, offering solutions to both present and future realities.

"SALVATION IS the application of the work of Christ to the life of the individual."

Finally, one other inherent concept in this simple definition relates directly to humanity as a whole. Salvation, as used in its absolute sense in our definition, suggests a common universal condition of "lostness," as well as a singular, cosmic scheme of recovery. Hence, the Christian understanding of salvation is not simply one of man's salvific theories, but is rather one truth to which all must conform.

Within Erickson's definition, we see many sparkles in the facets of Christian theology. We see the origin and transmission of sin, the finality of Christ's work on the cross, the extent of human responsibility, and the comprehensive nature of salvation. We see the time of salvation, its physical dimensions, direction and futuristic associations. The very depths of the crucifixion itself are supported by Erickson's definition. Christ's substitutionary act, his representative work, the triumph over Satan, and the supreme demonstration of servanthood are whispered through this simple sentence.

"Salvation is the application of the work of Christ to the life of the individual."

TOWARD A BRIEF BIBLICAL THEOLOGY
OF SALVATION IN THE OLD TESTAMENT

Traditionally, Christian doctrines such as salvation have been defined through, primarily, a deductive approach to interpreting scripture termed "systematic theology." In this methodology, one begins with a working definition of the doctrine and then draws out related Biblical texts that give support of the said meaning. While there are many merits to this form of systematic organization, often Scripture is forced into addressing issues apart from its original context. One's theological orientation (for instance, Calvinism or Arminianism) may give a prior bias to a Biblical concept that is then read into the text. This approach does not allow the concept to be defined by its contextual argument. It is my contention that more than a few theological impasses have been created due to a refusal to surrender these presupposed definitions.[5]

On the other hand, systematic theology must not be wholly discarded, for it does point us toward a tentative conclusion. Ultimately, however, each passage, and all of Scripture, must be read through a more exegetical examination. Otherwise, the original intent of the author would be lost to the scalpels of proof-texting.

In recent years, however, a more inductive methodology of doctrinal formulation has risen to the forefront in theological circles. This more exegetical approach, termed "biblical theology," is chronologically based. Beginning with the early chapters of the Old Testament, doctrines are allowed to emerge from the progressive pages of revelation. This approach assumes a fundamental unity of the Scriptures (e.g. two testaments, one Bible) while allowing for diversity and development of a biblical theme, especially as it achieves its culmination in the New Testament.

158

The particular merit of this "biblical theology" is well articulated by Walter Kaiser, who sees the Old Testament as a book of "promise" (a theme exegetically suggested by New Testament writers). Yet this book of promise is multi-faceted and complex, rather than one generic idea.[6] Throughout time, God has revealed more and more of His intent concerning the fulfillment of this promise, namely, the redemption of humanity. Kaiser refers to this as an epigenetic approach, much like the development of a tree from seedling to shoot to a full tree with a panoply of branches, twigs, and leaves. Epigenetic biblical theology allows us to chronologically locate, then develop, our doctrine of salvation, which Erickson thus summarizes as the application of Christ's work to the life of the believer. The rich, personal implications of this definition will then be seen in a totality and expanse which is often overlooked by systematic theology. This comprehensive approach may help to unite many of the supposed "conflicts" that have arisen between theological traditions, and thereby lead toward future unity in today's fragmented church.

The doctrine of salvation cannot be properly understood apart from the first three chapters of Genesis. Theologians from the twentieth century have rightly emphasized the Bible as a book of salvation history. The Bible is a specific, purposeful communication of God's saving intentions toward mankind, NOT a volume addressing the particulars of history, geography, science, or the like.[7] In the past, such a recognition has often been given with an author's suspicion concerning the historical credibility of the Scriptures. Many authors have an almost anti-supernatural bias (one this author, as well as other evangelical authors, does not share). Rather, the Bible should be seen as "holy history." The Bible is accurate, yet it is primarily concerned with historic events in the context of man's relationship with God.

Thus, the opening account of creation must be seen in the framework of salvation history. It sets the stage, the groundwork, and reason for the subsequent chapters in the Bible. The creation account boldly declares that man was NOT a mistake or accident in an impersonal universe (which is certainly the perception we all receive at some time or another). Rather, we see the unique creation of a personal, yet transcendent, God who cares for his creation and blesses the man and woman he makes (Gen. 1:28).

Genesis 1:26-31 declares that humanity was created in the "image of God." Rooting all of humanity's anthropology in two created persons, Adam and Eve, we are shown a God who transcends sexism, racism, or any other kind of cultural or ethnic elitism.[8] Humankind is given the unique mandate to rule over God's creation (1:26), fill the earth and subdue it (1:28), and enjoy its bountiful harvest (1:29, 30). The Bible immediately challenges the world views of Near Eastern animists or westerners who would reduce humanity to machine or animal. In the time of Moses, when Genesis is understood to have been written and compiled, there was a challenge in these words to the Egyptian racism that enslaved the Hebrews. Here is also a challenge to the "slave mentality" that had developed during the reigns of oppressive Pharaohs who "did not know Joseph" (Exod. 1:8).[9] Who can believe themselves to be of "lesser stock" while realizing they are the intentional creation of the Almighty?

The creation account is, in and of itself, a salvation statement. It announces to the beleagured pilgrims of the Exodus, both Hebrew and "Gentile" (cf. Exod. 12:38; 48, 49), that people were created to dominate the earth, not each other (a fundamental concept which only God Himself could reveal).

Furthermore, the Genesis author declares to these early Israelites that Man gave the birds and animals their identity (2:19, 20), not vice versa, as in Near Eastern animism. And only after the woman was created did creation receive the final divine assessment as "good" (2:18).

The Genesis 1-2 narrative would have been liberating enough, if all these former Egyptian slaves suffered from was a knowledge problem (a diagnosis given by many; modern educators). However, the human character revealed a propensity to do evil which Genesis 3 identifies as rebellion against God. In the well known account of the Fall of humanity, Eve, followed by Adam, chose to believe the lie of the serpent (Satan), eat of the forbidden fruit, then found themselves estranged from their Creator. The consequence of such disobedience ("death," 2:17) is a comprehensive fragmentation between man and every relationship he previously experienced. Open, free, and loving communication with God is now replaced by fear (3:9) and futile attempts to hide oneself from God. This initial point of separation of man from God then reverberates into a psychological dissonance as Adam cannot accept responsibility for his own action ("The woman whom You gave to be with me, she gave me the fruit!" 3:12). Furthermore, such inner conflict is certain to bring social disintegration. It began with Adam and his wife, yet later it translated to the tragic episode between their sons, Cain and Abel (4:1-8). Man's relationship to his environment also underwent a severe change, for the entrance of rebellion against God brought a cosmos in revolt against the planning, as well as the planting, of man (3:17-19). Scripture later goes on to classify this foundationally theological separation as sin (*hamartia* = Greek; the Hebrew sin vocabulary is expressed by a number of words: *asaq, awon, pesa, chata*. All words connote a volitional nature).

The Hebrew experience in Egyptian idolatry and human deprivation certainly served as prime evidences of the Genesis 3 Fall to Moses' original audience. However, these people who had borne the crushing weight of slavery had also tasted of the liberating emancipation from Pharaoh's cruelty through the Lord's intervention (plagues, parting of the Red Sea, etc). This experience of social and political freedom was aptly put in its true "spiritual" context by the prophetic words of Genesis 3:15:

> And I will put enmity between you and the woman, and between your seed and her seed. He shall bruise you on the head, and you shall bruise him on the heel.

In the midst of sin threatening to undo God's desire to bless His human creation, as well as the whole of His creation (1:22), the Lord speaks this word of curse upon the serpent and salvation upon humanity. Jewish (and later, Christian) exegetes saw in this promise a messianic deliverer who would come in the fullness of time (Gal. 4:4).[11] Many commentators have noted the grammatical idiosyncrasies and strange "genealogy" of this passage. Even the casual reader can see the future implications inherent in this verse, including the virgin's conception, the cross of Christ, and the resurrection. What is often missed is the fact that the word "seed" is a collective noun (Hebrew = *zera*) which can both refer to a single descendant or a multitude.[12] While the crushing of Satan is obviously the work of the unique Deliverer, the beneficiaries of such a victory include an entire human race which allies itself with the Messiah. Conversely, there is a "line" of Satan as well, consisting of those who choose to reject God's saving work and continue on in the lies from the Garden. They will likewise share in the defeat of the serpent. This initial messianic announcement contains much more than simply prophetic trivia. Rather, it announces and broadly defines God's salvific intentions, a paradigm which will essentially govern the flow of redemptive history.

Therefore, as we have seen, humanity's rebellion has brought alienation in all aspects of existence. Whether the conflicts are sociological, psychological, or ecological, all such enmity finds its source in this schism. Second, sin is an intruder upon God's intention to bless humanity, bringing with it a separation so consequential that everlasting life has been lost to eternal condemnation. Third, God refuses to have His plan thwarted and promises that He Himself will bring forth a deliverer, the seed of a woman, who will, at a costly price (bruised heel), defeat the serpent to the everlasting benefit of others. Consequently, because sin disorders the entire matrix of human relationships, we should then expect that the salvation act will be effective for this same wide range of fragmentation. Although fundamentally theological, the seed's (and seeds') salvation will bring "blessing" to individual, societal, and environmental contexts. This is a holism that subsequent Scripture reveals as it shares its history of salvation.

If one were to doubt that blessing man was an obsession with God, particularly after the Cain/Abel travesty of Genesis 4, the opening words of Genesis 5 dispel any uncertainties by stating, once again, the creation narrative (yet this time in a post-Fall context):

> He created them male and female, and He blessed them and named them man in the day when they were created, (Gen. 5:2).

This statement reminds us that God's created intentions have not been terminated by sin, and implies that if blessing is in order, God must already be at the work of bringing the salvation act to pass.

Genesis 6 narrates that sin had once again reared its ugly head in unprecedented dimensions of evil. God expresses regret in making humanity and announces that He will bring judgment upon the entire earth. The resulting destruction, however, contains a further reminder that the blessing plan will not fail, for in 6:8 we are told that Noah finds favor with God. While for forty days and nights, rain devastates the earth and its inhabitants (both human and animal), Noah and the selected beasts find safety and well-being (6-8). Noah experiences a taste of the promised redemption (3:15). While he and his family are physically rescued from death, it is in the context of Noah's relationship with God that deliverance is wrought. Once again we see the creation mandate repeated, "Be fruitful and multiply, and fill the earth" (9:1), as well as a reaffirmation of man's fundamental nature as God's image (9:6). Finally, the Noahic narrative is brought to a close as we read that God Himself (not Japheth, as many modern translations imply) will dwell in the tents of Shem. One day, we are promised, God will indeed enjoy a harmonious relationship with man, and the location of His dwelling place will be with a certain people — in reality, "as the seed of the woman." Not by accident does the fourth gospel declare that the Word became flesh and tabernacled (Greek = *eskenosen*) among us (John 1:14). Nor should it be surprising that the "tent of Shem" is later identified with Abraham and his descendants, the nation of Israel. And furthermore, while God's dwelling is placed among a certain people, Japheth and even a repentant Ham or Canaan are not kept out of its folds. Surely, the "table of nations" (Gen. 10) strongly insinuates God's desire to save *all* of the repopulated earth.

Salvation history's next major encounter occurs in Genesis 11, when human sin manifests itself in a great feat of technological arrogance. The precursor of all contemporary secular salvation theories is given apt expression, when united (evil) humanity boasts that MAN will make a great name for himself (11:4). The Lord's subsequent scattering of their population and confusion of their language is in itself an act of salvation. Such human arrogance left to its own design would have certainly moved the world toward a pre-Flood wickedness. One cannot help but enjoy the irony between God's promise to bless all of humanity through one line of people (Shem; 9:27), while man's intention was to bless one race through a massive collection of peoples.

As we have already come to expect, a word of promise is soon to follow. The next such declaration is spoken to Abraham in Genesis 12:1-3. In this keystone covenant, God promises Abram a new land, a seed (a collective noun), and declares that through his line all the nations of the world will be blessed. The connecting links between Genesis 3:15 and 12:1-3 are inescapable: the seed (the deliverer and the delivered), the theme of multiplication ("great nation," and "all families," corresponding to the "be fruitful" mandate), and the fundamental divine purpose to bestow blessing. To these salvific facets is added a place of God-blessed "residence" (recalling 9:27), a location that will progressively take on a more spiritual or "heavenly" understanding in Old Testament theology. The Abrahamic blessing, first enunciated in Genesis 12, becomes the essential program of salvation which "interprets" the remainder of the biblical record. Since humanity is lost in sin, God chooses to bless a human line (Abraham) so that this humanity will, in turn, proclaim His salvation to all other nations. This salvation promise is given almost verbatim to the successive generations of the Abrahamic family, to Isaac (28:13, 14) and Jacob (28:13, 14). Indeed, these salvation reaffirmations are given in situations much like the original promise (Gen. 3, 9, and 12), contexts which describe human rebellion against God and its related disorders. As Genesis lays out its foundational doctrine of salvation, one thing is abundantly clear: the restoration of man's broken relationship with God is solely God-initiated. Man clearly cannot save himself.

Before we depart from this cursory discussion of salvation in Genesis, we would be remiss if we failed to note the individual application of the salvation promise. In Genesis 15:6, following yet another recapitulation of God's intention to deliver a blessing, we are told that Abram "believed in the LORD; and it was reckoned to him as righteousness." This statement becomes a model, too, for defining the general concept of human reception of salvation's blessing: belief, or faith (cf. Rom. 4:3, 9, 22; Gal. 3:6; James. 2:23). Salvation, as individually appropriated by faith, will thematically carry throughout the Bible, albeit the specific details of this belief may vary from epoch to epoch. However, lest one be tempted to ascribe this faith to human merit (as later Jewish rabbis, in fact, did), let it be noted that the righteousness given was due solely to God's decision to "credit" such belief.

As we have previously noted, the Genesis record of the beginnings of sin and salvation was originally written to a nation of former slaves, their deliverance expressed in concrete, if not miraculous, events. The Genesis account gave the necessary theological backdrop to the plagues, Passover, the Red Sea crossing, etc. They were not to see these mighty acts as mere power displays or displays of favoritism, but rather as the outworking of the Genesis 3:15 promise and its further articulation in 12:1-3. And yet these real life experiences of deliverance made it clear that salvation was not some ethereal or merely philosophic emancipation, but a meaningful "event" that touched one in space/time history. The concrete realities of the Exodus then, became the framework through which the consummate deliverance would be anticipated and understood (cf. Matt. 2:13-15; 4:1-11, etc.), thus reaffirming that humanity's redemption from sin before God brought holistic consequences.

The Exodus account is resplendent in its portrayal of God as savior. From His name "Yahweh" (which is given in the context of redemption, Exod. 6:2-8) to His demands to Pharaoh to release His people (Exod. 7:16, et al.), the Creator of Genesis is seen to be active in His character as Redeemer. As the people of Israel stood at the banks of the Red Sea, threatened by Pharaoh's oncoming chariots, Moses called their attention to the "salvation of the LORD" which would be seen in their midst that day (14:13). Later, he sang of how God had become his salvation (15:2) and redeemed His people (15:13).

Israel's oldest and most prolific confessional recognized Yahweh's identity in primarily salvific terms, as He was remembered as the "LORD, your God, who brought you out of the land of Egypt, out of the house of slavery" (Exod. 20:2).[14] Moreover, the Sinaitic Covenant itself (Ten Commandments) is set within the context of this prior redemption (see above). The decalogue was never intended to provide Israel with an instrument by which she might earn her salvation, as some Christian writers have suggested, but rather it established a covenant relationship with its constituent stipulations to govern those who had already been "saved." Furthermore, due to sinful humanity's incessant ability to both disobey God and forget His previous grace, a way of redemption (sacrifices) was given through which the divine/human relationship could be restored, albeit in light of the future, full sacrificial death of Jesus (Rom. 3:25; see also Heb. 10:4). This salvation was not to be conceived in some provincial manner as the Lord's intent was to bring proclamation of His name throughout the earth (Exod. 9:16). "Strangers" (non-Hebrews) were to be welcomed into the camp of the redeemed on the same *faith* basis, without discrimination (Exod. 12:49; Lev. 24:22; Num. 15:15, 16). The faith in God shown by the Canaanite prostitute Rahab (Josh. 6:17-25) was not to be an unusual phenomenon, but was rather the response the Lord desired as He performed His saving works before the world.

The Exodus, then, picks up the Genesis salvation history and, in concrete, space-time demonstrations, further identifies the God of both Creation and Promise as the Deliverer. The blessing forfeited by human sin is redeemed through a series of mighty acts in the Mosaic period. Authentic holistic experiences of salvation are given, although their ultimate effectiveness still resides in the future atoning death of the seed of the woman.

The remaining Old Testament history of salvation reflects, advances, and anticipates the final fulfillment of the saving program of the saving God, so well defined in Genesis and Exodus. Moses' successor was significantly named Joshua (Yoshua), related to the Hebrew word "Yeshua," or "Yahweh saves." Yahweh promised Joshua and his nation "blessing" if they would obey (not "works salvation," but rather behavior that is consistent with *being saved*) their redeeming God (Deut. 28:1-14), yet also promised judgment if their hearts were marked by ingratitude (28:15-68). Clearly the Lord's salvation is both conditional (beneficial only in the context of on-going faith) and something to be regarded with utmost seriousness!

The Moses/Joshua era was followed by a time of great disobedience on the part of the nation, particularly evidenced by their pursuit of idols in preference to the Lord, "the God of their fathers who had brought them out of the land of Egypt" (Judges 2:12). Consequently, pagan, militaristic empires which should have been evangelized by the saved nation were allowed by God to continually intimidate His ungrateful people. This was in order that Israel might be "tested" and come to recognize their dependence upon Him (Judges 2:22, 23). When the sons of Israel cried out of their misery to the Lord he raised up a deliverer (Hebrew = *yasha*; 3:9). This cycle was continually repeated, as a series of judges, both male and female, were sent to deliver the nation. This was not only in a militaristic sense, but with a salvation that fundamentally "restored" the people to the rule of God alone (Judges 8:23).

The book of Ruth offers another "salvation portrait" of God in its description of the noble Boaz as the widow Ruth's redeemer/kinsman (Hebrew = *goel*). Boaz provides us with a practical human model of God's redemptive blessing being shared with a "foreign" woman, signifying once again, both the holistic nature of salvation and its global inclusiveness.

The Davidic-Solomonic era provided insights into God's ultimate king (II Sam. 7; Psa. 89, 110, etc.), as well as comprehensive riches (materially, as well as spiritually) of divine blessing. While God had promised the nation a king of his own choosing many years prior (Deut. 17:14-20), human sin attempted to usurp the divinely appointed monarch with its own fallen agenda (a king like all the nations, I Sam. 8:5) and its own fallible deliverer (Saul). God does, however, succeed in placing a man of "His own heart" (I Sam. 16:7) upon the throne (the shepherd/warrior David) who, alternately, incarnates the radiance of God's salvation and the ugliness of human rebellion. From David's hand comes some of the most haunting expressions of human suffering due to debilitating sin (Psa. 22:1-18; 51:3-5) as well as some of the most joyful reveling in the forgiveness and restored relationship with God (22:22-31; 5:10-19 et al.). The psalmist knows that "peace" (Hebrew = *shalom*) and "rest" (Hebrew = *menuchah*) are far more than military cessation or material wealth. It is, fundamentally, to be in a harmonious relationship with the Shepherd-Friend, God (Psa. 23). It is the Lord who is David's "light," "salvation," and "refuge" (Psa. 27:l), whose face of blessing David is to seek in every situation of life. Solomon's material splendor would seem to emphasize the "physical" dimensions of God's deliverance, yet this man of wisdom understood that one's salvation was a theological issue, once again, appropriated by heart faith, or "fear of the LORD" (Prov. 1:7, et al.).

The prophets, like the judges before them, attempted to keep Israel focused on the truth that her physical well-being was secondary to, and in many instances, related to her spiritual health. This was a precept that the nation tragically ignored, resulting in her division, destruction, and eventual deportation. In this approximate five hundred year period of internal decline and external crises, the prophets more and more turned their attention to the ultimate day of deliverance and the appearance of the divine savior, described as both the kingly "Son of Man" (Dan. 7:13, 14), as well as the suffering servant of Isaiah, whose consummate act of salvation is accomplished by His death and humiliation (Isa. 53: 4-9).

This final act of salvation, the promised crushing of Satan's head (Gen. 3:15), would then usher in a redemption of cosmic consequences: restored nature (Isa. 11:6, 7), restored cities (Isa. 61:4), and a literally new heavens and earth (Isa. 65:17), devoid of human sorrow and pain. Salvation's ultimate fulfillment would bring about the final restoration of all the beauty and harmony that was inherent in pre-Fall Eden. This ultimate, comprehensive response to the Fall's multi-faceted disordering would come about primarily because the source of the problem, humanity's sin, had received its cure, both objectively and existentially. Ezekiel saw, in this final act of salvation, the transformation of the wicked human heart.

> I will sprinkle clean water on you, and you will be clean. . . . moreover, I will give you a new heart. . . . I will remove the heart of stone from your flesh, and give you a heart of flesh (Ezek. 36:24-26)

Furthermore, this "clean heart" was to become the dwelling place of the Holy Spirit (v. 27) who would in turn recreate the recipient's attitude toward God and His ordinances. The redeemed believer would now desire to consistently walk in the ways of the Lord.[15]

This same theme is seen in Jeremiah 31:31-37 as Ezekiel's prophetic contemporary sees this "new birth" in the context of the "new covenant" (Hebrew = *berith chadashah*). What makes this covenant new is not some fundamental change in the salvific promise and plan of God, but rather a spiritual transformation of the undependable human recipient. This covenant, in contrast to the former one, cannot be humanly broken (31:32) and will be experienced by an unrestricted universal audience, no longer relying upon Israel's faithfulness to her call to be the "light of the nations" (Isa. 49:6). All mankind will "know the LORD," as persons of all cultures choose to respond to this salvation, and all are promised that in that day, their sins will be remembered no more (v. 34). This is a full and complete spiritual redemption!

The prophetic anticipation of this great day of salvation brings to a close the Old Testament's history of salvation and provides the climactic context for the New Testament's proclamation of the coming of Jesus — God's "visit," with its accompanying redemption for His people (Luke 1:68). Salvation history has now reached its promised hour; the "time is fulfilled" (Mark 1:15).

THE FULFILLMENT OF GOD'S SALVATION PLAN

> For as numerous as the promises of God may be, in Him they are yes . . . (II Cor. 1:20a).

In light of our cursory study of Old Testament theology and its progressive development and clarification of God's salvific plan (a repeated promise to "bless" the fallen human race), Paul's declaration above brings the great "Amen" to a drama which has been eagerly anticipating its final event for two thousand years.[16] Applying a common New Testament summation of Old Testament salvation history promise (Greek = *epangelia*), Paul asserts that Christ Jesus (v. 19) is the focal point of the scheme of redemption. Implicitly, He is the singular seed of the woman which would triumph over Satan. It should not surprise us that Paul, the consummate evangelist and missionary, is also the New Testament's consummate salvation theologian. His understanding of Jesus' completion, as well as validation of the Old Testament's redemption story, compelled him to unabashedly preach this good news to both Jew and Greek (cf. Rom. 1:14-16; Acts 26:22, 23). What could be more exciting to a committed Jew than to know that the crucial "omega point" of salvation, the crushing of the serpent's head, had occurred and all the promises of God regarding man's salvation (past, present, and future) were now officially made good?

The story of this Christ Jesus of Nazareth is one which Paul could assume that his audience had a rudimentary knowledge of, or at least access to such, through the living apostles. Toward the latter part of the first century A.D. as the Faith moved into its second and third generations, the Spirit of God provided the narrative material about this Person in four gospels (plus the Lucan sequel, Acts). These evangelistic biographies brought to a conclusion the salvation history that began in Genesis. Read in conjunction with their Old Testament counterparts, these "Christ chronicles" brought to completion the promise theme in all its component parts, as well as provided the life details of the God-man, which brought the Pauline and other epistolory reflection.

The Gospels set forth the person Jesus (Greek = *Iesous*: savior) as one who is the genealogical "seed" of Abraham and its kingly expression in David (Matt. 1:1-17), as well as that of Adam (Luke 3:23-38).[17] The pre-existent and divine nature of Christ (the Word) is declared in the opening chapter of John's gospel (1:1-5), while the second evangelist, Mark, identifies Jesus as the subject of God's "good news" (Mark 1:1, 14). He is depicted as the focal point of John the Baptizer's preaching ("Make ready the way of the Lord," 1:2), the obedient "beloved son" who assents to His salvation mission in His baptism (1:9-11), and a preacher Himself who announces that His ministry brings the fulfillment of God's salvific promise as well as the Kingdom of God's intervention and rule (1:15). This aspect of the Kingdom's presence is crucial to understanding the message and activity of Jesus, for in His self-identification as the Kingdom-broker, He is making the startling claim that the Old Testament's anticipated day of salvation and punishment (the day when the full and final deliverance from sin would be made and the Fall's decay remedied) was in fact occurring in that first century context.[18] The ministry of Jesus also brought into clarity the "two-advent" dimension of the Kingdom: (1) the immediate presence of salvation in His healing miracles, exorcisms of demons (Mark 1:2lff), and most importantly, authority to forgive sin (Mark 2:5-10), as well as (2) a future manifestation in which the "Son of Man" would be universally recognized as He returned to earth in all His glory to finally complete His deliverance (Mark 13). The Kingdom of God reaffirms the holistic and concrete nature of salvation (introduced in Genesis and Exodus) by attacking the problem at its theological root, separation from God. Indeed, Mark spends virtually half of his gospel (8:31ff) declaring that Christ's fundamental mission is to "suffer many things and be rejected by the elders and the chief priests and the scribes and be killed." Later, Jesus declares it is His purpose to give His life as a ransom for many (10:45). Matthew, Luke, and John devote an unusually large amount of their narratives to the final week of Jesus' life, for it is in His death that the age-old promise of salvation is most decisively delivered. In each gospel account, the crucifixion of Jesus is consciously related to significant Old Testament passages which give clarification and prediction to the Genesis 3:15 salvific event (cf. Zech. 11, 12; Psa. 22, 31, 34, and 39).

Jesus' dramatic, final words recorded by John, "It is fin-

THE DOCTRINE OF SALVATION

ished!" (Greek = *tetelestai*) provide a fitting exclamation mark to a redemption program that has been centuries in the making. This ultimate sacrifice, coupled with its subsequent resurrection, declares that the seed of the woman has crushed the serpent's head, the payment of sin has been fully secured, the effects of the Fall (consequences of sin) will be fully repaired, and the faith of generations of believers, from Adam and Eve (presumably), to Noah, Abraham, Moses, et al., has been well-placed. It is not surprising that Old Testament saints are raised and appear to many in Jerusalem, subsequent to Jesus' resurrection (Matt. 27:52, 53) for in this, we see their trust in God's redemptive promise powerfully vindicated — a public declaration, so to speak, that those who pursued God's salvific path, recounted in the pages of the Old Testament, pursued the right way. The tearing of the temple veil (Matt. 27:51) was also a visual demonstration from God that the barrier of human sin had been removed, thus ushering in a new age of divine-human relationship and blessing.

Thus from the announcement of Jesus' birth through His ministry, to His death and resurrection, this Person is inextricably linked to the promised consummate deliverer from sin, in whom the Old Testament anchored its understanding, hope, and ultimate reality of salvation.

The Acts narrative, which in essence completes Luke's "orderly account" for Theophilus (Luke 1:3, 4; Acts 1:1), records the subsequent interpretation of and response to the gospel's portrayal of Jesus, notably His death and resurrection (Acts 2:22ff). In Peter's foundational Pentecost sermon (Acts 2:14-36), the apostle clearly ties Jesus' betrayal and death to the "predetermined plan and foreknowledge of God" (v. 23), His resurrection and exaltation to Davidic prophecy (vv. 25-31; 34, 35), and the supernatural demonstration of tongue-speaking (vv. 3-13) to Joel's "Day of the Lord" oracle, which in turn grounded such phenomena in a last days outpouring of the Holy Spirit (vv. 17, 18). On this great day, "everyone who called upon the name of the Lord would be saved" (v. 21; cf. Joel 2:32). Peter leaves no doubt that in Jesus, he sees the promised mediator of God's salvation plan. Furthermore, he boldly indicts each member of his audience as being guilty in the crucifixion of Christ ("whom you crucified," v. 36), an accusation that ultimately refers to basic human sinfulness and its required redemption price. Obviously, many of Peter's hearers were pilgrims in Jerusalem, rather than actual partici-pants in the sentencing and death of Jesus (2:5-11). Yet they were equally yoked with those guilty of the actual crime. Peter's connection between Jesus and the Old Testament's promised deliverer elicits the well-known invitation to apply the finished work of Christ to one's life: repent and be bap-tized so that sin would be forgiven and the gift of the Holy Spirit's indwelling received (2:38). This Pentecost definition of saving faith (i.e. belief, repentance, and baptism) would then become a model for the apostolic church (see conversion accounts in Acts, e.g. 8:12, 13, 35-37; 9:5-18; 10:44-48, et al.), although the exact sequence of these faith elements might differ. There is no exegetical clue in Acts (or the epistles, for that matter) that this faith model has ever been altered.

The book of Acts goes on to tell us of how this initial multi-national response to the gospel was replicated through-out the known world, from Jerusalem to Antioch to Rome. It records several sermons that were preached to a variety of audiences, exhortations, which like Peter's in chapter 2, relate Jesus to the promises made to the fathers (13:32) and thus call on their hearers to have their sins forgiven and be freed (13:38, 39). The cross and resurrection, then, is clearly the redemptive goal of Old Testament salvation history and, importantly, the sole means by which people of all cultures may be saved.[19] In Acts 4:12, Peter declares without any qualification that "there is salvation in no one else and that there is no other name under heaven that has been given among men, by which we must be saved."

The immediate context of this last statement offers a final observation about the nature of this Christocentric salvation: it is holistic. As people were brought into contact with the Savior, Jesus, their diseases were cured (3:2-10), their demons were exorcised (16:16-18), and less miraculously, but perhaps just as supernaturally, their social consciences were pricked (4:32-35; 6:1, 2). While salvation in Christ repaired a fundamentally theological, or spiritual, separation, this vertical healing had clear horizontal dimensions as well. Certainly the real-life experiences of God's deliverance which were so much a part of the Old Testament, were no less real in the New (especially Acts). Salvation in Scripture is uniformly holistic.

While the Acts described the preaching of and response to the Christ event in the first century, it was the writers of the epistles who related the theological implications of salvation.

The consummate New Testament salvation theologian is undoubtedly the Apostle Paul. As he writes his missionary letters to a diversity of churches and concerns, the "bondservant of Jesus Christ" clearly identifies his gospel as that which was promised beforehand through His prophets in the Holy Scriptures. That promise is the incarnation, death, and resurrection of God's Son, Jesus (Rom. 1:2-4). This Christ-centered gospel is the power of God for salvation (Greek = *soteria*) for everyone who believes (1:16), revealing both the righteous nature and "righteousness-working" of God, as well as His wrath against rebellious, truth-suppressing human nature (1:17, 18). ALL humanity is hopelessly lost, both those who possess God's Law and those without it (Rom. 2:1-3:19). Christ alone brings salvation to the sinner, and this deliverance is appropriated by faith (1:5, 17). The genius of Paul's soteriology emerges at this point as he sets salvation in an unique time framework: past, present, and future.

Salvation as a past event is seen in the apostle's use of several key terms. The first, *apolutrosis*, commonly translated in English as redemption, means deliverance from captivity at the payment of a price.[20] In Paul's writings, redemption has, as its primary object, the historic deliverance from sin and its penalty by the sacrificial death of Christ in A.D. 30. This death is itself viewed through the *hilaskomai* vocabulary (English rendered *propitiation*, or atoning sacrifice) which, as Leon Morris contends, suggests that God's wrath stands in need of appeasement, the required death of an innocent victim in order to satisfy the demands of holiness which, in turn, cannot tolerate sin.[21] Unlike the often perverted "appeasement" tales in Greek mythology, this propitiatory sacrifice is made by God Himself. The past-time delivering act of Jesus Christ is also characterized as a reconciliation (Greek = *katallasso*) in which the prior enmity between God and humanity, brought on by sin, is now overcome and healed.[22]

Another past time reference is seen in Paul's employment of the *dikaio* word group ("justification") which nuances a law court scenario and a judicial decree of "freedom" from guilt and condemnation.[23] Justification, then, is God's gracious gift to a powerless sinner. It is an objective declaration of the latter's release from the deserved penalty of sin (death) due to the Judge's own satisfactory payment on one's behalf (Rom. 3:24). This substitutionary payment for human sin allows God to become "just with Himself" (v. 26), for His prior (Old Testament) works of salvation were, in actuality, the passing over of sin (v. 25). While these sacrifices brought a real sense of healing to the Old Testament believer, nonetheless justification did not actually come until the work of the cross. The shedding of Christ's blood authorizes and validates all prior divine verdicts of "saved."

For Paul, however, salvation is not merely the past drama of the cross. Although Jesus' death is the central event of all history, the resulting life in Christ and future hope is of key importance as well.

As noted in the prophecies of Ezekiel and Jeremiah, the day of salvation was to bring with it a new, regenerated heart (mind) toward righteousness. Paul's sanctification (Greek = *hagiazo*) vocabulary picks up this new heart" imagery as the necessary correlation of Christ's justifying act. Sanctification involves the application of Jesus' resurrection to the life of the believer, through the person and power of the same Holy Spirit "who raised Jesus from the dead" (Rom. 8:11). We who are baptized into the death of Christ (6:3, 4) are also united with Him in His resurrection, to a "newness of life" (v. 4), which rejects the old mastery of sin (6:6, 14). This holiness process is an ongoing one: a struggle, which at times can be frustrating (Rom. 7:14ff) but one which can/should be completed through the power of the indwelling Spirit (8:9-11). The Spirit's saving work in the life of the individual is not to be seen in a purely individualistic context, however, for the sanctified person is incorporated into a new society of people who share the same redemptive experience, past and present. They are to be identified by the Christ-like characteristics of humility, gentleness, patience, and unity (Eph. 4:1-3). This corporate body of the saved ("saints," or more generally, the church; Greek = *ekklesia*) is to approach life through the same attitude which was in Christ, a mind which eschews selfishness and self-exaltation and prefers instead to minister to the needs of others (cf. Phil. 2:5ff). The reconciliation effected at the cross between God and man is now to be evidenced in human relationships, especially to those who are also in Christ, as well as unsaved humanity; as a whole (Rom. 12:9-21). This latter observation, peace with non-Christians, suggests a further dimension to the "being saved" experience: evangelism. Redeemed social relationships, both in and outside the church, declare the "manifold wisdom of God" to unbelieving humanity and heavenly principalities (Eph. 3:10), which in turn brings about further human conversion, shaming those who deny the saving work of God (Rom. 12:20). Indeed, Paul gives special commendation to congregations such as the one in Thessalonica, which faithfully witnessed to the world through its redeemed lifestyle (I Thess. 1:9).

The Holy Spirit further assists the church's growth, maturity, and witness through the giving of diverse spiritual gifts (Greek = *charismata*; cf. Rom. 12:6ff; I Cor. 12; Eph. 4:11ff). These gifts, some spectacular, others not, should also be seen as the Spirit's "first fruits" (Greek = *aparche*; Rom. 8:23), which suggests a third dimension to the salvation time frame: future.[24] The death and resurrection of Christ promise a complete renewal of God's created order, from inanimate creation to every aspect of human existence (Rom. 8:18ff). The Spirit who is now at work sanctifying our minds and attitudes will also, one day, raise our mortal bodies, as He did earlier with Jesus (8:10, 11). On that final day of the Lord, the persevering believer will not only be spared the wrath of God (5:9, 10), but also experience the completion of his/her salvation in the redemption of the body (8:23). This future day of Christ's visitation (Greek = *parousia*) for judgment and salvation, becomes a major source of Christian comfort (I Thess. 5:13-18), ethical motivation (Rom. 13:11-13), and hope (Greek = *elpis*) that enables us to experience our present-day tribulations without despair and grow toward spiritual maturity (Rom. 5:3-5).[25] This future redemption cannot be stymied by death (Rom. 8:35-39; I Thess. 5:13, 14), although physical death will touch every human until the return of Christ.

The three-fold time framework (past, present, and future) that is so integral to Paul's salvation doctrine is well summarized by John under the formulation of "ETERNAL life" (Greek = *zoe aionion*; cf. John 3:16; 17:3; I John 5:11). It is a God-given quality of life which is experienced now in the present, as well as throughout eternity itself.

While Paul's theology of salvation is heavily oriented around the individual's application of Christ's redemptive work, he is not remiss in articulating its cosmic implications. Christ's death and resurrection are God's public humiliation of Satan and his spiritual principalities, as well as the supreme statement of His triumph over them (Col. 1:15). Jesus' servant-like sacrifice has earned Him the title Lord, although there is no question of his pre-existent divinity, and the consequent worship and adoration due Him by all beings, in heaven, and on earth, and under the earth (Phil. 2:10-12). John, the Apocalypse writer, most creatively expresses this triumphant theme in Revelation 12, where in delightful symbolism, he describes the dragon's (Satan) pursuit of a pregnant woman and the male child she is giving birth to. Yet the child is caught up to God and to His throne (v. 5) and the woman is given refuge (v. 6). The dragon and his angels are defeated in a heavenly war and thrown down to the earth by Michael and his celestial cohorts (vv. 7-9). The subsequent loud voice in heaven supplies the meaning to this somewhat bizarre picture:

> Now the salvation, and the power, and the kingdom of our
> God and the authority of His Christ have come, for the accus-
> er of our brothers has been cast down, who accuses them
> before God day and night. And they overcame him (Greek =
> *enikesan*; aorist) because of the blood of the lamb. . . (Rev.
> 12:11, 12).

Christ's death on the cross has decisively defeated Satan's
heavenly pretensions and access. Indeed, so powerful is the
blood, that John can describe Satan's earthly plummet in
terms of an angelic victory. The cross has relinquished Satan
of his strength. The cosmic powers of Christ's accomplished
work are further reiterated in John's description of Satan's
"binding" (20:2, 3), which allows the good news of salvation
to be preached unmolested to all nations. And Satan's ultimate divestiture of power, his destruction, is recorded a few
short verses later (20:10). It is a fitting conclusion to the last
book of the Bible which admonishes its readers to overcome
through the Overcomer.

CONCLUDING REMARKS

From beginning to end, the Bible presents itself as a salvation document: in declaration, in historical record, in exhortation, and in invitation. God reveals that there is hope, and that
man is not hopelessly lost in an impersonal world. Our study
of Old Testament promise and its New Testament fulfillment
has suggested several summary observations about the Biblical doctrine of salvation:

(1) Salvation is essentially grounded in the creation narrative, for the Creator/personal God designs man, as well as the

universe, to His "blessing."

(2) The entrance of sin (Gen. 3) potentially threatens to undo this blessing, a rebellion so heinous that it not only breaks off God's relationship to man but also disorders every human relationship. Man is incapable of repairing this.

(3) In the light of this sin, God announces a "salvation plan," the seed of the woman that will ultimately destroy Satan and the effects of sin. It is a promise He reiterates throughout the entire Old Testament. Man becomes salvation's beneficiary by faith.

(4) Although fundamentally spiritual in nature (to restore the blessing of God to sin-ravaged man), salvation is holistic in its scope, relevant to the comprehensive effects of the Fall.

(5) In the Old Testament, God brings His deliverance in real, concrete space-time events, notably the emancipation of Israel from Egyptian slavery.

(6) The Old Testament, however, keeps the foundational expression of deliverance in balance. Physical relief is ultimately meaningless apart from a restored relationship with God.

(7) The later prophets eagerly anticipated the advent of the promised seed or mediator of salvation, for His deliverance will bring about a new heart in humanity and a restoration of all creation.

(8) The prime salvation act will involve the sacrificial death of God's Servant (Isaiah).

(9) The New Testament writers declare that the Deliverer is Jesus.

(10) Jesus' death on the cross:
    a. Pays the full price of human sin.
    b. Validates all of God's prior salvation promises and
       acts.

c. Reconciles God and man, formerly enemies.

d. Defeats Satan and his demonic legions.

(11) Jesus' resurrection brings:

a. A new quality and standard of life for the believer, a present transformation brought by the work of the Holy Spirit.

b. Promise of a future resurrected body.

c. Promise of a renewed heaven and earth.

(12) Salvation, while appropriated on an individual basis, is nonetheless corporate as well: a saved people.

(13) The proclamation of the good news of salvation has been, and always will be (at least in the present age), a fundamental purpose of those "saved. "

As we conclude our study of the biblical doctrine of salvation, let us realize afresh that the story and proclamation of God's redemption is not simply a piece of theological trivia finding relevance only in the classroom. God's saving activity, focused on Jesus, is the key to understanding all of human history, whether that which is recorded or that which is to come. The only hope for the nations of the world, whether the newly democratic CIS or the staggering USA, is through the restoration of our relationships through Christ. Perhaps the failure of the secular saviors will merit this message a new hearing.

Endnotes

1. Reprinted in the *St. Louis Post-Dispatch* (Tuesday Dec. 31, 1991).

2. The following book provides an excellent critique of today's low intellectual climate, as well as our current moral decline. While not necessarily written from a Christian perspective, University of Chicago professor Bloom nonetheless deplores the loss of absolutism of the biblical tradition in contemporary education to the relativism of "progressive humanism."

The book's title reveals the "success" of this endeavor.

Bloom, Allan. *The Closing of the American Mind* (New York:Simon & Schuster, 1987).

3. The recent cult/New Age/Occult explosion is discussed in a very competent and readable manner in the following:

Tucker, Ruth. *Another gospel: Cults, Alternative Religions, and the New Age Movement* (Grand Rapids: Zondervan, 1989).

Henry, Carl F. H. *Twilight of a Great Civilization; The Drift Toward Neo-Paganism* (Westchester, IL: Crossway Books, 1989).

4. Erickson, Millard J. *Christian Theology* (Grand Rapids: Baker, 1986), p. 887.

5. For several recent attempts to define key Biblical words according to their contexts, rather than presupposing meanings from systematic theology, the following books are recommended. These volumes contain key studies of salvation-related language: election, predestination, foreknowledge, etc., countering presupposed Calvinistic understandings (as found in John Murray's *Redemption Accomplished and Applied*).

Forster, Roger, and Marston. *God's Strategy in Human History* (Minneapolis: Bethany House, 1984).

Pinnock, Clark. *Grace Unlimited* (Bethany, 1975).

Shank, Robert. *Elect In The Son: A Study of the Doctrine of Election* (Springfield, MO: Westcott, 1970).

6. Kaiser, Walter D., Jr. *Toward An Old Testament Theology* (Grand Rapids: Zondervan, 1978).

Kaiser develops a convincing, exegetically-based case for the concept of "promise" as the integrative center to the Old Testament. James Strauss has tended toward this approach as well, as is evidenced by his "promise-fulfillment" summation of the contents of Scripture. A similar, yet less formally developed, approach was presented in Robert Milligan's Restoration classic, *The Scheme of Redemption*.

7. While I do not share their non-historical biases, I am indebted to people like O. Cullman *(Christ and Time)*, G.E. Wright *(God Who Acts)*, and G. von Rad *(Old Testament Theology)* who remind us that the Bible is fundamentally a proclamation of the mighty acts of God. Consequently, we must be cautious about making the Bible address every sphere of knowledge. The Bible's fundamental intention is to proclaim the saving activity of the Creator God.

8. The implications of the Genesis presentation of man, every male and female, as the "Image of God" are enormous. D.J.A. Clines notes the "confrontational" nature of this doctrine (i.e. Hebrew *tselem* was a common Semitic term that was normally attached to nobility and representations or idols of pagan deities. See Clines, "The Image of God in Man," *Tyndale Bulletin* 19 (1968), pp. 55-103.

9. Gunter, W. and Bauder, W. "Sin." *New International Dictionary of*

New Testament Theology (Grand Rapids: Zondervan, 1975-1978), vol. 3, pp. 573-86.

Quell, G., Bertram, G., Stahlin, G., and Grundmann, W. *"Hamartano, Hamartema, Hamartia." Theological Dictionary of the New Testament.* Ed. G. Kittel (Grand Rapids: Eerdmans, 1964), vol. 1, pp. 267-316.

10. Hedlund, Roger. *The Mission of the Church in the World* (Grand Rapids: Baker, 1991).

Van Rheenan, G. *Communicating Christ in Animistic Contexts* (Grand Rapids: Baker, 1991).

A brief, but very good discussion of Egyptian animism (as well as the general animistic confrontation by biblical revelation) can be found in Hedlund's work. Van Rheenan's book has provided some needed understanding of the religious environment in biblical times.

11. See Martin, R.A. "The Earliest Messianic Interpretation of Genesis 3:15." *Journal of Biblical Literature,* 84 (1965): 427.

12. See Brown, F., Driver, S.R., and Briggs, C.A. *A Hebrew and English Lexicon of the Old Testament* (Oxford: Clarendon Press, 1972), p. 282. See Kaiser, pp. 36-37.

13. See von Orelli, C. *Old Testament Prophecy,* pp. 98ff; cited by Kaiser, pp. 37-39.

14. This is the contention in von Rad's book:

Von Rad, Gerhard. *Old Testament Theology,* Vol. 1 (New York: Harper, 1962), p. 121.

15. Jesus "marveled" that the teacher of Israel, Nicodemus, did not understand this teaching on "new birth" (John 3:3-10), for the Ezekiel passage should have been well-known to the Pharisee (and subsequently taught to people).

16. The New Testament identifies these promises (actually, one unified promise) as:

    a. that given to the fathers (Rom. 15:8, 9).

    b. a blessing for the Gentiles (Gal. 3:8, 14, 29; Eph. 1:13; 2:12; 3:6, 7).

    c. the resurrection from the dead (Acts 26:6-8; II Tim. 1:1; Heb. 9:15, 10:36; II Pet. 3:4, 9; I John 2:24, 25).

    d. the promise of the Holy Spirit in a new fullness (Luke 24:49; Acts 2:33-39; Gal. 3:14).

    e. redemption from sin and its consequences through the promise of Jesus the Messiah (Acts 2:38-39; 3:25, 26; 7:2, 17, 18; 13:23, 32, 33; Gal. 3:12).

All of these "promise aspects" are oriented to salvation: God's creation-intention to "bless" and His successful rescue.

17. Some evangelical apologists have attempted to "harmonize" the two genealogies by suggesting that Luke is presenting the lineage of Mary. While this is somewhat dubious, it must be admitted that Luke writes his birth narrative from Mary's point of view ("the woman;" Gen 3:15), whereas Matthew's reflects Joseph's. For further study consult the following:

Johnson, M.D. *The Purpose of the Biblical Genealogies.* Cambridge: University Press, 1969.

18. The old Testament antecedents of the New Testament Kingdom of God (Hebrew = *malkut*) included an expectation of an end-time divine visitation in which:

a. the promises of David's heir would be fulfilled.

b. the Day of the Lord would arrive (usually with strong overtones of judgment).

c. Israel would be regathered.

d. new covenant would be inaugurated.

e. new heavens and earth.

See II Sam. 7:13-14; Isa. 1;24-28; 9:6, 7; 11:1-10; 64-66; Jer. 23:56; 31:31-34; Ezek. 37:24; Dan. 2:44; 7:13, 14.

19. A growing debate in evangelical circles concerning the fate of those who have never heard the gospel is evidenced in such recent publications as follows:

Crockett, W.V., and Sigountos, J.G., Eds. *Through No Fault of Their Own?* (Grand Rapids: Baker, 1991).

Pinnock, Clark. *A Wilderness in God's Mercy* (Grand Rapids: Zondervan, 1992).

The "issue" does not appear to center around a pluralistic view of salvation, but rather about the extent of "natural revelation" in a world of religions. Certainly, the somewhat controversial Pinnock does not deny the "finality of Jesus Christ." His particular inquiry is more directed toward how the work of God's last word is applied to these diverse contexts. It is my contention that we might best lay aside "fate of the lost" speculation for the New Testament priority: How do we tell them God's saving news? I have carefully searched the Scripture, especially Paul's writings, for any hint of the lost not hearing. There is no such clue, presuming that Romans 2 is talking about evangelized Gentiles rather than "God-conscious pagans."

20. Morris, Leon. *The Apostolic Preaching of the Cross* (Grand Rapids: Eerdmans, 1965), pp. 11-64.

21. Morris, pp. 144-213.

See Link and Brown, C. "Reconciliation." *New International Dictionary of New Testament Theology.* Vol. 3:148-65.

While our study on New Testament soteriology has primarily been concerned with Paul's doctrinal formulation, we would be remiss not to mention the apostle's "equal" as an atonement theologian: the author of the Hebrews epistle. Using the Old Testament background of sacrificing for sins, the Hebrews author reminds us that there is no forgiveness without the shedding of blood (9:22); the blood of bulls and goats cannot "take away sins" (10:4); by one offering (His death), Jesus has made the perfect sacrifice for all time (9:28; 10:14). Consequently, we now have confidence as believers to enter into God's "holy place" because of Christ's blood. As the faithful high priest, Jesus makes "propitiation" (Greek = *hilaskesthai*) for the sins of the people (an allusion to and fulfillment of the Old Testament Day of Atonement).

22. Morris, pp. 214-50.

See H. Vorlander, and C. Brown, "Reconciliation." *New International Dictionary of New Testament Theology.* Vol. 3:166-176.

23. Morris, pp. 224-74.

See C. Brown, "Righteousness, Justification." *New International Dictionary of New Testament Theology.* Vol. 3:352-76.

See Alister McGrath, *Justification by Faith* (Grand Rapids: Zondervan, 1988).

McGrath has brought a much needed emphasis upon the "experience" of justification similar to our emphasis upon "salvation" in this essay. His book attempts to rescue the doctrine from the dusty shelves of theological abstraction and put it into the life situation of the church member—and generally succeeds.

24. The Holy Spirit Himself is called "arrabon," or downpayment, or earnest, on future salvation (Eph. 1:13, 14).

25. The related doctrine of "perseverance" is beyond the scope of this brief essay. However, the following book contains a good exegetical treatment of "eternal security." We have noted previously, in the text of this essay, the conditionality of salvation in the Old Testament. Perhaps the best example of conditionality is the wilderness generation not being permitted to enter the "rest" of the promised land (Psa. 95:11; Heb. 3:11, 4:3). The Hebrews author certainly appears to continue this same note of conditionality (or the possibility of "falling away") as he structures his "exhortation" (13:22) around six major warning sections: 2:1-4; 3:1-19; 4:1-13; 5:11-6:12; 10:19-39; and 12:1-7.

Marshall, I. Howard. *Kept by the Power of God* (Minneapolis: Bethany Fellowship, 1969).

See also G. Osborne, "Soteriology in the Epistle to the Hebrews," *Grace Unlimited,* C. Pinnock, ed. (Minneapolis: Bethany Fellowship, 1975), pp. 144-66.

The Lord's Supper

Andrew Paris

The cross of Christ stands supreme as the grand monument of God's love for us. Although sin had devastated the world and made it one sad junkyard, the cross towers above the shattered rubble. The cross remains the indestructible beacon pointing sinners to God's forgiveness.

This fact certainly impressed Sir John Bowring (1792-1872). Having been twice elected a member of Parliament, this eminent English statesman became both governor of Hong Kong and British knight all in the same year (1854). Shortly after this appointment, he embarked on a tour of southern China. As he was sailing along the southeastern coast, he saw in the far distance the city of Macao. It had just recently suffered the fury of a devastating earthquake. But on the shore, high on a hill, he noticed the ruins of a mission church building. A huge cross towered above the shattered debris. The sight thrilled his soul. In a flash, he took out pen and paper and wrote: "In the cross of Christ I glory; towering o'er the wrecks of time."

And at the Lord's Supper the glory of Calvary shines forth in all its divine splendor. There we see how brilliantly "all the light of sacred story gathers round" the cross of Christ. As we partake of broken bread and fruit of the vine, we remember with love the Christ of the cross whose death rescues us from the pollution, power, and penalty of sin.

For that is the main idea in the Lord's Supper. By definition, the Lord's Supper is a sacred meal instituted by Christ that reminds us of His death for our sins on the cross. The bread symbolizes His body broken, and the fruit of the vine symbolizes His blood shed. This memorial feast stimulates our minds to remember how He saved us from sin and hell. Far more than being a mere memorial, the Supper truly feeds the soul.

Although the church receives a multitude of blessings from this simple yet profound means of grace, the Table of the Lord is no magical charm that works automatically. It is not a grace machine. The worshippers must come fully prepared to meet their Lord. The mind and heart must be actively involved. We need to understand what this holy banquet means in order to receive grace and power for holy living. This chapter will meet that need. To help us understand the essential features of the Lord's Supper, we will study: 1) Christ's Presence at the Lord's Supper, 2) the Meaning of the Lord's Supper, and 3) the Frequency of the Lord's Supper.

CHRIST'S PRESENCE AT THE LORD'S SUPPER

The Lord's Supper was not invented by mankind; Jesus

Himself created it. He gave this precious gift to His Church. He commanded His people to celebrate this meal "in remembrance of Me" (Luke 22:19; I Cor. 11:24-25). On the night He was betrayed, He and His disciples met together in an upper room somewhere in Jerusalem. There they celebrated the Jewish Passover. At the conclusion of that holy ritual, the Master took some unleavened Passover bread, broke it, gave it to His disciples and said, "This is My body" (Matt. 26:26); then he took a cup filled with the fruit of the vine and told them, "This is My blood of the covenant" (Matt. 26:28). Thus was born the Lord's Supper.

But what did Jesus mean by those words, "This is My body," "This is My blood"? Obviously Jesus meant that in some real sense He is PRESENT at the Lord's Table. But HOW is He present? In what sense are the bread and cup His body and blood? These difficult questions have divided Christianity for centuries. The manner of Christ's presence in the Lord's Supper has been a battleground of debate and strife among Christians throughout the ages. Although this issue is complex and controversial, we must study it if we would understand the essential nature of the Lord's Supper.

The battle lines have been drawn between three views: the Roman Catholic, the Lutheran, and the Memorial interpretations of Christ's presence in the Lord's Supper.

The Roman Catholic Church declares that Jesus is PHYSICALLY present in the bread and cup. They believe that in the Mass when the Catholic priest speaks the words of institution ("this is My body," "this is My blood"), the inner invisible nature of bread and wine is transformed into Christ's physical flesh and blood. The outer nature of bread and wine, however, remains bread and wine. Although the elements look, taste, and smell like bread and wine, they are really the physical body and blood of Jesus.

Lutherans also believe that Jesus is PHYSICALLY present in the Lord's Supper. They maintain that after the Lutheran priest speaks the Words of institution ("this is My body," "this is My blood"), the physical flesh and blood of Jesus become present "in, with, and under" the bread and wine. This view differs from the Catholic position. For the Lutheran declares there is no change in the elements: the inner and outer nature of bread and wine remains. The flesh and blood of Jesus are simply added to the elements. In, with, and under the bread and wine are the body and blood of Christ.

The Memorial view affirms that Christ is not physically present in the bread and cup, but is SPIRITUALLY present in the ACTION of the Lord's Supper. The bread and cup symbolize Christ's body and blood as He is dying on the cross. They serve as blessed MEMORIALS of Calvary. So when the Christian participates in the entire action of receiving these emblems and meditating on the death of Christ which they symbolize, Jesus spiritually comes to us and feeds our souls.

But which one is the Biblical view? The physical presence theory advocated by Catholics and Lutherans contains two serious flaws: 1) it cannot be proved from Scripture; and 2) it is repugnant to Scripture.

First of all, the physical view cannot be proved from Scripture. John 6:63 condemns any physical theory—Catholic or Lutheran. When Jesus proclaimed, "The flesh profits nothing," He at least meant His physical flesh and blood cannot benefit our souls. Eating Christ's physical body would be irrelevant to our soul's deep need. "The Spirit gives life"— not Christ's physical body. If we are to receive any blessing from the Lord's Supper, it must come from the spiritual presence of Christ. Thus His physical presence is unnecessary.

Jesus announced, "This IS My body"; He never said, "This BECOMES or is TRANSFORMED into My body," as the Catholic claims. Nothing in Scripture suggests that the verb "is" must mean the bread "is changed into" Christ's flesh. But the verb "is" sometimes carries the figurative idea ("to symbolize") in such texts as John 15:1 ("I am the vine"), John 10:7 ("I am the good shepherd"), and Matthew 13:38-39 ("the field is the world"). And it can mean that in the Lord's Supper accounts also.

I Corinthians 11:26 teaches that we are to observe the Lord's Supper "until He comes." This shows that in His physical presence Jesus is absent from the earth until His Second Coming occurs. Now He is here spiritually, but not physically. His flesh and blood do not come down into the bread and cup at the Lord's Supper.

Secondly, the physical view is repugnant to Scripture. It is absent from and opposed to the clear teachings of God's Word. Scripture condemns all cannibalism; drinking blood is strictly forbidden (Gen. 9:4; Lev. 7:26-27; I Samuel 14:32-34; Acts 15:20, 29; 21:25). If believers eat Christ's flesh and blood in the Supper, they commit the disgusting sin of cannibalism. And that is repugnant to what the Bible teaches.

On the other hand, the Memorial view is supported by Scripture. First of all, consider Exodus 12:11. Since many of the words and actions Jesus used in the upper room are closely patterned after the Jewish Passover (see Exod. 12), we can go to the Passover to understand the Lord's Supper. The words of explanation for the Passover (Exod. 12:11, "it is the Lord's Passover") are strikingly similar to the words of explanation for the Lord's Supper (Matt. 26:26, "This is My body"). Exodus 12:11 thus helps explain Matthew 26:26. In Exodus 12:11 the verb "is" means "to symbolize": "it is the

Lord's Passover" must mean this Feast SYMBOLIZES Yahweh's "passing over" the Israelite houses and killing all Egyptian first-born sons. No other view fits. Therefore "is" carries the same symbolic meaning in Christ's words at the Supper: "this is My body" means the Lord's Supper SYMBOLIZES Christ's death for our sins. This supports the Memorial view of Christ's spiritual presence at His Table.

Secondly, Scripture supports the Memorial view by showing how the disciples reacted to Christ's words in the upper room. He had just told them to eat His body and drink His blood. In light of the Jewish abhorrence to drinking blood, this statement would have caused them tremendous problems, if the disciples had interpreted His words literally. Yet Scripture does not record any such questioning by them in the upper room. They seem to have accepted it calmly; why? Obviously because they did not interpret His words literally. They believed the bread and cup symbolize their Lord's body and blood.

Therefore the Bible teaches the spiritual presence of Christ at the Lord's Supper. For this is the only kind of presence our souls desperately need. It is a spiritual presence, yet a true presence.

THE MEANING OF THE LORD'S SUPPER

What should the Lord's Supper mean to the Christian? How can we receive its rich blessings? What should we think about as we partake of the broken bread and fruit of the vine? To answer these questions, consider the four "C's" of the Lord's Supper: Commemoration, Confession, Communion, and Covenant.

Commemoration

What does the Lord's Supper mean? First of all, it means commemoration. "Do this in remembrance of Me" (Luke 22:19) is the blessed motto for this holy banquet. It reminds us that He loved us and died to save us from sin. We remember or commemorate this glorious fact every time we gather at the Lord's Table. By receiving the bread and cup, we remember "Christ and Him crucified." As we break the bread in our own hands and eat it, we think of Christ's body broken on the cross; and as we drink from the cup, we meditate on Christ's blood poured out. These sacred emblems, like a celestial time-machine, take us back to that time when the Lord of Glory gave His life for sinners at Calvary. It reveals to us the glories of Calvary in all their radiant splendor. How does the Lord's Supper do this?

At the Lord's Supper we remember the horrific evil of sin. Our sin was the reason He died. Our sin nailed Him to the accursed tree. And sin never appeared uglier than at Calvary. As we eat the broken bread and drink from the cup, we remember that Jesus was wounded for OUR transgressions and was crushed for OUR sins (Isa. 53:5). The Supper reveals to us how much God hates our sins but loves our souls.

At the Lord's Supper we remember the justice of God. It reminds us that at the cross God punishes sin. There God the Judge appears in all His justice and righteous wrath against evil. But there is more to it than simply this. For at the cross God solves a problem that involves His justice and our sins. Because of His justice, God requires the eternal punishment of sinners in hell. Because of His love, God desires the eternal salvation of sinners in heaven. But how can God do both? How can He punish sin but save sinners? He solves this problem at Calvary. For there Jesus becomes the "PROPITIA-TION" for our sins (Rom. 3:25; I John 2:2; 4:10). This term means that Christ's death turns away the wrath of God from us. At the cross Jesus endured the full punishment of eternal hell that we deserved for our sins, bearing God's wrath and justice as our Sin-Substitute (II Cor. 5:21; Gal. 3:13-14; Isa. 53:6). Therefore Christ's death satisfies both the justice and love of God. At the Table of the Lord, we see how perfectly God's justice solved the problem of sin.

At the Lord's Supper we remember the love of Jesus. We certainly see the Father's love at the cross (John 3:16; Rom. 5:6-8). But more than this, the cross reveals Christ's love for sinners. It shows us His divine love, supernatural compassion, and miraculous grace. He loved us even while we were His enemies, and died on the cross to save us. And as we meet around the Lord's Table, we behold with joy the wondrous grace of our loving Lord.

At the Lord's Supper we remember the defeat of Satan. At Calvary Jesus destroyed the devil's works (I John 3:8) and made him powerless (Heb. 2:14-15). There our Savior disarmed the demonic powers, making a public display of them, triumphing over them through the cross (Col. 2:14-15). Since Christ's death cleanses us of sin (I John 1:7), Satan the accuser (Rev. 12:10-11) cannot condemn us before God (Rom. 8:33-34). We commemorate this victory at this feast.

At the Lord's Supper we remember the infinite worth of a human person. All people become extremely valuable when seen from the perspective of the cross. For we judge the value of something by the price a wise person gives for it. He who created us offered for our salvation not "perishable things like silver or gold," but the "precious blood . . . of Christ" (I Pet. 1:18-19). Jesus laid down His life to be a ransom for ours, when nothing else was sufficient to answer the price. In the Lord's Supper, we see how much we are truly worth; we are worth the very blood of Jesus.

Thus the Lord's Supper is a commemoration; through it we remember Christ's crucifixion. This meal compels us to see Christ crucified—His agony, His glory, His love. The more we desire to receive the Supper reverently, the more we will want to know about the cross; and the more we learn about Calvary, the more we will want to partake of this food from heaven.

Confession

What does the Lord's Supper mean? Secondly, it means confession. "For as often as you eat this bread and drink the cup, you proclaim the Lord's death until He comes" (I Cor. 11:26). Here we confess or proclaim to all around us that Jesus has saved us from all sin and will return for us. We confess that we are not ashamed of the name "Christian" (I Pet. 4:16) or of the Christ to whom we belong. Thus the Lord's Supper is a token or badge of our faith. Through it we confess to remain faithful servants and soldiers of His cross until death (Rev. 2:10). What does this involve?

At the Lord's Supper we confess and praise Christ crucified. We glorify the Christ who died for us. We glory and boast in His cross (Gal. 6:14). We hold it in high esteem as the grand mark of our salvation. Although to Jews it was a stumbling-block and to Greeks it was sheer foolishness, to us the cross is the very wisdom and power of God (I Cor. 1:18-21). We are proud of the Christ and His cross. Rather than being some ridiculous insult to Christianity, the cross of Christ is the one true sign of our victory over sin, death, and hell. This we reverently declare every time we partake of the Lord's Supper.

At the Lord's Supper we confess the Return of Jesus. There we proclaim the Lord's death UNTIL HE COMES (I Cor. 11:26). The Second Coming—that "blessed hope" (Titus 2:13)—is what this meal emphasizes. For it stimulates our minds to go backward to the past (commemoration) and forward to the future (confession). We look back to the Cross and commemorate its saving power; we look forward to the Second Coming and confess it to be the grand finale when Christ's cross will reach its full and perfect climax. And like a majestic bridge stands the Lord's Supper, linking the past with the future. So as we eat the broken bread and drink from the cup, we confess that Jesus is returning for us. Rather than frightening us, this fills our hearts with peace. Because the Lord's Supper shows us that through Christ's death we have been reconciled to God and are now His dear friends (see Rom. 5:1-2; Col. 1:21-22). He is coming to bless us. There is nothing to fear. One day Jesus will split the skies and descend in glory to redeem us from sin and its deadly effects. He will raise us from death, giving us new glorified bodies that will never suffer or die or decay. He will take us home to the New Jerusalem where we will reign with Him forever. This we confess at the Supper.

Finally, at the Lord's Supper we confess our sins to God. This is an obvious and natural result of meditating on Christ's death. Realizing that our sins nailed Him to the cross, we confess them with broken and contrite hearts. This calls for earnest self-examination. Without it, we "shall be guilty of the body and blood of the Lord" (I Cor. 11:28). As a result of this self-examination and confession, the Father forgives us (I John 1:8-10). However, the Lord's Supper is not primarily designed to give us forgiveness, but rather to remind us how we have been saved. The Christian receives forgiveness whenever he asks for it; any time we confess our sins to God, He pardons them—not just at the Lord's Supper. Some people think that unless we take the Supper every week, the sins committed in the previous week are left unforgiven; this notion is unbiblical, and it ruins the grace of God.

Communion

What does the Lord's Supper mean? Thirdly, it means communion. This term refers to the act of sharing something in common among two or more persons. In the King James Version of I Corinthians 10:16, Paul declares the Lord's Supper to be a "communion" of Christ's body and blood (other versions say "sharing" or "participation"). At His Table we share together the blessings Christ gives. He feeds our souls as we partake of the bread and cup. Together we share the sweet knowledge that Christ's death has saved us from all sin. So this feast is far more than merely a memorial; it strengthens and revives with power divine.

In what way do we commune with Christ's "body and blood" (I Cor. 10:16)? Not in any physical manner (that would be unnecessary and absurd), but through His spiritual power streaming down from heaven. Christ's "body and blood" are His life and strength. Consider the sun. To receive its blessings, we do not need the sun's physical presence. Though 93 million miles away, it enlightens and warms by its rays and sunbeams streaming down upon us. So it is at the Lord's Supper. There we receive the power of Christ's life, and in this way we commune with His body and blood. What benefits come to us as that power beams down from the "Sun of Righteousness"? Consider these five wonderful blessings.

We receive the blessed assurance that we are forgiven. Truly the greatest blessing of the New Covenant in Christ is the cleansing of our transgressions (I Cor. 6:11; Eph. 1:7-8; I John 1:7; Col. 1:13-14; Heb. 8:8, 12; 10:17). All our sins are gone. The New Testament constantly assures us this is so, but at the Communion we receive a special assurance of this fact. As we remember Christ's saving death, He confirms and guarantees to us that all our sins are pardoned. There we hear the voice of joy from our loving Father: "Be of good cheer; your sins have been forgiven."

We receive the blessed assurance that we are God's adopted children. We, who were once lost and alienated from God, are now His adopted sons and daughters (Rom. 8:14-17, 23; Gal. 4:5; Eph. 1:5; I John 3:1). In Christ not only our sins are gone, but our status is changed. No longer aliens and strangers, we are now the very family of God. Because we are God's adopted children, many precious privileges are ours. At the Lord's Table our sonship is confirmed and sealed to us. For there we see that Christ's death has made us His Father's adopted children.

We receive peace and satisfaction. One of the most enjoyable gifts of God's grace to His Church is peace. As the God of hope, He fills us "with all joy and peace in believing" (Rom. 15:13). And at the Lord's Supper, Jesus showers us with this divine peace. We need this desperately, and He gives it abundantly when we remember His death for us. For this meal shows that God's wrath has been turned away from us through the cross—the Propitiation. The mind that once was disturbed with the dread of God's wrath is now quieted by the signs of His favor and love—the bread and cup.

We receive power for holy living. Jesus is not only our

Savior, but also our Life and Holiness (I Cor. 1:30). He empowers His Church to live the victorious Christian life. His death justifies us (forgives our sins) and sanctifies us (equips us to be pure and holy). We need both. And as we remember His death at the Communion, Jesus strengthens us to live the righteous life. We ought to come to the Feast with anticipation, expecting rich blessings to revive our weak souls.

Finally, we receive the blessed assurance that we are going to heaven. For that glorious place is our true and final home. All Christ's blessings are intended to lead us onward and upward to those pearly gates where we shall see His face and serve Him forever. As we commune around the Lord's Table, He blesses us with the sweet assurance that we are bound for the "Promised Land." This meal reminds us that Christ's blood both saves from sin and opens to us the gates of heaven. It brings before our eyes the pleasures and glories of that better world. It makes us hunger for heaven.

Covenant

What does the Lord's Supper mean? Finally it means covenant. We see this in our Savior's words at the Last Supper: "This cup is the new covenant in My blood" (Luke 22:20). What is a "covenant," and what did Jesus mean by these words? The term itself as used in the New Testament is a formal contract or agreement containing pledges and promises between two parties. All its terms are prepared by one party possessing full authority (Christ) who then offers it to another party (mankind). That second party may accept or reject it, but can never alter it. In Luke 22:20, Jesus means that the Lord's Supper cup symbolizes the New Covenant which He ratified or confirmed by His blood at Calvary.

Therefore in some sense the Lord's Supper is connected with the New Covenant in Christ. But how? What covenant pledges and promises between God and His Church are renewed at this meal?

God promises to be our God. At the Lord's Table, God renews His covenant pledge to guide us forever. His wisdom will direct us; His power will protect us; His justice will justify us; His holiness will sanctify us; His goodness will bless us. He will be to us a "Father," a "Shepherd," a "Husband."

The Church promises to be God's people. At the Lord's Table, we renew our covenant pledge to surrender and dedicate ourselves to God alone. We promise to serve Him faithfully and walk closely with Him in all holy obedience all our days. What specifically does this involve?

We solemnly promise to oppose all sin. As we enjoy this sacred banquet, we pledge to be the enemies of sin and to offer our bodies as a living sacrifice, holy and pleasing to Christ. We will fight and struggle against any sins that may assault us. We pledge to be more prepared this coming week to conquer the Prince of Darkness. Never will we yield to those "pet sins" that get the best of us so easily (Heb. 12:1-2).

We solemnly promise to make inward godliness the very rule of our lives. We will seek to cultivate a holy heart. We pledge to live in constant communion with God, to set Him always before us, fixing our eyes on Him with love and gratitude as the first cause and last end of all things that concern us. When I receive the Lord's Supper, I dedicate myself to live more earnestly a life of confidence in God, in His beauty, bounty, and blessing; a life of dependence upon God, upon His power, providence, and promise; a life of devotion to God, to His Word's commands, to His Spirit's leading, and to His will.

We solemnly promise to abound "in work that keeps faith sweet and strong." At this sacred feast, we promise that we will not be lazy, but red-hot, zealous, always living for Him who died for us (Rom. 12:10-11). We will be obedient children of God.

We solemnly promise to pray more earnestly, asking God to help us fulfil the covenant promises we have made at the Lord's Table (I Chron. 29:18; II Thess. 1:11).

We solemnly promise to love one another fervently from the heart (I Pet. 1:22-23; 4:8-9). At the Lord's Supper we see how dearly Jesus loved the Church, for He purchased her with His blood (Acts 20:28). And here we see how dear they should be to us. Church unity is a theme the Lord's Supper emphasizes always (I Cor. 10:16-17). If I have made a solemn covenant to obey God, this is His command: "love one another" (John 13:34-35; I John 3:23-24; Heb. 13:1).

THE IMPORTANCE OF THE LORD'S SUPPER

The Lord's Supper was certainly important to our Lord. He instituted it and commanded His Church to celebrate it in His memory. For this simple meal dramatically portrays the way He saves sinners—through His death. And to follow in her Master's footsteps, the Church of Jesus should also show forth the grand importance of this meal. But how can this be done?

Weekly Communion

We show forth the importance of the Lord's Supper by observing it every week. Although Jesus declared, "This do in remembrance of Me" (Luke 22:19), neither He nor His Apostles ever explicitly said how often we should do it. Ample evidence exists, however, to prove God wants us to observe it weekly.

First, consider the Biblical evidence. Since the Apostles were guided into all truth by the Holy Spirit (see John 14:25-26; 15:26-27; 16:12-15), they in turn guided their churches into all truth. Whatever the early churches did by the appointment or approval of the Apostles, they did by the command of Jesus Himself. By studying the Book of Acts, we find that the early Christians celebrated the Lord's Supper every Sunday. This appears by viewing two texts together: Acts 2:42 and 20:7.

Acts 2:42 says, "And they were continually devoting themselves to the apostles' teaching and to fellowship, to the breaking of bread and to prayer." Thus the Jerusalem church observed the Lord's Supper as regularly and faithfully as they did any other part of Christian worship. All four items fit together like one giant chain. As often as they met together for sermons and fellowship and prayers, the Jerusalem Christians met together to receive the Lord's Supper.

Acts 20:7 says, "And on the first day of the week, when we were gathered together to break bread, Paul began talking to them." The early Christians at Troas met together on Sunday to receive the Lord's Supper. Nowhere does Luke suggest that this was a special Communion Sunday, as if to say they did not take it each Sunday. No; the text implies they received it every Sunday.

By joining these two texts together, notice what we get: 1) from Acts 2:42 we learn that the Lord's Supper was a regular, stated part of Christian worship in their meetings; and 2) from Acts 20:7 we learn that Sunday was the stated time and the Lord's Supper was the stated purpose for those meetings. This provides solid Biblical evidence for weekly Communion.

Secondly, consider the historical evidence. The early Christians (in the first three centuries of Christianity) celebrated this banquet every Sunday. The consistent testimony of the early Church and of church historians demonstrates this fact. Weekly observance remained in the Greek church until the seventh century. Weekly communion ceased after pride, carnal indifference, and superstition infected the churches.

Finally, consider the theological evidence. Many churches today object to weekly communion. They claim if we received it that often, it would lose much of its meaning. This common objection reflects a theological confusion about the real meaning of the Lord's Supper. Once we understand the theology of this meal, we see that weekly celebrations make it all the more meaningful; taking it less often really ruins its effectiveness. The Lord's Supper is a COMMEMORATION of Christ's death: can we honor His death too often? Does it make sense to celebrate His resurrection every Sunday, but His death only half as often? The Lord's Supper is a CONFESSION that Christ's blood has already saved us from sin: can we declare this too often? The Lord's Supper is a COMMUNION: do we not need frequent and weekly communion with our Lord? Are we not spiritually weak and in need of Christ's strengthening grace and power each week? The Lord's Supper is a COVENANT: how we need a formal renewing of our covenant with God every week. Besides all this, why should weekly observance make the Supper less meaningful, when it does not do the same for prayer, singing, the offering, or preaching! We go to church every week; we receive an offering every week; we hear preaching every week. Yet I do not hear any churches saying how much more meaningful the offering would be if we received it once every three months.

Therefore, from the evidence of Scripture, history, and theology, we see that God wants His people to take the Lord's Supper every week. This holy practice will certainly show forth the importance of this feast.

Breaking the Bread

Another way to underline the importance of the Lord's Supper is for every participant to BREAK the bread. The following four reasons prove this is essential: 1) the name of the feast, the "Breaking of the Bread," demands it; that majestic name suggests we ought to break the bread. Is it an empty name or does it reveal the action to be done? 2) Jesus broke the bread at the Last Supper (Matt. 26:26; Mark 14:22; Luke 22:19; I Cor. 11:24). All the Biblical accounts of the Supper include this statement. 3) The early church followed the blessed example of their Lord (Acts 2:42; 20:7; I Cor. 10:16). 4) Breaking the bread fits the purpose for which bread is given at Communion. It vividly portrays to us the wounded, pierced, broken body of Jesus on the cross. When the bread is not broken by the worshipper, much of its beautiful and edifying symbolism is ruined or at least diminished.

Therefore I am opposed to the modern practice of distributing the bread in the form of "celestial chiclets." This error prevents the worshippers from breaking the bread. It ruins the symbolism the bread is designed to portray. No one gets to see the bread broken. Anyway, convenience is the only reason we use these "pellets"; Scripture has nothing to do with it. May we return to the Biblical method that our Savior laid down centuries ago and the early Christians followed diligently. If we of the "Restoration Movement" endeavor to do things the same way the first-century Christians did them, then we will restore the Biblical practice of breaking the bread at the Lord's Table. This will surely show forth the importance of the Supper.

In conclusion, this chapter reveals what the Bible says about the Lord's Supper. Christ is truly present, but in a spiritual manner through the action of the ceremony. This holy meal means four things to the reverent participant: commemoration, confession, communion, and covenant. Its importance shines forth when we partake weekly and personally break the bread. This precious means of grace is far more than a "mere memorial"; it truly feeds us as we receive it in a worthy manner. May this be true of us all.

Living in the Shadow of Christ's Final Coming

Robert Lowery

Antichrist and Armageddon. Tribulation and timetables. Rapture and resurrection. Millennium and the Middle East. Israel and the imminent return of Christ. Speculation and sensationalism. For many Christians, these are the words often associated with Christ's final coming. But should they be the dominant ones?

It is evident from the books of the New Testament that the first Christians expected Christ to return. Indeed, the entire New Testament is dominated by this eager expectation. All but two (III John and Philemon) of the twenty-seven books of the New Testament contain one or more passages about Christ's final coming. Each author (Matthew, Mark, Luke, Paul, Peter, James, Jude, the unknown author of Hebrews, and John) at some point or at numerous points refers to the final coming of Christ (see Matt. 24:36ff.; Mark 13:32ff.; Acts 1:11; I Cor. 1:4ff.; I Pet. 1:6ff.; James 5:7ff.; Jude 21; Heb. 9:27ff.; John 21:22ff.).

THE FINAL COMING OF CHRIST: SEEING THE BIG PICTURE

A survey of some of the relevant passages reveals a broad outline of the events that will precede, accompany, and follow Christ's final return, while at the same time room is left for some surprises. As God took the world by surprise when Jesus came the first time, so there will be surprises when Christ comes the final time. The surprises, however, should not obscure the certainties Scripture teaches about Christ's return. We know the direction history moves: at Christ's return God will become all in all, dwelling at last with us as our God (I Cor. 15:28; Rev. 21:3; cf. Eph. 1:22-23; Col. 3:11). The future can be anticipated with confidence. Nevertheless, future events associated with the final coming of Christ must be approached with diffidence and caution.

What can we be certain about concerning the manner of Christ's final coming? Four characteristics are set forth in the New Testament.[1] First, Christ's final coming will be visible: "Every eye will see Him" (Rev. 1:7; cf. Matt. 24:30; Acts 1:11; Titus 2:13; I Pet. 5:4; I John 3:2). Second, Christ will come suddenly and unexpectedly: "For the Son of Man is coming at an hour when you do not think He will" (Matt. 24:44; cf. Matt. 24:50; Luke 12:39ff.; I Thess. 5:2; II Pet. 3:10). Third, Christ's coming has universal significance as indicated by certain cosmic phenomena which will precede or accompany it: "But the day of the Lord will come like a thief, in which the heavens will pass away with a roar and the elements will be destroyed with intense heat, and the earth and its works will be burned up" (II Pet. 3:10; cf. Matt. 24:29; Rev. 6:12-17). Finally, Christ's coming will be in glory: "at the name of Jesus every knee should bow . . . and every tongue should confess that Jesus Christ is Lord, to the glory of God the Father" (Phil. 2:10-11; cf. Matt. 24:30; Col. 3:3-4; Titus 2:13).

What about the purpose of Christ's coming?[2] While Christians know that Christ has already won the decisive battle against the powers of evil and that He is already King (Matt. 28:18; Col. 2:10,15; Rev. 1:5; 5:5), His victory awaits to be revealed to those who negate or ignore Christ's present lordship. At His coming unbelievers will cry out: "Fall on us and hide us from the presence of Him who sits on the throne, and from the wrath of the Lamb; for the great day of their wrath has come; and who is able to stand?" (Rev. 6:16-17; cf. Rev. 11:15; Phil. 2:10-11). In contrast, at His coming the servants of God will be disclosed as being victorious, obedient, and trustworthy. They will someday stand "before the throne and before the Lamb, clothed in white robes," and they will cry out: "Salvation to our God who sits on the throne, and to the Lamb" (Rev. 7:9-10; cf. Col. 3:3-4; Rom. 8:19).

Furthermore, at His coming judgment will be rendered. For Christians, what happens at judgment will be the disclosure of their acceptance by God through Jesus Christ while living on earth: "For you have died and your life is hidden with Christ in God. When Christ, who is our life, is revealed, then you also will be revealed with Him in glory" (Col. 3:3-4; cf. John 3:16,18,36; Rom. 8:1). Both Christians and unbelievers will be judged with regard to the manner in which they lived as either followers or rejecters of Christ: "Do not marvel at this;

211

for an hour is coming, in which all who are in the tombs shall hear His voice, and shall come forth; those who did the good deeds to a resurrection of life, those who committed the evil deeds to a resurrection of judgment" (John 5:28-29; cf. John 3:18,36; I Cor. 3:15; II Thess. 1:5-10; I John 5:12; Rev. 20:12-15; 22:12).

Finally, with Christ's final return there will be the resurrection of the body and the new heaven and the new earth. In contrast with our earthly bodies, our glorified bodies will be imperishable, glorious, powerful, and immortal: "For our citizenship is in heaven, from which also we eagerly wait for a Savior, the Lord Jesus Christ; who will transform the body of our humble state into conformity with the body of His glory" (Phil. 3:20-21; cf. I Cor. 15:35ff.; I Thess. 4:13ff.). We shall be raised to live in heaven, since heaven is the place where God lives: "Behold, the tabernacle of God is among men, and He shall dwell among them, and they shall be His people, and God Himself will be among them" (Rev. 21:3; cf. Rev. 22:3-5; II Pet. 3:9ff.).

Some brief observations need to be offered with regard to two other topics: (1) the signs preceding and/or accompanying Christ's final coming, and (2) the imminent return of Christ.[3] The signs associated with Christ's coming must never be viewed as history in advance so that Christians can predict when Christ will come. Such signs as the preaching of the gospel, earthquakes and wars, and persecution of Christians have been present throughout the history of the Church. Indeed, in the major passages where signs are given, the call is for vigilance and faithfulness: "Therefore be on the alert, for you do not know which day your Lord is coming" (Matt. 24:42; cf. Matt. 24:44; 25:13; Mark 13:23,33-37; Luke 21:34,36; I Cor. 15:52; I Thess. 5:2-3,8). The New Testament is consistent in its warnings about any attempt to calculate the time of Christ's final appearance: "But of that day and hour no one knows, not even the angels of heaven, nor the Son, but the Father alone" (Matt. 24:36; cf. Matt. 24:42,44,50; 25:13; I Thess. 5:2ff.; II Pet. 3:10ff.). Hence, the signs call us to readiness and vigilance. No New Testament author commits himself to any time scale. Speculation is absolutely forbidden.

With regard to the imminent return of Christ, throughout the centuries the Church has been called upon to continually preach Christ's near return. Indeed, the signs serve as a continual reminder that Christ's return is always near.[4] Because Christ is always nearby there is always a sense of immediacy and relevance for Christians: "Therefore, beloved, since you look for these things, be diligent to be found by Him in peace, spotless and blameless" (II Pet. 3:14; cf. II Pet. 3:3-13; Matt. 24:33; Rom. 13:12; Phil. 4:5; Heb. 10:37).[5]

If we are to allow God to accomplish His purposes whenever His Word addresses the topic of Christ's final coming, there may very well be the need for a paradigm shift. Paradigms are individual rules that establish boundaries and influence our judgment and perceptions. Paradigms have the ability to keep us from accepting new ideas or from viewing an issue from a proper perspective. For example, in a business people traditionally keep to patterns of operation that have proved adequate but that may now need to be examined in a new light or from a different perspective. For many Christians there is the need to view Christ's final coming from a different angle. If we study the doctrine of the final coming of Christ, hoping to determine how close we are to that event, we are, quite simply, misreading and misusing Scripture. For example, we should not read the newspaper in one hand and the Book of Revelation in the other, trying to figure out where we are on God's time-line or some human-made time-line. Rather, we should read the Bible in one hand and the newspaper in the other and be reminded about the challenges, opportunities, and mission we face as Christians. The numerous passages in the Bible which deal with Christ's final coming are not to be consulted like a crystal ball, thinking that we have revealed for us in great detail the events leading up to Christ's final coming. As Christ's first coming affects our daily living, so should Christ's final coming.

The writings of the New Testament teach that the present and future are secure in the hands of Christ. What more did the original recipients need to know? And what more do we need to know? What matters is the certainty of God's triumph, when Christ is universally confessed as Lord, not its timing. The surety that Christ is going to come a final time and the certainties associated with that coming—its manner and purpose as well as the signs and the issue of imminence—must not obscure the central purpose God has when He inspired the various authors to address the subject. Christ's final coming is a truth that must change our lives now. Keeping in mind that the numerous references in Scripture to His return are not there in order to merely satisfy our curiosity about the future or enable us to work out in great detail a schedule leading up to the end, what is their main purpose? The following thesis is proposed for consideration: whenever and wherever the Bible speaks about Christ's final coming, its purpose is always to challenge Christians with regard to belief and behavior. Christians are to live lives which reflect that Christ has come and that Christ is coming.[6]

In supporting this thesis it will be impossible to examine every passage in the New Testament which deals with the doctrine of the final coming. Therefore, a case study approach has been adopted.[7] As a teaching tool, a case study is the writing up of an actual situation and studying it in order to determine what lessons may be gleaned. Two New Testament documents, I Thessalonians and the Book of Revelation, will be examined in order to see what can be learned about how the doctrine of Christ's final coming is used to affect Christian living. Both books are reminders that the theology of the New Testament writings was constructed in the context of practical problem-solving rather than pure theoretical speculation. Theology (or doctrine) must "work" in the Church; it must enable people to deal with their day-to-day reality.

Before an overview of the two books is offered, it is appropriate to offer the rationale for focusing on these two particular documents.[8] First, Paul and John are the authors who, perhaps more than any others in the New Testament, have shaped our understanding of the doctrine under consideration. Second, in both books the doctrine of Christ's final coming is pervasive. Third, it is instructive to observe how both a first generation of Christians (I Thessalonians was written shortly after the establishment of the church) and second and third generation of believers (the Christians in Asia Minor received Revelation around 95 A.D.) are challenged to live responsibly in light of Christ's final coming.[9]

I THESSALONIANS: HOPEFUL LIVING IN A HOSTILE WORLD

Paul's first letter to the Thessalonians was probably written around 50 A.D., within a year of the establishment of the church.[10] Acts 17:1ff. reveals that the church was born in the midst of conflict (see vs. 5-10) involving Jewish and Roman opposition. There are several passages in I Thessalonians which refer to the suffering of either Paul and his fellow-workers or the Thessalonian believers themselves (2:14-16; 3:2-7; 5:14-15). Furthermore, with many of the Thessalonian Christians coming from a pagan background (1:9-10; cf. Acts 17:4), there was the ever-present temptation to compromise with the culture (4:1ff.) or face rejection (5:15). Generally speaking, I Thessalonians is practical and pastoral. The first three chapters are essentially narrative in which Paul reminds his readers of their conversion and evangelistic efforts and his and his colleagues' conduct during their visit and subsequently. Chapters four and five are hortatory in nature, dealing with such issues as sexual ethics, work, death, and holy living.

Not only does I Thessalonians refer frequently to Christ's first coming (1:5,10; 2:2,4,8,9; 3:2; 4:14; 5:9), there are repeated references to His final coming. Indeed, each chapter ends with a reference to it (1:10; 2:19-20; 3:11-13; 4:13-18; 5:24; cf. 5:1-11).[11] These references and others suggest that the doctrine is of more than marginal importance. The pervasiveness of this doctrine in the letter testifies to the essential part which this forward-looking note plays in Christian living.

In addition to the references to the final coming being found at the end of each chapter, there are two other ways in which Paul relates Christ's coming to Christian living. First, two words often associated with this doctrine play a significant role in the letter. The word "hope" appears in 1:3; 2:19; 4:13; 5:8 (cf. II Thess. 2:16). This important term refers to the certainty or the confidence a Christian may have with regard to the future because of God's faithfulness. It is, indeed, "the joyful expectation of good things to come."[12]

The Greek word *parousia*, meaning "coming, arrival, presence," occurs twenty-four times in the New Testament, with seventeen of those occurrences referring to the final coming of Christ.[13] Four of the seventeen occurrences are found in I Thessalonians (2:19; 3:13; 4:15; 5:23). The word was used often in the Greco-Roman world to refer to the official visits by the emperors.[14] The New Testament writers use it to refer to the final coming of Jesus and how that coming ought to affect Christian living. In particular, in light of the *parousia*, the Thessalonians are exhorted to remain faithful (2:19), challenged to love and be blameless and holy (3:12-13; 5:23), and encouraged to face death and life confidently (4:15).

In addition to the above ways Paul uses the themes of hope and the *parousia* to exhort, there are several sections of the book which wed the doctrine to Christian living.

1. In light of Christian hope there is to be perseverance in Christian living (1:3; cf. 5:8ff.).

2. Serving God is called for in light of conversion and the final coming (1:9-10; 2:12).

3. According to 2:19-20, the effectiveness of Paul's ministry among the Thessalonians will be confirmed at the coming of Christ.

4. Paul prays that they will be found blameless and holy to the end (3:11-13; 5:23).

5. The exhortations to work in 4:9-12 (cf. II Thess. 3:6ff.) may have been included because of an obsession with the *parousia.*

6. Christians can have confidence when confronting death because of Christ's resurrection and His promised return (4:13-16).

7. A vision of a victorious future provides encouragement (4:18; cf. 5:11).

8. Christians must not be obsessed with date-fixing (5:1-3). Instead, Paul reminds his readers in 5:4-11 who they are (sons

of the light and of the day) and what they are to be doing (to be alert, to be self-controlled, and reflecting faith, love, and hope).

9. The various exhortations affecting the Christian community in 5:12-22 are demanded in light of the call to be found blameless and holy at His coming (5:23).

10. From a negative perspective, at Christ's *parousia* judgment will come to those who have opposed the gospel and its proclaimers (2:16) as well as to those Christians who have been sexually immoral (4:3-6).

All in all, Christ's final coming affects the Christian's view of life and death. The mission of the church as well as the ministry and morals of her members are to be lived out in light of Christ's final coming. Paul presents the doctrine of the final coming with practical soundness, using it as an incentive to Christian faith, love, fellowship, and holiness, and as a strong encouragement in the face of death and the power of evil.[15] He realized that beliefs concerning Christ's final coming determine the actions of Christians.

THE BOOK OF REVELATION:
HOLY LIVING IN AN UNHOLY WORLD

Of all the New Testament authors none is more well-known for his contributions to the Church's understanding of the doctrine of Christ's return than the apostle John. And none is more misunderstood! In the history of Bible study there probably has never been a book provoking more delirium and foolishness without any relationship to Jesus Christ than Revelation. Accordingly, one should approach the book with caution, studying it properly and painstakingly in order to expound it accurately and obediently live out its exhortations.[16]

With Revelation, as with any book of the Bible, we must be sensitive to the historical setting of the original recipients before we can know how it spoke to them and how it speaks to Christians today. As with I Thessalonians, the term "conflict" describes in a general way the situation of the Christians living in Asia Minor. With regard to threats from without, two major antagonists stand out: the Jews and the Romans. Jewish opposition is referred to in Rev. 2:9 and 3:8-9. With regard to Roman opposition, Revelation appears to suggest that Roman toleration of Christians was disappearing and being replaced by growing suspicion and vindictiveness. Politically, Christianity endangered the unity of the empire by its refusal to pay allegiance to the emperors, some of whom claimed to be divine. Religiously, it repudiated the legitimacy of other religions as well as the absolute power of the Roman state religion, namely, the worship of the emperor as a god. Socially, it rejected the libertine lifestyle of the Roman citizens. By its very nature Christianity provoked attack. Rejection and oppression of faithful Christians were unavoidable. In general, Revelation marks the transition from the earlier permissive attitudes of Roman society toward Christianity to the more suspicious and hostile responses that were to be manifested in the second and third centuries.[17]

Ultimately, the greatest menace the Christians confronted was not direct persecution from without, but rather it was the temptation to compromise with their culture, specifically the syncretistic adaption to their pagan culture. Like Babylon of old, Satan used Rome to act as seductress, calling on all of her moral, social, economic, religious, political, and military might to lure Christians into compromising relationships and complacency. Resisting the power of cultural seduction is sounded again and again in the book.

Accordingly, the repeated references to Christ's final coming (including the events that are to precede, accompany, or follow it) are normally found in close connection with exhortations to be faithful in a seductive and oppressive world. John challenges the Christians of Asia Minor who had clearly capitulated to culture to repent and be faithful. He encourages the Christians who had conspicuously remained ardent in their loyalty to Christ. He challenges those who need to be shaken from their spiritual lethargy, reminding them of the cost of discipleship.

Indeed, Christ's final coming and its inherent connection with responsible Christian living is found at the very beginning: "Blessed is he who reads and those who hear the words of this prophecy, and heed the things which are written in it; for the time is near" (1:3). The emphasis is found at the end as well: "And behold, I am coming quickly. Blessed is he who heeds the words of the prophecy of this book" (22:7; cf. 22:11-12,14). What is to be kept or obeyed? What strategies did John adopt in seeking to produce certain changes in the attitudes and actions of his audience?

An abiding value of Revelation is how the book through a variety of modes of exhortations addresses the theme of what it means to live a Christian life in light of Christ's final coming. John intends to be persuasive in that he appeals to an authority higher than his own; God is the author of the revelation (1:3) with Christ and the Holy Spirit playing roles as well (2:1,7). He is comprehensive in that the visionary and hortatory aspects are intricately linked. Indeed, exhortations are found in every major section in Revelation. In demonstrating his pastoral concern to guide the Christians in light of Christ's final coming, John is specific and pertinent. He reveals throughout the book that God does not desire His servants to be left on their own, using their own imagination or intuition to determine how they should be living in a pagan culture which oppresses and seduces. The Revelation was given to aid the Christians in Asia not only by giving them confidence because God and His servants will ultimately prevail over the forces of evil but also by helping them decide what is good and what is evil. There is no hint whatsoever that The Revelation was given in order to provide a blueprint to the future, enabling later generations to determine with precision events to come.

In what specific ways does John exhort the Christians to holy living in an unholy world while they await Christ's return? Several strategies may be observed. First, he exhorts through numerous imperatives. For example, Christians are exhorted to repent (2:16), to remember (2:5), to do deeds (2:5), not to fear (2:10), to be faithful (2:10), to be watchful (3:2), to be righteous and holy (22:11), and to hear (2:7).[18]

Second, in using several labels to describe Christians, John reminds Christians who they are and/or what they are to be doing. They are: a kingdom (1:6; 5:10), priests (1:6; 5:10; 20:6), the people of God (18:4; 21:3; cf. 5:9; 7:9), conquerors (2:7,11,17,26; 3:5,12,21; 15:2; 21:7), servants (1:1; 2:20; 6:11; 7:3; 11:18; 19:2,5; 22:3,6), fellow-servants (6:11; 19:10; 22:9), saints (5:8; 8:3-4; 11:18; 13:7,10; 14:12; 16:6; 17:6; 18:20,24; 19:8; 20:9; 22:11), and the called, chosen, and faithful (17:14).[19]

Two closely related ways of exhorting the Christians are found in the words of commendation and rebuke. For example, Christians are commended for their work (2:2), toil (2:2), perseverance (2:3), love (2:19), ministry (2:19), and commitment to Jesus (2:13).[20] On the other hand, they are rebuked for their neglect of love (2:4), their acceptance of false teachers (2:14-15), their idolatry and immorality (2:14), their false reputation (3:1-2), and their apathy (3:16).

Threats of judgment and promises of reward are used to exhort Christians. Judgment will come not only upon unbelievers but upon faithless Christians as well (2:16,21-23; 3:3,16). In later sections of the book, believers are reminded that those who abandon their allegiance to Christ and ally themselves with Satan will be judged (14:9-16; 16:15; 18:4; 20:11-15). The promises of reward found in chapters two and three (2:7,10b-11,17a,29; 3:4-5,11-12,21) are consistently linked with the call to be an overcomer. As with the theme of judgment, the concept of rewards is found in later sections of the book (7:9ff.; 11:18; 14:1ff.; 17:14; 19:1ff; 21:1ff.). Only God's faithful servants will participate in paradise restored (22:1ff.). John consistently links privileges and responsibility in his depiction of the rewards to be given to those who serve God. At no point are the two separated. The character of the Christian life while on the present earth anticipates or reflects the nature of the Christian life in the new heaven and new earth.

Even the emphasis on the imminence of Christ's final coming is used to challenge Christians to responsible living: "And behold, I am coming quickly. Blessed is he who heeds the words of the prophecy of this book" (22:7). God desires that His servants know what must soon (or suddenly) take place so that they may be encouraged and exhorted to respond accordingly (1:1,3; 2:16; 3:11; 11:14; 22:7,12,20). The nearness of Christ's final coming does not denote a chronological brevity, but the always-impending intervention of God with a strong exhortation to holy living. To live in the conviction that the final coming is imminent means, according to Revelation, that the servant of God is concerned with doing the will of God so that when Christ does come the Christian will be found ready.

Another way in which John exhorts Christians in light of Christ's final coming should be noted. Privilege and responsibility are brought out in the well-known seven beatitudes (1:3; 14:13; 16:15; 19:9; 20:6; 22:7,14). Christians are blessed if they remain faithful to God and Christ. Their commitment is described in various ways (e.g., keeping the words found in the book, refusing to worship false gods, etc.). Furthermore, each beatitude is linked with the believer's privileges that come either upon death (14:13; cf. 20:6)[21] or at Christ's final coming (1:3; 16:15; 19:9; 22:7,14).

Finally, John uses lists of virtues and vices to challenge the Christians to remain faithful (14:4-5; 21:8,27; 22:15). The lists compel the listeners to examine their lives, to recognize their own conditions, and to repent if necessary. In particular, Christians are those who have not defiled themselves either sexually or spiritually; they are disciples of the Lamb; they belong to God and to the Lamb; they possess integrity in their speech; and they are blameless (14:4-5). The lists of vices in 21:8 contrasts those who are "the cowardly and unbelieving and abominable and murderers and immoral persons and sorcerers and idolaters and all liars" with the ones who overcome (21:7). The list in 22:15 is very close to that found in 21:8. Similarly, John contrasts those who shall dwell with God with those who shall not in 21:27.

The above survey reveals how thoroughly hortatory the entire Revelation truly is. Rather than limiting the exhortations to a handful of passages, our survey has revealed that there is a marbling effect, an intermixture of the visionary and the hortatory. The two are interwoven throughout the book to the extent that the various visions are never far removed from the exhortations.[22]

In concluding the survey of Revelation, it must be said that the cleavage between good and evil is placed within the framework of the Church and her members as they await Christ's final coming. The reward of the righteous and the fate of the wicked are brought to attention in terms of striking contrasts and often within hortatory contexts. Furthermore, John's exhortations to Christians throughout Revelation fall within the sphere of encouragement and exhortation to make the right decisions, especially in view of the accomplished victory of the Lamb.

CONCLUSION: LIVING WITH THE FORWARD LOOK

Our brief survey of Paul's first letter to the Thessalonians and John's Revelation offer a united picture in the way Christ's final coming is presented. Both authors clearly set forth the call to uncompromising fidelity which is necessary for true believers as they await Christ's return. Insofar as this steadfast loyalty to God was the pressing need of the hour, the churches addressed by Paul and John were being challenged to be faithful until Christ returned. It may be added that insofar as the contemporary Church is confronted with a similar choice of allegiance, it can follow no other course than that demanded by Paul and John and the other writers of the New Testament.

Both writers reminded their fellow Christians that their behavior would indicate whether they had compromised with the values of a society which could not last or whether they were faithful servants of the Lord who is ruling the universe and who at the end of time would reward each person according to that person's conduct (I Thess. 4:6; Rev. 22:12). If their readers took their Christianity with consistent seriousness, realizing that both Christ's first and final comings were to radically affect their lifestyles, they would remain cultural exiles within their societies. Both writers, therefore, sought to guide their readers. They did this directly by specifically instructing them concerning the proper path of behavior for a Christian in light of Christ's final coming.

By placing their exhortations in the context of Christ's first and final comings they impressed upon their audiences an awareness of the Christian life. It was a context in which Christians were called upon to choose between holy living and unholy living, between the path which would lead to the New Jerusalem and that which would lead to the lake of fire. No compromise was allowed. There were no shades of gray in their teachings. Throughout their writings John and Paul set up stark contrasts between good and evil and invited the believers to make a choice. They exhorted the Christians to choose between clearly opposed sides.

To use Oscar Cullmann's language, D-Day is past, but V-Day is still future.[23] Meanwhile we who live "between the times" not only know Christ's presence with us here and now as Victor and Deliverer, but also hold fast to the well-founded hope that the future—both our personal future and the whole world's future—belongs to Him.

Thus, what words should dominate our thinking as we ponder Christ's final coming? The list would include: faith and faithfulness; mission and ministry; purity and perseverance; service and sacrifice; work and worship; prayer and patience; righteousness and repentance. In contrast with those words which opened this essay, these words suggest a far more demanding response to His promised return.

We need to take the final coming of Christ as seriously as we do the first; it ought to play a controlling part in our day-to-day living. When He returns may He find us a people thankful because we have been a people faithfully living in the shadow of His coming. As C.S. Lewis warned, the doctrine of Christ's final coming must never preclude

> sober work for the future within the limits of ordinary morality and prudence. . . . For what comes is judgment: happy are those whom it finds laboring in their vocations, whether they are merely going out to feed the pigs or laying good plans to deliver humanity a hundred years hence from some great evil. The curtain has indeed now fallen. Those pigs will never in fact be fed, the great campaign against white slavery or governmental tyranny will never in fact proceed to victory. No matter; you were at your post when the inspection came. . . . Women sometimes have the problem of trying to judge by artificial light how a dress will look by daylight. That is very like the problem of all of us: to dress our souls not for the electric lights of the present world but for the daylight of the next. The good dress is the one that will face that light. For that light will last longer.[24]

ENDNOTES

1. For helpful, detailed discussions of these characteristics, please see S. Travis' two books, *The Jesus Hope* (Downers Grove: IVP, 1974), pp. 46-56; and *I Believe In the Second Coming of Jesus* (London: Hodder and Stoughton, 1982), pp. 100-06; and A.A. Hoekema, *The Bible and the Future* (Grand Rapids: Eerdmans, 1979), pp. 164-72.

2. See Travis' *I Believe In the Second Coming of Jesus,* pp. 106-09, 157-83, 184-208; *The Jesus Hope,* pp. 57-79; *Christ and the Judgment of God: Divine Retribution in the New Testament* (London: Marshall Picker-

ing, 1986); and Hoekema's *The Bible and the Future,* pp. 239-87.

3. See Hoekema, *The Bible and the Future,* pp. 129-63; Travis' *The Jesus Hope,* pp. 34-45, 80-91; and *I Believe In the Second Coming of Jesus,* pp. 116-56.

4. We have good authority for not measuring God's time by our human clocks: "with the Lord one day is as a thousand years" (II Pet. 3:8).

5. We should be ready for the coming of the Lord at any time. J.H. Newman suggests that for the Christian it is always five minutes to midnight:

> For so it was, that up to Christ's coming in the flesh, the course of things ran straight towards that end, nearing it by every step; but now, under the Gospel, that course has (if I may so speak) altered its direction, as regards His second coming, and runs, not towards the end, but along it, and on the brink of it; and is at all times near that great event, which, did it run towards it, it would at once run into. Christ, then, is ever at our door.

See his sermon, "Waiting for Christ," in *Parochial and Plain Sermons,* London: Rivington, 1869, Vol. 6, p. 241.

6. Others who emphasize that there must not be a divorce between Christian living and the final coming are: J.R. Ross, "Living Between Two Ages," in *Dreams, Visions and Oracles,* ed. by C.E. Armerding and W.W. Gasque (Grand Rapids: Baker, 1977), pp. 231-41; Travis' *The Jesus Hope,* pp. 9-21, 92-128 and *I Believe In the Second Coming of Jesus,* pp. 209-52; and K. Staton, *What To Do Till Jesus Comes* (Cincinnati: Standard, 1982).

7. As an essay, there is no intention on the part of the author to be exhaustive and comprehensive. A full-blown study would pay stricter attention to the relevant primary sources and would provide detailed support for positions taken. The various books and articles cited will aid the reader in exploring numerous issues in more detail.

8. Because Revelation is the book most clearly associated with Christ's final coming and because its purpose is often misunderstood, more attention will be devoted to it.

9. This essay focuses mainly on structure and content of the two books. For helpful discussions of other issues (e.g., authorship, date, etc.), please consult the works listed in notes 10 and 16.

10. Some helpful commentaries dealing with both interpretive and introductory issues like date and purpose are:

F.F. Bruce *I & II Thessalonians,* Word Biblical Commentary, 45 (Waco: Word, 1982);

I.H. Marshall, *I and II Thessalonians,* The New Century Bible Commentary (Grand Rapids: Eerdmans, 1983); and

J.R.W. Stott, *The Gospel and the End of Time: The Message of Thessa-*

Ionians (Downers Grove: IVP, 1991).

11. All three chapters of II Thessalonians contain allusions to Christ's final coming as well (II Thess. 1:9-10,12; 2:1-17; 3:6-15).

12. See H.K. Moulton, *The Challenge of the Concordance: Some New Testament Words Studies In Depth* (Greenwood, S.C.: Attic Press, 1977), p. 240.

13. Excluding its appearances in I Thessalonians, the word refers to the final coming in the following instances: II Thess. 2:1,8; Matt. 24:3,27,37,39; I Cor. 15:23; James 5:7,8; II Pet. 1:16; 3:4,12; I John 2:28. It does not do so in II Thess. 2:9; I Cor. 16:17; II Cor. 7:6,7; 10:10; Phil. 1:26; 2:12.

14. See G. Braumann "Presence," in *New International Dictionary of New Testament Theology* (1976) 2:898.

15. Even the notoriously difficult passage dealing with the Man of Lawlessness in II Thess. 2:1ff. ends on a hortatory note. In facing evil at its worst Christians are to give thanks "for salvation through sanctification by the Spirit and faith in the truth" and are to "stand firm and hold to the traditions which you were taught" (2:13,15).

16. Among the more helpful commentaries and special studies (and ones which this author would support in their overall understanding of Revelation) are the following:

H.R. Boer, *The Book of Revelation* (Grand Rapids: Eerdmans, 1979);

M.E. Boring, *Revelation*. Interpretation (Louisville: John Knox Press, 1989);

G. Goldsworthy, *The Lamb and the Lion: The Gospel in Revelation.* (Nashville: Thomas Nelson, 1984);

L. Morris, *Revelation*. Revised edition. Tyndale New Testament Commentaries (Grand Rapids: Eerdmans, 1987); and

E.H. Peterson, *Reversed Thunder: The Revelation of John and the Praying Imagination* (San Francisco: Harper & Row, Publishers, 1988).

Quite often misunderstanding of Revelation takes place because of a failure to follow proper principles of interpretation. The following works provide guidance in this area:

J.B. Green, *How to Read Prophecy* (Downers Grove: IVP, 1984);

P.E. Hughes, *Interpreting Prophecy* (Grand Rapids: Eerdmans, 1978);

L. Ryken, *How To Read the Bible As Literature* (Grand Rapids: Zondervan, 1984). See especially pp. 165-75; and

D. Stuart and G. Fee, *How to Read the Bible For All Its Worth* (Grand Rapids: Zondervan, 1982). See especially pp. 205-17.

17. A note of caution concerning the degree of Roman opposition to Christians in the first century needs to be sounded. One must beware of reading the various descriptions of hostility found in Revelation with the assumption that the book is primarily describing situations already happening at the time of writing. Texts should be examined individually to determine whether or not past, present, or future hostile acts are envisioned. Contrary to popular belief, there is no evidence that first century Christians were being persecuted on a systematic, wide-scale basis. Persecution had been or was in John's day, at most, occasional and selective. John does foresee an era in which Christians would be persecuted. Hence, Revelation recalls past periods of conflict, responds to current periods of conflict, and anticipates a future era of even greater conflict.

18. For other commandments directed toward Christians, see 2:7,11,17,29; 3:6,13,22; 12:12; 13:9; 18:4; 19:5,7; 22:7,11.

19. Numerous other places describe Christians (1:3; 2:26; 12:17; 14:12; 22:7,9, etc.). Negative designations are found in 3:17 and in the list of vices in 21:8 (cf. 22:11).

20. A careful reading of Rev. 2—3 reveals many words of commendation as well as rebuke.

21. For a very helpful discussion of the beatitude found in Rev. 20:4-6, see E.C. Caldwell, "The Millennium: An Exegetical Study of Revelation, Chapter 20, in the Light of the Book as a Whole," *Union Seminary Review* 31 (1919): 207-34.

22. Of the 107 paragraphs found in the 26th edition of the Nestle-Aland Greek text of Revelation, at least seventy-four contain one or more of the hortatory techniques discussed in this essay.

23. See his book, *Christ and Time* (Philadelphia: The Westminster Press, 1950), pp. 81ff.

24. C.S. Lewis, "The Christian Hope." *Eternity* (March, 1954), p. 50.

Heaven and Hell

Andrew Paris

The ultimate question of questions is, "If a man dies, will he live again?" (Job 14:14). And all cultures in all ages have hungered and thirsted for the answer. Since our Maker has "set eternity in the hearts of men" (Eccl. 3:11), we desire to know if there is life after death; and if there is, what it will be like and how long it will last. Philosophers have debated this question. Many religions, both primitive and advanced, have advocated wildly and widely diverse notions about it. However, mankind alone can never answer this issue; in our best attempts all is uncertain and dark. We need clear light from the Father of lights. Because Jesus "has brought life and immortality to light through the gospel" (II Timothy 1:10), only in Christianity do we find the absolute and assured answer about life after death. The Bible reveals that all people

231

live on forever after death, the righteous enjoying glory in heaven and the wicked suffering torment in hell. This chapter will bring out the essential features of that doctrine.

HEAVEN

The Blessings of Studying Heaven

Unfortunately, we do not hear much about heaven any more. Even though the Bible emphasizes it and Christians will live there forever, the church today rarely talks about it. This sad silence robs the saints of precious blessings. Jesus made much of heaven and as His people so should we. Whether living in happy or gloomy times, Christians should have heaven on their minds. Preachers need to proclaim it; classes need to discuss it; and all Christians need to study it. For when we do, rich blessings will abound: 1) it will fill you with joy (Luke 10:17-20; Isa. 65:17-19); 2) it will make you firm and steadfast in difficult times (Heb. 6:18-20; 10:34-36; Rom. 5:2-5); 3) it will stimulate you to do good works (Heb. 4:9-11; II Pet. 1:4-11; Phil. 3:14; Matt. 6:19-21); and 4) it will encourage you to overcome sin (Rev. 2:7, 11, 26-28; 3:5, 12, 21; 21:7). Studying heaven is good for you.

Heaven Is a Definite Place

Some people say heaven is not a place, but a condition or state of being. To them it is something rather than some-where. They are half right. Heaven is a spiritual condition, but it is more than just that. Since God created heaven (Heb.

232

11:10, 14, 16), how could He make something that cannot be located? Since Jesus ascended into heaven with a resurrection body and now reigns in that glorified body occupying heavenly space (Phil. 3:20-21), heaven must be a place. If Jesus promised His disciples, "In My Father's house are many mansions . . . I go to prepare a place for you" (John 14:2-3), how could He go to prepare what cannot be located? God in heaven sits enthroned on "a high and holy place" (Isa. 57:15). Heaven is a real place.

Heaven Prior to Christ's Return

In Scripture the term "heaven" can refer to three different places: 1) the sky or atmosphere (Deut. 33:26); 2) the stars and planets (Neh. 9:6); and 3) the dwelling-place of God Himself (I Pet. 3:22; the "third heaven" in II Cor. 12:2). But even when the Bible talks about the heaven where God lives, it makes a distinction between heaven prior to Christ's Return (intermediate heaven) and after Christ's Return (infinite heaven). What does the Word of God say about the intermediate heaven?

Scripture teaches that all Christians go to heaven immediately when they die. Some people believe we go to Paradise, which they say is not really the heaven where God dwells but is instead a blissful waiting room where we live until our bodies are resurrected; then we enter the real heaven to be with God. This notion does not appear in the Bible. Scripture teaches that at death Christians go immediately to be with Christ (II Cor. 5:6-10; Phil. 1:21-23; Luke 23:43). And where is Christ? In heaven with His Father. Therefore the righteous dead are in heaven with Jesus right now. There is no waiting room. For Paradise is heaven. Paul calls Paradise "the third heaven" (II Cor. 12:2-4). John declares that the Tree of Life in the Paradise of God (Rev. 2:7) is in the New Jerusalem (Rev. 22:2, 14, 19). Thus Paradise is the name for heaven intermediate and infinite, but it is no waiting room. Right now in heaven the saints are "before the throne of God" serving "in His Temple" (Rev. 7:15).

Scripture also teaches that the righteous dead are fully conscious in heaven right now. Some people maintain the doctrine of "soul-sleep," in which the righteous dead dose off into a dreamless sleep (like Rip Van Winkle), to wake up at the resurrection when Jesus calls them forth. This notion does not appear in the Bible either. Paul announced triumphantly that "to die is gain," to depart from this life is to "be with Christ," which is "better by far" (Phil. 1:21-24). These statements make no sense if the saints in heaven are unconscious. For how could death be "gain" and "better by far" if the Christian lapses into a coma? What blessing comes from being "with Christ" if the dead are unaware of His presence? Since we are "at home with the Lord" when we die (II Cor. 5:8), there is no "sleeping" between death and resurrection. When Jesus talked about the Rich Man and Lazarus (Luke 16:19-31), He proved the dead are conscious immediately after death.

Scripture teaches that the righteous dead enjoy many rich blessings in heaven right now. The intermediate heaven is a place far better than anything they had experienced on earth. The book of Revelation vividly describes this heavenly joy in three majestic scenes. The first scene reveals that right now in heaven the saints REST FROM THEIR LABORS (Rev. 14:13). They enjoy sweet relief from Satan and sin, sorrow and pain, toil and trouble. However, do not think this heavenly rest means doing nothing, as if we will be in neutral gear. For the second scene reveals that right now in heaven the saints SERVE GOD DAY AND NIGHT IN HIS TEMPLE (Rev. 7:15). This probably describes heaven prior to Christ's Return because in the final, infinite heaven there will be no Temple (Rev. 21:22) and no night (Rev. 21:25; 22:5). So in heaven right now the saints enjoy intimate fellowship with God as they serve in His Temple. Doing what? Probably many of the same things they did for Christ on earth—only in a more excellent manner. In the parables of the talents (Matt. 25:14-30) and the minas (Luke 19:11-26), Jesus teaches that the special abilities we developed here on earth will determine our service in heaven. The spiritual gifts God gave us on earth will not be put on the shelf in heaven. Saints like Stephen, who were cut off early in their earthly ministry, will continue their service in greater effectiveness. Finally, the third scene reveals that right now in heaven the saints FOLLOW THE LAMB (Rev. 7:15). They see the beautiful face of Jesus. As "that great Shepherd of the sheep" (Heb. 13:20), Jesus leads His celestial flock to "springs of living water" where they never hunger or thirst. God wipes every tear from their eyes. These three scenes from Revelation show that in heaven right now we enjoy God's presence, and we see the face of Jesus.

However, as wonderful as this heaven is, it is not as perfect as the final, infinite heaven (New Jerusalem) for at least two reasons: 1) in heaven right now the saints are without their glorified, resurrection bodies. This abnormal state, which is against God's eternal purpose for mankind, will be corrected when the Second Coming occurs (I Cor. 15:23-24; I Thess. 4:16-17). And 2) they do not see the Father's face in all His glory until they enter the New Jerusalem (Rev. 22:4).

Heaven After Christ's Return

What will heaven be like after Christ's return, after the resurrection of the dead and the rapture of the living, after the Judgment Day, after God has made the new heavens and new earth? What does Scripture tell us about the final, infinite heaven—the "New Jerusalem"?

—*Its Physical Dimensions.* What will heaven look like? Notice what Revelation 21 tells us. The physical dimensions of the Holy City are awesome. Laid out like a perfect cube (just as the Most Holy Place in the tabernacle and the temple), the city measures about 1400 or 1500 miles long, wide, and high (v. 16). The walls are about 200 feet thick (v. 17 NIV). The four walls, twelve gates, and twelve foundation stones are made of the finest precious stones known to mankind (vv. 18-21). The city and its streets are made of pure gold, clear as glass (vv. 18, 21). The whole city glows with the glory of God, much like precious jasper (diamond?), clear as crystal (v. 11). Since Jesus is its lamp (v. 23), the sun and moon are not needed.

Many people believe heaven has one pearly gate where Peter stands to admit some and exclude others. However, Jesus reveals there are twelve pearl-gates (three in each direction, v. 13) attended by twelve angels—not Peter (vv. 12, 21).

I believe the precise measurements and graphic descriptions in Revelation 21 are to be taken literally. They convey how grand, how glorious and lavish life will be in heaven. Our mortal minds cannot comprehend such magnificence; it boggles the imagination even to attempt it. Truly heaven is out of this world!

—*Its Spiritual Dimensions.* When the New Jerusalem descends from heaven, John sees more than simply a physical city with walls and gates; he observes the bride of Christ—the redeemed, resurrected, righteous people of God living within that city (Rev. 21:9-10). An angel calls the Holy City "the bride, the wife of the Lamb" (v. 9). The vision emphasizes the saints living forever with God in the New Jerusalem. Never get so caught up in the physical side of heaven that you fail to see its spiritual glory. The city is big and beautiful; but more important still is the fact that the people of God will live there forever. We will enjoy intimate fellowship with God.

Notice also that heaven's physical appearance carries deep spiritual meaning. On the gates are written the names of the twelve tribes of Israel (v. 12), and on the foundations are the names of the twelve Apostles (v. 14). The number twelve thus symbolizes the continuity of the New Testament church and the Old Testament people of God. They form one chosen nation. The Holy Spirit-inspired teachings of the Old Testament prophets and of the New Testament Apostles will be remembered, honored, and obeyed in heaven. Probably the variety of gigantic gems named after the Apostles suggests the overwhelming wealth buried in their teachings (vv. 14-20). The Tree of Life and the River of Life (Rev. 22:1-2) provide both physical and spiritual health to all who live in the Eternal City. It truly is a wonderful place!

—*Its Location.* Where will heaven be located after Christ's Return? Will it be on the earth or somewhere else? Some people maintain that heaven will not be on the earth; they contend that God made the world merely as a temporary residence for mankind, and after the Judgment Day He will annihilate it. The Bible, however, does not support this view.

God declares the earth was designed to be man's home forever (Psa. 78:69; 93:1; 104:5; Matt. 5:5). Because sin has polluted the present heavens and earth, God will transform them into a new and perfect state where only righteousness lives (Rom. 8:19-23; II Pet. 3:13; Isa. 65:17; 66:22; Rev. 21:1-2). When Peter proclaims the earth will be destroyed by fire (II Pet. 3:7, 10, 12), he means the earth's outer crust or land—not the entire planet. The fire will melt and purify—not annihilate. Thus heaven will be on the earth. Heaven and earth will be one.

—*Life in Heaven.* What will we do in the New Jerusalem after Christ returns? Sad to say, most people today picture heaven as merely a place of eternal boredom. They conjure up images of saints in serene stupor, floating on fluffy clouds and doing nothing more than holy contemplation forever. The Bible certainly opposes such an idea. It indicates we will be busy serving God in the New Jerusalem (Rev. 22:3). Our "rest" in heaven will not take the form of couch-potato idleness, but rather work without weariness, work so enjoyable and invigorating it will actually be rest. Work and rest will be identical there. Heaven will become the ultimate workarama.

Of course, many jobs on earth will be eliminated when Jesus returns: no police or alarm systems, no spies, no funeral directors, no life insurance agents, no medical workers, no psychiatrists or sex therapists, no street repair or waterworks employees, and no car mechanics. Our golden harps and crowns will never need polishing (Scripture never mentions halos). To fit into the new work setting, some saints will need to learn a new job in heaven.

But what will we do in heaven? Our ministry to God will involve at least four duties: serving, singing, ruling, and growing.

In heaven we will SERVE forever. And we will never be weary of the work or in the work. Each of us will do the job that fits our talent and taste. There will be more than enough work to do. Consider the millions of angels. They "do His bidding," "obey His word," and "do His will" (Psa. 103:20-21). In this vast universe, many countless tasks require their constant attention. And the angels take care of them. If God has somehow managed to keep His many angels busy accomplishing those ministries throughout the many galaxies, surely He will see to it that we have plenty of work to do forever!

In heaven we will SING forever. Singing ranks as one of the creative activities of heaven. It is one of the few experiences of this life that will carry over into the next. The book of Revelation emphasizes this heavenly occupation more than any other. The redeemed, the angels, the four living creatures, the twenty-four elders, they all sing praise-hymns to God (Rev. 4:8-11; 5:8-14; 7:10-12; 14:2-3; 15:1-4; 19:1-6). Their anthems proclaim God's majesty, splendor, power, justice, holiness, victory, and love. In the New Jerusalem we will do the same. It will be our favorite activity for all eternity.

In heaven we will RULE the earth forever (Rev. 5:9-10; 22:2, 5). Jesus will give us "authority over the nations" (Rev. 2:26-27). Some of Christ's parables teach that when He returns to judge the world, He will reward His loyal servants by giving them ruling power. In the parable of the talents, the two faithful servants are put in charge of many things by their master (Matt. 25:21, 23; see also 24:45-47). In the parable of the minas, the king gives to his two good servants the authority to rule over various cities (Luke 19:17, 19). These parables teach two facts: 1) in heaven we will rule with God; and 2) the more we develop now the abilities God has given us, the better we will be able to serve Him in heaven.

Finally, in heaven we will GROW forever. Hell may reek of sameness and stagnant monotony, but heaven never. We will develop and mature under our divine Trainer and

Teacher. The very nature of heaven requires this conclusion. Heaven is eternal LIFE (Matt. 19:29). The Tree of Life and River of Life will be there (Rev. 22:1-2). The Father of Life will be there; Jesus, the Resurrection and the Life, will be there; the Spirit of Life will be there. And since all life involves progress and development, these must abound in heaven as well. Because sin cannot exist in the New Jerusalem, no obstacles will keep us from rapid and astounding growth. Ever learning and advancing as we receive new truths each day, we will climb higher and higher as the Father leads us throughout eternity.

HELL

If the church rarely talks about heaven these days, it mentions hell even less. Bombarded by unbelievers who ridicule the whole idea of eternal punishment, the church seems ashamed to proclaim that hell really exists. We feel uncomfortable and stammer lamely when critics ask, "How can a loving God send people to hell forever?"

The Biblical writers took a different attitude, however. The Old Testament frequently predicted the eternal doom of those who forget God. The Apostles of Jesus often included "the wrath to come" in their writings. Far from being ashamed to bring up the subject, they unabashedly portrayed hell as the dark background that makes the cross of Christ glow with glory divine. They boldly preached that hell is as certain as heaven. Their Master taught them this truth. He not only promised heavenly glory for believers, but also warned of eternal punishment for unbelievers. And the Apostles preached Christ as the only way to escape that punishment.

To them, the Gospel is "good news" only if it rescues sinners from a real Lake of Fire. So if hell is a fantasy, the New Testament becomes irrelevant drivel. The rest of this chapter will explain this unpopular topic from God's point of view.

The Fact of Eternal Punishment

The Bible clearly teaches that a place called hell really exists. There sinners suffer eternal punishment without relief or chance of parole. This doctrine appears in the following five Biblical facts.

1. Certain sinners will NOT enter the kingdom of heaven: see Matt. 7:13, 21-23; 18:3; Mark 10:23-27; Luke 13:24, 26; John 3:3-5; I Cor. 6:9-10; Gal. 5:19-21; Eph. 5:5; Heb. 3:19; 4:1, 13.

2. There is a CONTRAST between the final state of the righteous and the wicked: see Dan. 12:1-2; Matt. 3:12; 8:11-12; 24:46-51; 25:46; Mark 16:16; Luke 6:23-24; 6:47-49; John 3:16; 5:29; Rom. 6:21-23; Gal. 6:7-8; Phil. 3:17-21; II Thess. 1:5-12; II Tim. 2:19-20; Heb. 6:8-9.

3. Hell-punishment is "everlasting," "eternal," "forever," and "forever and ever": see Dan. 12:1-2; Matt. 18:8; 25:46; II Thess. 1:8-10; II Peter 2:17; Jude 6-7, 13; Rev. 14:10-13; 19:3; 20:10.

4. A change of heart and preparation for heaven are confined to THIS LIFE alone: see Isa. 55:6-7; Matt. 25:5-13; Luke 13:24-29; John 12:36; II Cor. 6:1-2; Heb. 3:1-10; 13:15-22; Rev. 22:11.

5. All will PERISH who reject the gospel of Jesus: see Acts 13:40-46; 20:26; 28:26-27; Rom. 10:12; I Cor. 1:18; II Cor. 2:15-16; 4:3; I Thess. 5:3; II Thess. 1:8; 2:10-12; Heb. 2:1-3; 4:1-11; 10:26-31, 38-39; 12:25-29; II Pet. 3:7.

The Conditions of Hell

What is hell really like? What will sinners experience once they enter its awful gates?

What Hell Is Not. Before we can understand what hell is, we need to clear away two misconceptions about it. First, this present life is not hell. People often say hell is any intensely painful experience you go through in this world: a bad marriage, a lost job, a terminal illness. But they are wrong. We may suffer greatly in this life, but it is not hell. That infernal region is not to be found in the here and now on a Rand/McNally map. The lost go to hell and experience its horrors only AFTER they die—never before (Luke 16:22-23).

Second, hell is not Satan's throne. Some think the devil now rules there and loves it, as if hell were his own comfortable home. No way! He is neither in hell now, nor will he enjoy it once he does get there. Although nothing in Scripture tells us he is now in hell, Revelation 20:1-3 may indicate he is presently chained in the "Abyss" (Rev. 9:1-11), along with some of his demons (Luke 8:31; II Pet. 2:4; Jude 6). On the Judgment Day, Jesus will condemn the Prince of Darkness and all evil spirits to suffer eternal torment in hell (Rev. 20:10; Matt. 25:41). It will never become his pleasure penthouse, nor will he ever rule there. God alone rules over heaven, earth, and hell.

What Hell Is. Hell is obviously a place of everlasting punishment for those who reject God. But what is the nature of that punishment? Consider some of the Biblical descriptions.

Hell is eternal separation from God's love and favor. This describes the most dreadful and painful of all hell's horrors. The wicked are "shut out" from (II Thess. 1:9), sent "away from" (Matt. 7:23; Luke 13:27), and "thrown out" of God's loving fellowship (Luke 13:28; Matt. 8:12). They will "depart from" His holy presence (Matt. 25:41). God is perfectly just and fair to do this; for the people in hell are those who had already chosen to separate themselves from God while on earth. Therefore it is only right to send them to the one place where they will continue to be separated from God. After all, they prepared themselves for it. They would not be ready for any other place.

In hell, people suffer intense pains in body and soul forever. To describe the PHYSICAL torments, Scripture sometimes uses the word "fire" (see Matt. 5:22; 18:8; 25:41; Mark 9:43, 48). We should not press this term too far. Maybe hell's physical tortures will be far worse than any literal fire on earth, but Jesus used this word because it conveys the most intense form of physical suffering mankind knows. Those in hell will suffer such intense physical anguish they will be weeping and gnashing their teeth (Matt. 8:12; 13:42, 50; 24:51; 25:30; Luke 13:28). There will also be intense SPIRITUAL agony there. Pangs of conscience, despair, loneliness, hopelessness, and memory of what might have been, are just a few of hell's spiritual pains. Its spiritual misery never ends (Rev. 14:9-13; 20:10; Matt. 25:46). Dante may have been right when he said that over hell's portals are these words: "Abandon ye all hope."

Hell means wastefulness. It is a garbage dump. Jesus often described hell by using the word "Gehenna." This Greek term referred to the "Valley of Hinnom," a garbage heap into which the Jews of Jerusalem threw their filth and thrash. A fire burned there constantly to keep the valley clean. Whenever Jesus used this word, He meant that hell is the eternal trash dump, a place of wastefulness where "unquenchable fire" burns forever. To every person God has given the precious gift of life along with myriads of blessings, opportunities, and warnings. But when we discard these gifts and disobey God's word, life becomes wasted; it turns into a garbage heap. And hell is the place where God sends those who have thus wasted and ruined their lives. It is filled with people who once were made to walk with God, but now have been so disobedient they are no good—useless.

There are degrees of punishment in hell. Jesus taught this truth in His parable of the faithful and unfaithful servants. The one who knew His master's will but did not obey will be beaten with "many blows," while the other who did not know His master's will and did things worthy of punishment will be beaten with "few blows" (Luke 12:47-48). Jesus predicted Tyre and Sidon would receive less punishment on the Judgment Day than the Galilean cities of Chorazin, Bethsaida, and Capernaum (Matt. 11:22). Sodom would receive less punishment than Capernaum (Matt. 11:24). The degrees of punishment in hell will be determined by the amount of light that a person possessed on earth. For people see, sin, and suffer differently.

Alternatives to Eternal Conscious Torments in Hell

We have seen the Biblical view that everyone in hell will suffer conscious torment forever. However, some sincere Bible students deny that Scripture actually teaches this. They have suggested two alternatives: Restorationism and Annihilationism.

Restorationism. This alternative maintains that those in hell will eventually return to God ("be restored") and go to heaven. God will use the intense sufferings of hell to cause people to turn from sin and believe the gospel of Jesus. Many find this alternative attractive and appealing.

However, this view contains several serious flaws. First of all, numerous Biblical passages reveal hell to be eternal torment without relief or escape (see Matt. 25:46). These texts appear in the section entitled, "The Fact of Eternal Punishment." Secondly, this theory violates human freedom. For according to it, God employs the fires of hell to force people to love Him against their own will. Scripture plainly teaches that the unsaved go to hell, and the saved go to heaven. Never will the two groups meet.

Annihilationism. This alternative contends that the wicked will not suffer in hell eternally. They will endure a temporary duration of conscious torment (or none at all, as Jehovah's Witnesses believe). Then God will annihilate them. They will be completely erased and wiped out from existence. Since the advocates of this view believe the human soul is not immortal, they maintain that only Christians will receive an immortal soul after the Judgment Day. But all non-Christians must be annihilated sooner or later because their mortal souls cannot last forever in hell. This alternative raises certain serious objections to the idea of eternal conscious torment in hell. I will respond to some of those objections.

1. The Annihilationist objects that man does not now have an immortal soul; only God is immortal (I Tim. 6:16). Therefore there is no necessity for keeping humans in hell-torment FOREVER.

But the problem here is that the Bible is silent on the entire issue. Nowhere does it discuss the immortality of the soul, but only the immortality of the resurrection body (I Cor. 15:53-54). And for the Annihilationist to stress the supposed mortality of the soul, making it the main foundation of his argument, is a rather flimsy base. Anyway, if God can make the mortal souls of the devil, the beast, and the false prophet suffer eternal torment in hell (Rev. 20:10; 14:9-11), why can't He do the same for all the wicked?

2. The Annihilationist objects that eternal conscious suffering in hell violates God's nature; it is contrary to His love: how can He stand to let His creatures suffer endlessly? It is contrary to His justice: how can any sin be so terrible as to deserve eternal suffering?

However, we must be careful not to approach Scripture with our own preconceived ideas of what God ought to be like. We must let Scripture tell us what is consistent and inconsistent with His nature. Maybe eternal torment is consistent with both His love and justice. Is eternal suffering really against God's justice? Who are we to decide what is fair and what is not? See Romans 9:19-23; Habakkuk 1. Perhaps sin against the INFINITE God does deserve INFINITE torment. Eternal suffering for one sinful act done in a moment of time is justified because the sin of a moment will cause RESULTS (spiritual death) that we by our own power cannot undo.

3. The Annihilationist objects that the Biblical words used to describe hell do not require eternal torment. In fact, most of the terms suggest an end to the torment. Thus, the wicked will in the end be annihilated.

However, this argument contains several flaws. First, the term translated "eternal" or "forever" as it appears in the New Testament always means "unending duration"—never a temporary period. It describes the nature of: God (Rom. 16:26), the Spirit of Jesus (Heb. 9:14), our inheritance (Heb. 9:15), our glory (II Tim. 2:10; I Pet. 5:10), our life (I Tim. 6:12), the kingdom (II Peter 1:11), the gospel (Rev. 14:6), the judgment (Heb. 6:2). And that same term portrays hell as eternal punishment (Matt. 25:46), eternal destruction (II Thess. 1:9), and eternal fire (Matt. 25:41).

Even in Jude 6-7, this term means "eternal." True, the PHYSICAL buildings and streets of Sodom and Gomorrah were not burning forever. But the PEOPLE LIVING IN THOSE CITIES are what Jude refers to here. They died physically in the flames on earth and then passed into eternal torment in hell.

Also the Annihilationist claims that only when the compound phrase ("forever and ever") appears, does it ever mean "unending duration of time." But when only one "forever" is used, it may not mean eternality. Thus, since only the devil, the beast, and the false prophet suffer hell-torment "forever and ever" (Rev. 14:9-11; 20:10), all the rest of the wicked suffer temporarily and then are annihilated.

However, if this were true, no one who LISTENED to Jesus describe heaven and the Christian life with a single "forever" would ever think He meant Christians live "forever" in heaven (John 3:15, 16, 36; 4:14, 36; 5:24, 39; 6:27, 40, 47, 54, 68; 10:28; Matt. 25:46; Mark 10:30). They would have to WAIT until Paul and other Bible writers wrote in the New Testament that heaven is "forever and ever." And obviously we know that cannot be true. A single "forever" can mean exactly what the compound phrase ("forever and ever") does. Also, notice in Matthew 25:41 that all the wicked will suffer the same duration of hell-torment as the "devil and his angels" will. It is "eternal fire prepared for the devil and his angels" to which all the wicked will go. All who worship the beast will be tormented without rest "forever and ever" (the compound phrase!) (Rev. 14:9-11).

Does any term in the New Testament require the doctrine of eternal TORMENT in hell? Yes: "punishment" in Matthew 25:46. There the word describes the state of the wicked after the Judgment Day. This word never means annihilation, but always CONSCIOUS SUFFERING and sometimes death. The only other place in the New Testament it occurs also carries this same idea: I John 4:18 (the verb appears in Acts 4:21; II Pet. 2:9). Throughout all ancient Greek literature, this word never refers to UNCONSCIOUS punishment or suffering. Therefore, "punishment" in Matthew 25:46 cannot be annihilation. How can punishment continue where there is no longer any person to be punished? The term surely refers to the process of "punishing" rather than to the results of the punishment. That process of "punishing" is said to be "eternal."

The terms "death," "perish," and "destruction" do not describe annihilation; rather they refer to a NEGATIVE CONDITION OF HOPELESS RUIN. The word "destruction" as used in the New Testament and ancient Greek literature always means "ruin, loss, curse, beyond all chance of repair," but never annihilation. "Death" never means annihilation either, but rather refers to the SEPARATION of the vital element. Physical death is the separation of the spirit from the body (James 2:26); spiritual death is the separation of the spirit or soul from loving fellowship with God (Eph. 2:1, 5); eternal death is the eternal state of final separation from God (Rev. 20:14). The difference between "death" and "life" is not that of non-existence (annihilation) versus existence. For the term "life," as used in the New Testament to describe the Christian life on earth and in heaven ("eternal life"), never means merely unending existence. Instead it refers to a specific KIND or QUALITY of life with God (Matt. 19:29; 25:46; Mark 10:30; John 3:15, 16, 36; 4:14, 36; 5:24, 39; 6:27, 40, 47, 54, 68; 10:28; 12:25, 50; 17:2; Rom. 2:7; 5:21; 6:22-23; I John 5:11, 13, 20). Therefore, death is not the extinction of being, but of WELL-BEING.

Thus no New Testament term for the conditions in hell REQUIRES annihilation.

4. Finally, the Annihilationist objects by saying that the concept of Jesus dying in our place for our sins rules out eternal suffering. The essence of His atonement was that He DIED—not that He suffered forever on the cross.

However, the Annihilationist has missed an important truth. Christ's suffering was not merely quantitative—suffering endlessly, on and on; it was also qualitative. When Scripture declares He died for our sins, it means He paid the penalty our sins deserved (Gal. 3:13; II Cor. 5:21). And what was that penalty? Merely physical death? Not! Eternal torment/death was what He suffered on the cross. Because Jesus by nature was INFINTE (being God in the flesh), He suffered in a finite period of time the equivalent of ETERNAL TORMENT for finite creatures. Calvary was a miracle in which God placed the eternal pains of hell for all sinners upon His Son within the short space of six hours.

Thus the QUALITY of His sufferings was equal to that of all sinners suffering forever in hell. The INTENSITY of His anguish was so heightened that this could occur. The cross was the time when Jesus was eternally separated from the Father. For that is what hell essentially is.

Annihilationism cannot fit this Biblical teaching about the cross of Jesus. If the sinner's punishment is annihilation, then Christ actually was annihilated on the cross. He ceased to exist; He was obliterated. If so, then it is wrong for the Bible to speak about His resurrection; if at the cross Jesus suffered ANNIHILATION, then His reappearance from the tomb ought to have been called a whole new creation. This seems to border on heresy. It is the achilles heel of Annihilationism.

Therefore, both alternatives—Restorationism and Annihilation—contain flaws so serious they cannot be Biblical. The Bible teaches that hell is eternal conscious torment. This view has been faithfully maintained by the church throughout the centuries. It still stands as the only Biblical position.

In conclusion, we have studied the essential features of what the Bible teaches about heaven and hell. "This day I call heaven and earth as witnesses against you that I have set before you life and death, blessings and curses. Now choose life"—eternal life in heaven with God (Deut. 30:19).

The Christian and the Old Testament

Gary Hall

From the early church fathers to modern times, Christians and the church have had a great deal of difficulty with the Old Testament. The basic problem is this: since the Old Testament was written for another time, culture, and people (ancient Israel) how can it be of any authority and value for the Christian? A basis for this problem is often found within the New Testament itself. It seems to suggest that the Law (often understood by many as the whole Old Testament): does not justify the sinner, is a prompter of sin, was canceled by the death of Jesus Christ (Rom. 3, 4, 7; Gal. 3-4; Col. 2), and serves mostly as a source of types for Christian antitypes (Heb. 7-10).

Further the Old Testament is long and complicated and difficult to understand. In addition to this, the church is a New

Testament institution and therefore the Old Testament appears irrelevant. Moreover, its ethics and morals seem sub-Christian and are an embarrassment to the church. Those who want to utilize the Old Testament despite the problems find it almost impossible to take at face value. They generally adopt a "what it means to me approach" or use the Old Testament as a source of moral instruction. Although these methods are an admirable attempt to take the Old Testament seriously, they are still a denial of its authority for they ignore the text in its original context and meaning.

The issue has been stated in various ways but it is always the same: the major problem for understanding the Bible in the church is what to do with the Old Testament. The crux is hermeneutical: that is, what method of interpretation should be adopted to best make sense of the Old Testament.

THE OLD TESTAMENT IN THE NEW

The problem of the Old Testament would not be so critical if the New Testament had ignored it. But that is not the case. In fact the New Testament either quotes from or alludes to the Old Testament on almost every page. This relationship between the Testaments can be demonstrated statistically.[1] Out of all the New Testament books, only Philemon, a short book, has no direct quote or allusion to the Old Testament. Shires lists 437 quotes that are either introduced with a formula, or are of such verbal affinity and length to be classified as direct quotes. He adds to this number 1,167 instances where the Old Testament is either reworded or directly referred to in the New Testament (classified as extensive allusions). The grand total is 1,604 citations of the Old Testament. One remarkable chapter, Acts 7, has 105 references to 15 Old Testament books. When the thousands of allusions that include one or more words are added, only one conclusion can be reached: the influence of the Old Testament on the New was profound and pervasive. This fact is quite remarkable when one considers that the New Testament was written in Greek, not Hebrew, and that it was written mostly for Gentiles on Gentile soil. Yet the writers apparently expected the readers to know the source of the quotes, make the proper interpretation, and respect the authority and relevance of the Old Testament. It is also clear the writers could not write about the Gospel and Christ without an Old Testament foundation.

Further research into the quotes and allusions has shown that there were various Old Testament passages that were favorites of the New Testament writers. Though these writers quoted from a variety of texts they seemed to agree on the importance of a number of Old Testament chapters.[2] C. H. Dodd has classified the most quoted and alluded to texts into four categories. 1) Apocalyptic-eschatological scriptures such as Joel 2-3, Zechariah 9-14, parts of Daniel 2, 7, 9, and 12, and Malachi 3 and 4. 2) Scriptures of the New Israel including several texts from Hosea, Isaiah 6-9:7; 11, 28, 29, 40; Jeremiah 7 and 31, and Habakkuk 2. 3) Scriptures of the servant of the Lord and the righteous sufferer, most of which come from Isaiah and the Psalms, including Isaiah 42-44; 49-51; 52-53; 61 and Psalms 22, 31, 34, 41, 42-43, 69, 118. 4) There are several texts that don't fit a neat category but are referred to often. These include Psalm 2, 8, 110; Genesis 12; and Deuteronomy 18.

Dodd suggested that the early church had produced a collection of these texts and circulated them among the churches.

The creative mind behind this effort was Jesus himself as he taught the disciples which Old Testament passages spoke most clearly of him (see Luke 24:44-49). Though there is no evidence for such a gathering of texts, the concentration of quotes and allusions on a few Old Testament texts lends support to the theory of a collection, whether written or oral. Dodd's observations show that the New Testament writers did not just search out at random isolated texts to apply to Jesus, but shared a common theological outlook based on the general context of several large sections from the Old Testament.

Recognizing such a concentration of a few chapters in the Old Testament must not lead us to a false conclusion. Working backward from the New Testament it might be easy to conclude that only part of the Old Testament was important to the New Testament writers. This, however, is not the case as individual quotes and allusions to all parts of the Old Testament occur in the New.

THE OLD TESTAMENT IN THE HISTORY OF THE CHURCH

Although the New Testament authors were convinced of the authority of the Old Testament and how it should be used, the church has not always been so confident. A survey of the history of the use of the Old Testament by Christians through the ages shows that a multitude of attitudes and approaches have been employed. A brief look at this history will help clarify the issues and provide a foundation for developing a viable methodology for using the Old Testament in the church without repeating past mistakes.

1. The Early Church to the Reformation

The earliest of the church fathers in the early second century were mostly concerned to use the Old Testament as guidance for living. Using the Old Testament characters as examples for faith, that is moralizing, was regularly done. The Old Testament Law was not binding on the Christian, but spiritual principles were drawn from it.

A real threat to the Old Testament in the church came from the second century Christian, Marcion. Marcion was strongly influenced by Gnosticism, which taught that God could have no direct contact with a material world. Therefore, he concluded that the God portrayed in the Old Testament could not be the same as the God in the New Testament. Their characters and means of communication with mankind were too different. Marcion's solution to this problem was to call for the jettisoning of the whole Old Testament. But since parts of the New Testament seemed to rely heavily on the Old Testament, he had to call for those passages to be excised also. Marcion was branded a heretic and driven out of the church in 144 A.D.

Justin Martyr (100-165 A.D.) responded to Marcion's heresy by taking a tack that has been used often in the subsequent history of the church. Justin looked for references to Jesus Christ in the Old Testament in passages other than the familiar Messianic texts. Consequently he found appearances of Jesus in Genesis 18 and 32, Exodus 3, Psalm 45, and Proverbs 8. He went so far as to accuse the Jews of removing Christological passages from the Hebrew Bible.

The early church father who had the most influence on later Christian use of the Old Testament was Origen (185-254 A.D.) who resided in Alexandria, Egypt. He developed the allegorical method of interpreting the Old Testament. He was able to build on the tradition begun in Alexandria by the Jew, Philo (25 B.C. to 45 A.D.). Although Origen took some of the Old Testament at face value, especially the law, he looked for hidden meanings for several reasons. He thought that parts of the Old Testament read at face value contradicted common sense and reason. Also he wished to avoid the charge that Marcion had raised that the God of the Old Testament was immoral and different in character from the God in the New. Further, he wanted to reject any language about God that gave Him human characteristics. Finally he was convinced that when read spiritually the whole Bible was in harmony and the difficulties disappeared. Therefore, the literal meaning as ascertained by studying the historical setting and context was of little value to Origen. The spiritual meaning that one could place on the text that would lead to higher ideas and edifying thoughts was to be preferred. References to Jerusalem, for example, were not best understood as references to the real city, but as pointers to the heavenly abode of God's people. Origen was a towering intellectual giant of his day and the method he perfected ruled the Christian's use of the Old Testament for over a thousand years. His aim and the aim of those that followed him was to save the Old Testament from Marcionite type attacks and make it relevant to the life of the church.

Augustine (354-430 A.D.) wrote one of the greatest expositions of the Old Testament produced by a Christian, the *City of God*. He accepted allegorical spiritualizing and explained away anthropomorphisms. But he also made a major breakthrough by seeing the Old Testament as prophetic history: it showed how God's purposes had been worked out in the history of Israel and in the advent of Christ. There was an essential unity to the Bible and the Old Testament was incomplete, anticipating the coming of Christ.

After Augustine little new thinking was introduced into Old Testament studies until the eleventh-twelfth centuries. In that period a school arose in Paris at the abbey of St. Victor. Hugh and Andrew, the most famous scholars who resided there, demonstrated a renewed interest in the history and culture of the Old Testament, and even expressed interest in the intention of the author. Both consulted Jewish scholars to learn Hebrew (a major innovation) and to learn of Jewish interpretations.

Aquinas (1225-1274 A.D.), the great medieval scholar, was the first to distinguish between the moral, ceremonial, and judicial content of the Old Testament law. He taught that only the moral law was binding. In this he has been followed by many Christians from the Reformation until today.

2. The Reformation

The Reformation era was a watershed period in the history of interpretation and is noted for its complete abandonment of the allegorical method.

Martin Luther (1483-1546) is given credit for rescuing Christians from the dilemma that had plagued them to this time: if the Old Testament was interpreted only historically it was to Israel and irrelevant for the church; if it was interpreted spiritually then it became subservient to the New Testament and was easily abandoned.

Luther is well known for his antithesis between law and gospel, but by this he did not mean the Old Testament was totally law and the New Testament totally gospel. Luther taught there was law and gospel in both testaments. Of course the Old Testament was mostly law, but there was gospel there and this is what made the Old Testament relevant for the

Christian. What provided the unity of the Testaments was that the new covenant was found in the Old. This new covenant had existed secretly from Genesis 3 on and was recognized by believers and the prophets. Christ was at work in the Old Testament as well. There was a hidden church in the Old Testament and hidden Christians, for whoever believed in the coming Christ was already a Christian. Events of Israelite history were significant for the believer for they were the visible Word of Faith and eternal examples of faith. Although the old covenant was completely annulled by God, to the extent that it prophesied of the new covenant, it was confirmed and fulfilled in the New Testament.

However, Luther still taught that the Old Testament was mainly the teaching of laws, the showing up of sin, and the demanding of good. In contrast the New Testament was mainly gospel or a book of grace in which was found the power to fulfill the law. Luther differed from the earlier church fathers in seeing a much sharper break between the Testaments. The earlier scholars saw a gradual theological development moving from the Old into the New Testament. Luther saw a definite contrast between the two. What gave the Old Testament its value were the Christological references throughout. These references were on the same level as gospel.

Although the law in the Old Testament was antithetical to the gospel, Luther saw its value. The Ten Commandments were important for the Christian because they agreed with natural law and were therefore to be observed. In this he agreed with earlier church scholars. The promises and pledges the laws contained concerning Christ were important. The rest of the law was useful because one could see there beautiful examples of love and faith, and examples of how God treated the Godless. The primary purpose of the law was to bring people to the realization that only through the gracious word of the gospel could they have forgiveness and hope.

Though Luther rescued the Old Testament from useless symbolism his strong dichotomy between the law and gospel easily led to a denigration of the Old Testament by his followers. If the law convicted of sin and led to Christ, then of what use was it after one became a Christian?

John Calvin (1509-1564) had a totally different approach to the Old Testament. Since the Bible was the source of all religious insight, for him all parts of the Bible had equal authority. Since the Holy Spirit was the author of the whole Bible, what seemed to be of lower morals, etc. were accommodations of the Holy Spirit, not contradictions. All history was under the eschatological promise of Christ.

Calvin held the law to be central. Since Jesus cannot contradict the Father, the New Testament must be understood on the basis of the Old. The unity of the Bible was based on the covenant. Both Testaments witnessed to the same covenant. The difference between the two was that of administration. In the Old Testament the administration of the covenant was incomplete. The pious in the Old Testament could receive an anticipation of salvation through Christ. Since the Ten Commandments were in agreement with natural law the Christian should observe them, but not be bound by legalism.

Calvin's starting point was how the New Testament used the Old. Jesus' sayings on the new covenant were interpreted to mean that it only became new and eternal in its truth, but it was the same covenant. Since the Old Testament had knowledge of Christ as mediator the newness of the Gospel was almost lost for Calvin. For him the differences between the Testaments were only a matter of degrees of clarity. The book of Hebrews had strong influence on him. It can be said that

Calvin Christianized the Old Testament and Judaized the New Testament to make them appear as one. On the other hand he rejected all allegory, even for homiletical purposes. Nor did he read Christ everywhere into the Old Testament as Luther did. Even the Messianic prophecies had to first have a meaning in their original context. The use made of them by the New Testament was in the nature of illustrative references and skillful adaptations.

The Reformation conceptualized the three functions of the law, best stated by Calvin. The first function was to bring knowledge of sin (Rom. 3:20) that should move one to seek grace. This idea was emphasized by Luther. The second function was to restrain evil doers with fear of punishment. A forced righteousness was necessary for the preservation of society and could lead to Christ. The third function was to help one learn better the nature of God's will and thus arouse one to obedience and good works. This was the major emphasis for Calvin and clarifies why he saw the Old Testament on the same level as the New. Jesus did not come to end the law but to remedy transgressions of it. Through Christ the teaching of the law remained inviolable. What was abrogated was that the law no longer condemned because Jesus bore its curse.

Calvin's methodology has wide influence today. But it seems to lose balance in its emphasis on the continuity of the covenants. There certainly are important discontinuities also, which Paul addresses. It appears Calvin saved the Old Testament at the expense of the New.

3. The Modern Era

The modern era had its beginning intellectually in the Enlightenment of the 17th century. The interest in ancient and original sources and the introduction of rationalism had profound effects for the place of the Old Testament in the church. The basic position was established by Grotius (1583-1645). He separated the Old and New Testaments and interpreted the former only in terms of its own times, not in relation to the New. The law was seen as archaic and incomplete. The Old Testament formed the background to the New Testament and had some spiritual value, but it was basically of no religious importance for the Christian. Thus the Old Testament became a historical document with historical interest, but since it was full of old material and primitive ideas it was totally superseded by the New and largely irrelevant. This also became the position of old Liberalism which captured the mainline churches world-wide and maintained control until the early 20th century. This was a time of eclipse of the authority of the Old Testament. The advent of rationalism removed any supernaturalism from both Testaments, so the Bible was no longer a record of God's revelation to mankind, but a record of mankind's search for God. The Bible had not been understood in this way before, and there is a great gulf between the modern era and previous approaches to the Old Testament. Now the Old Testament was of interest only to the ancient historian. If it came to have any value for the church it had to be as a foil for the elevated religious ideas of the New, or as a source of example for faith, either negative or positive—mostly the former.

With this denial of the supernatural came the analysis of most parts of the Old Testament into its supposed human sources. Search for the original sources, documents and authors became the avenue of study. The result was extreme fragmentation of the Old Testament, denial of traditional authorships, and eventual doubt of its historical reliability. If any value was to be found in this old book full of legends and stories, it had to be in its religious ideas. These ideas had no authority, however, but were mostly viewed as helpful and suggestive. Any religious ideas that did not measure up to the modern (read "superior") ideas were only of historical interest. The New Testament use of the Old was regarded as an antiquarian effort also. The New Testament writers were the product of their age and culture and since they believed in the inspiration of the Old Testament one could expect them to use it. But modern people know better so one cannot place any stock in the New Testament writers as authorities in this matter.

This revolution in thought freed the Old Testament from subservience to the New Testament and Christian dogma, but it raised an extremely critical issue. Was a free and critical spirit, guided by reason, sufficient for the correct interpretation of the Old Testament? If it relegated the Old Testament to a mere ancient historical document, then the answer would have to be, no.

The latter half of the 20th century has seen a resurgence in interest in the Old Testament as a literary document. Several new methods of its study all share the presupposition that the Old Testament is a literary production and should be studied as literature. These methods have produced a welcome antidote to the fragmentation of the Old Testament by emphasizing its literary unity. Attention is focused on its "final form," not the history of its composition. Some of these methods have produced rich insights into Old Testament texts and provided a basis for sound study.

4. Alexander Campbell

The Christian church has its own niche in the history of the interpretation of the Old Testament grounded in the method-ology of Alexander Campbell. He stands neither in line with traditional Protestant interpretation nor with the recent Enlightenment and liberal tradition.

Campbell first expressed his views on the Christian and the Old Testament in his "Sermon on the Law" delivered in 1816. This sermon earned him a heresy trial, which was eventually dismissed. It is remarkable that Campbell did not publish this sermon until 30 years after it was preached. The sermon takes issue with all the main points developed in the Calvinist tradi-tion out of which he came. Campbell defined the law as the whole legal dispensation of Moses, and denied the traditional division of it into 3 parts: moral, ceremonial, and judicial, for such a division was unbiblical. Trying to rescue the Ten Com-mandments for relevancy to the church by assigning them to a moral law category only created confusion when reading the New Testament, because it did not make such a distinction. Campbell pointed out the weaknesses of the law as expressed in the New Testament and stressed how God had remedied them through Jesus Christ.

Campbell came to 5 conclusions about the law and the Christian. 1) There was an essential difference between the law and the gospel and the Old and New Testaments. 2) There was no condemnation in Jesus Christ. To this should not be added a covenant of works or rule of life. 3) There was no need to preach the law in order to prepare men for the Gospel. This was a direct attack on the three uses of the law as devel-oped in the Reformation and Post-reformation period. 4) All arguments that drew from the Old Testament to urge Chris-tians to practice some form of Israelite customs or duties were repugnant. 5) Jesus Christ should be venerated in the highest degree.

From this sermon it is clear that Campbell staked out a position on the Old Testament that stood in sharp contrast with the traditional position of his day. Because of the polemical nature of the sermon we do not learn what sort of positive approach he might take in the Old Testament. In other scattered essays in the *Christian Baptist* and *Millennial Harbinger* Campbell rejected allegory and supported typological use of the Old Testament. Unfortunately the Campbellian understanding of the law, and emphasis on New Testament Christianity have led to a wide spread downplaying of and unease with the Old Testament among the Christian Churches and Churches of Christ.

THE CHRISTIAN AND THE OLD TESTAMENT

This survey of the history of the place of the Old Testament in the church has revealed several methods for making it relevant and useful, from allegory to mere historical interest. Each method has its strengths and weaknesses. None has been accepted by a broad spectrum of the church as the best method. Each method has been grounded in prior assumptions of the interpreters. Origen's allegorical method was grounded in the assumption that certain expressions violated the nature of God, and an allegorical level was more spiritual. The mere historical interest of the liberal was grounded in the assumption of the non-revelatory, purely human origin of the Bible. Many of the methods take as their starting point the New Testament and move backwards into the Old. Many also share another common trait, the inability to maintain the contextual meaning of the Old Testament in light of the perceived superior authority of the New Testament. The outcome often has been that in an effort to save the authority of the Old Testament for the church, a methodology has been utilized that ultimately contributed to its loss of significance.

It is crucial that the Christian formulate a methodology for study of the Old Testament that does justice to both its authority as God's word and its complex relationship to the New Testament.

The following proposals are suggested as a possible solution to the problem of the use of the Old Testament in the church. They should not be considered as definitive and final, but as guidelines for further reflection and thought.

1. Begin with the Old Testament, not the New.[3] The Old Testament is God's Word to His people delivered in a specific time and place. It must be understood first of all on its own terms. Its historical and cultural setting must be analyzed in order that its own unique message becomes clear in its own context. Only then can its main theological ideas and themes be properly understood. These theological themes provide the basis for its relevancy to the church. This common sense beginning, often ignored in the history of the church, will clear up many perceived problems immediately.

Further, understanding the Old Testament in its own context will allow the text to raise its own agenda, and prevent modern Christians from bringing theirs to it. A good example is Genesis 1 and 2, which are often mined by Christians looking for hints of modern science. But these chapters were written in an ancient Near East setting against the background of pervasive polytheistic paganism. In that setting they function as a polemic against the ancient misunderstanding of the world and must be first understood in that way.

2. After understanding the Old Testament in its own context through careful exegesis, determine what theological

themes and ideas are being presented. It is at this theological level that the Old and New Testaments most clearly connect. In fact the New Testament assumes many of the major Old Testament theological doctrines without discussion. One of the weaknesses of earlier methods that began with the New Testament and moved backward is that much of the Old Testament was left out of consideration. Important issues not explicitly taken up in the New Testament were missed.

Beginning with the theological teachings of the Old Testament does two helpful things: it deepens understanding of themes that the New Testament takes over from the Old[4] and it helps one to see the many direct connections between the testaments that are not made explicit in the New.

3. Do not moralize. Quite often Old Testament texts, especially narrative texts, are seen as some sort of indirect moral teaching. Old Testament people and events are used as either good or bad examples which Christians should emulate or avoid. These moralisms are not directly taught in the narrative passages, require imaginative reading between the lines, and ignore the basic theological theme of the narratives. The narrative texts are first of all about what God is doing in His world. If the Christian desires to derive moral teaching from the Old Testament, which is a very worthwhile task, then only texts that directly teach morals should be used.

4. Understand how the New Testament uses the Old Testament. The methods that began with this idea were not wrong in suggesting that this was an important issue. They erred in making it the first and major approach. It is rather one part of a multifaceted approach. One must begin by understanding the presuppositions of the New Testament writers.[5] They assumed the concept of corporate solidarity, that is, an individual could represent a larger group or nation or the larger

group was more important that the individual. Therefore, in the New Testament, Christ was seen as representing the true Israel of the Old Testament. Many passages addressed to Israel in the Old Testament were applied to Christ in the New. Secondly, they assumed a unified history under the sovereign plan of God which was not completed in the Old Testament and whose earlier parts provided a pattern for later events. Thirdly, they assumed that the eschatological fulfillment looked forward to in the Old Testament had come to completion in Christ. Fourthly, their basic assumption was that Christ was the key to interpreting the Old Testament and its promises, and the Old Testament derived its ultimate fullness of meaning from this fact.

5. Understanding the multiplicity of ways the New Testament writers used the Old Testament offers valuable guidelines for the Christian.[6] The most important are summarized here.

A. The New Testament writers believed that the Old Testament was fulfilled in the New. This is so well accepted it hardly needs stating. But it needs to be addressed because many seem to think this is the only relationship that exists between the Testaments. Many see the Old Testament as mostly prediction and the New Testament as mostly fulfilling those predictions. But that is not accurate. The Old Testament prophets were not mainly predictors of the future, but rather they were preachers of repentance who called for a return to God and warned of coming judgment. It was in this context that the promises for the future were made. Most of these promises fit the Messianic category, that is, the Old Testament promised a new age of salvation breaking in, sometimes connected with a Davidic type of royal figure. It is these texts that the New Testament claims were fulfilled in Jesus Christ.

267

The fulfillment motif suggests there is an open-endedness and incompleteness to the Old Testament. It is this incompleteness the New Testament points to as being filled up.

B. The New Testament writers used the Old Testament for dogmatic and theological purposes. Often complex theological presentations were buttressed by relying on Old Testament texts for support. Paul is best known for this procedure and his use of a wide variety of Old Testament texts in Romans 9-11 provides a good illustration. He assumed that God had revealed Himself and His will in the Old Testament and the theological implications of what was revealed there were conclusive support for Christian doctrine and thought. He understood that many of the theological teachings of the Old Testament and the church were a unified whole.

C. The New Testament writers believed the church to be on an historical continuum with the Old Testament (often called a salvation-historical perspective). They showed that the death and resurrection of Jesus Christ was a continuation of what God had begun in the Old Testament. This fact is best seen in many of the sermons recorded in Acts. Stephen's lengthy rehearsal of Israel's history (Acts 7) was two pronged: to show Israel's history of resisting God, and to show that Jesus Christ stood in a line with others such as Moses that God had used to save His people. The history of Jesus Christ and the church continued what God began in ancient times. There was one history of God's people, not two, and what God was doing through Jesus Christ had essential ties to the past.

D. The New Testament writers used the Old Testament for eschatological teaching. The language and ideas generated in the Old Testament to picture the future in-breaking of God in the world at the end of time was taken over in the New Testament to point to the future as well. The basis for this was found in Jesus' teaching (Mark 13:24-27). The word pictures were taken from several places in the Old Testament and were intended to describe the end of the world in familiar language. The use of Joel 2:28-32 by Peter in his sermon recorded in Acts 2:17-21 suggested that the end time the Old Testament anticipated began at Pentecost. Thus the New Testament portrays the future anticipated by the Old Testament as both now occurring in some way, but as also awaiting a more complete consummation in the future.

E. The New Testament writers used the Old Testament for apologetic purposes. Jesus and the early Christians found themselves in controversies with the Jews. The claim that Jesus was the promised Messiah raised opposition. Therefore, Old Testament texts that were interpreted as fulfilled by Jesus also had an apologetic purpose. They were intended to defend the Christian faith from the Jew's own Scripture. Good examples occur in many of Jesus' disputes with the Jewish leaders and in Peter's sermon in Acts 2:25-28 as well as in Stephen's sermon in Acts 7.

F. The New Testament writers used the Old Testament as a foundation for exhortation to Christian living. Old Testament passages that exhorted God's people to Godly living were applicable to the church as well. Thus these instructions were directly incorporated into teaching sections as if they had been directly addressed to Christians. For example, Jesus' beatitudes and other ethical teachings came from Old Testament texts. The repeated call to holiness in Leviticus (11:44; 19:2, etc.) was applied directly to Christians by Peter (I Pet. 1:15) and Proverbs 24:21, 22 became a direct word of exhortation for Paul (Rom. 12:20).

Moral conduct remained the same for all of God's people

and His revealed will for this conduct did not change.

G. The New Testament writers used the Old Testament in a typological way. They saw in the Old Testament a pattern of the ways God worked through institutions, people, and historical events and applied this pattern to issues raised in the life of the church. The best example of this, of course, is the book of Hebrews which found in many of the institutions of Israel's worship types of Christ. Great care must be taken to distinguish typology from allegory. The former is firmly grounded in history, and there is a formal pattern of relationship between type and antitype. Allegory is not concerned with history or with formal patterns. Very little allegory is used in the New Testament; Galatians 4:21-26 being the only explicit example. Typology, however, is a proper method of interpretation because it takes seriously how God worked and sees a continuation of that pattern in the church. Outside of Hebrews, Paul gives us an example of typology in I Corinthians 10 as a part of an exhortation to the Corinthians.[7]

CONCLUSION

The above brief analysis offers some guidelines for the Christian's use of the Old Testament. It must be a multifaceted approach, taking into account both the intention of the Old Testament text and the purpose for which it is used in the New Testament. It is improper to restrict the Christian's use of the Old Testament to just one or two categories. The Reformers' attempts to organize the use of the law into three propositions was too narrow. It was formulated in response to contemporary religious currents, not through a careful analysis of the Old and New Testaments. If we are to be Biblical we must adopt interpretive principles that will be broad enough to cover the wide range and the complexity of the relationship between the Testaments. On this basis a rich interchange with the Old Testament is possible. But we must not be limited to just how the New Testament makes use of the Old. We must also examine carefully the Old on its own merit to discover the ways it leads into the New. The Old Testament must be studied in its own historical cultural setting. This requires long and hard work. But the alternative to this hard work is unacceptable. To ignore or misuse 77% of the Bible is to fail to properly understand and use the New Testament itself. We cannot pay lip service to the authority of the Old Testament while ignoring it in practice. If the Old Testament is God's Word then it must be taken as seriously as the New.

The admonition of Paul to Timothy is especially appropriate, since the scripture he is referring to is the Old Testament. "All Scripture is inspired by God and profitable for teaching, for reproof, for correction, for training in righteousness: that the man of God may be adequate, equipped for every good work" (II Tim. 3:16-17, NASB).

ENDNOTES

1. Although different counts are given by different authorities, the following statistics are taken from H. M. Shires, *Finding the Old Testament in the New* (Philadelphia: Westminster, 1974), chapter 1.

2. C. H. Dodd's work in this area, though disputed at some points, offers us a good starting point to see how this works. See C. H. Dodd, *According to the Scripture* (New York: Scribners, 1953) and *The Old Testament in the New* (Philadelphia: Fortress, 1965).

3. See John Bright, *The Authority of the Old Testament.* Grand Rapids: Baker, 1976, chapter 3; Gerhard Hasel, *Old Testament Theology: Basic Issues in the Current Debate,* 4th ed. (Grand Rapids: Eerdmans, 1990), chapter 6.

4. See for example, F. F. Bruce. *The New Testament Development of Old Testament Themes* (Grand Rapids: Eerdmans, 1970).

5. See G. K. Beale. "Did Jesus and His Followers Preach the Right Doctrine From the Wrong Texts: An Examination of the Presuppositions of Jesus and the Apostles' Exegetical Method," *Themelios* 14, 3 (Apr. 1989): 89-96. The assumptions are grounded in Jesus' own teaching and ministry.

6. See Walter Kaiser, *The Uses of the Old Testament in the New* (Chicago: Moody Press, 1985).

7. Jack Weir, "Analogous Fulfillment: The Use of the Old Testament in the New Testament," *Perspectives in Religious Studies* 9 (1982): 65-76 suggests that a typological-like analysis can make the most sense out of the relationship between the testaments. This method, which he prefers to call analogy, he thinks can be used as an umbrella term to include all other methods. See also R. T. France. *Jesus and the Old Testament* (Grand Rapids: Baker, 1982), Chapter 3.

Bibliography

Achtemeier, Elizabeth. *Preaching From the Old Testament.* Louisville: Westminster/John Knox Press, 1989.

Although this book is aimed at the preacher it is very useful for the Sunday School teacher and others interested in how to apply the Old Testament to the Christian life. Achtemeier deals with each of the sections of the Old Testament: narrative, law, prophets, psalms, and wisdom literature. She also includes helpful suggestions of how to move into the New Testament from the Old.

Archer, Gleason. *Encyclopedia of Bible Difficulties.* Grand Rapids: Zondervan, 1982.

After a good introductory essay on Biblical inerrancy, this book examines the numerous alleged contradictions and discrepancies that critics through the ages have tried to find in the Bible. Beginning in Genesis one and continuing chapter by chapter through the Bible, Archer shows how the supposed errors have reasonable explanations. This is a faith-strengthening book that ought to be in every Christian worker's library.

Barclay, William. *The Lord's Supper*. Nashville, TN: Abingdon Press, 1967.

In this clear and concise presentation, a noted Edinburgh scholar explains what the Lord's Supper means for the church. This brief book combines historical, biblical, and devotional studies.

Basinger, David; and Randall Basinger, eds. *Predestination and Free Will: Four Views of Divine Sovereignty and Human Freedom*. Downers Grove, IL: InterVarsity Press, 1986.

Addressing the crucial issue of God's sovereignty and human free will, this book presents four different approaches by evangelical scholars, covering the spectrum from strong Calvinism (John Feinberg) to limited foreknowledge (Clark Pinnock). Norman Geisler presents a moderately Calvinistic view, while Bruce Reichenbach comes closest to the Biblical view.

Beasley-Murray, G. R. *Baptism in the New Testament*. Grand Rapids: Eerdmans, 1973. (Reprint from Macmillan, 1962.)

This scholarly work by a British Baptist is one of the most complete studies available today. His treatment of the meaning of the Biblical texts is thorough and objective, and his conclusions are very close to the ones presented in chapter seven of this book. Highly recommended.

Berkouwer, G. C. *The Work Of Christ*. Grand Rapids: Eerdmans, 1965.

This is a standard study, from a moderate Calvinist perspective, of "objective soteriology." The author's strengths include an ability to see doctrine in its widest context. His weakness is his verbosity. His chapter of "Aspects of the Work of Christ" is particularly helpful.

Bickersteth, Edward. *A Treatise on the Lord's Supper.* Two volumes. London, England: L.B. Seeley and Son, 1825.

Truly one of the best discussions of the Lord's Supper ever written. The first volume gives the biblical view, while the second volume offers numerous devotional studies. An excellent resource for church leaders seeking material for their Communion meditations.

Bruce, F.F. *New Testament Developments of Old Testament Themes.* Grand Rapids: Eerdmans, 1970.

A valuable book showing in detail how some major theological themes of the Bible begin in the Old Testament and develop into the New. The New Testament expansion of the theme is not understandable apart from the Old. He studies themes like: the rule of God, salvation, the people of God, and the servant Messiah.

Bruner, Frederick Dale. *A Theology of the Holy Spirit.* Grand Rapids: Eerdmans, 1970.

This classic critique of Pentecostal theologies is somewhat dated now, but still full of good exegesis and insights, especially on problems resulting from a spirit of "triumphalism" (acting as if one has already now achieved total spiritual perfection).

Campbell, Alexander. *The Christian System.* Joplin, MO: College Press, 1989. (Reprint from Standard, 1835).

Campbell's teaching set forth in a systematic format.

_____. *Christian Baptism, with Its Antecedents and Consequences.* Nashville: Gospel Advocate, 1951. (Reprint of 1851 edition.)

While not as precise on the meaning of baptism as we might wish, this is still an important and useful work for understanding the Restoration distinctives on the subject. The section on infant baptism is quite good.

Cottrell, Jack. *Baptism: A Biblical Study*. Joplin, MO: College Press, 1989.

This is an exegetical study of the twelve main New Testament passages that relate to the meaning of baptism. It provides a more thorough discussion of many of the points included in chapter seven and shows in more detail the clear Biblical basis for the view presented.

_____. *Solid: The Authority of God's Word*. Joplin, MO: College Press, 1991.

This is a reprint of a book first published in 1978. It is a brief, easy-to-read general study of the nature and purpose of the Bible. As a paperback divided into thirteen lessions, it is suitable for Sunday-school classes and other study groups.

_____. *What the Bible Says About God the Creator; . . . God the Ruler; . . . God the Redeemer.* Three volumes. Joplin, MO: College Press, 1983-1987.

These three large volumes cover every aspect of the Biblical doctrine of God. They include detailed studies of God's works and attributes, and of such subjects as the Trinity, sovereignty and free will, predestination, the problem of evil, miracles, the will of God, and prayer.

Ellis, E. Earle. *Paul's Use of the Old Testament*. Grand Rapids: Baker, 1957.

A standard work exploring how one New Testament writer quotes from and uses the Old Testament.

Elmore, Vernon O. *Man as God's Creation*. Nashville: Broadman Press, 1986.

Mr. Elmore offers a much-needed and generally successful approach at integrating into a holistic understanding the various aspects of man's existence, e.g., spiritual, sociological, psychological, ethnological, economical, industrial, and political. The book's greatest value is in the affirmation of man's worth as the special creation of God. It is a good condensing of an otherwise overwhelming array of topics.

Erickson, Millard J. *Christian Theology*. Grand Rapids: Baker, 1986.

Destined, perhaps, to be THE evangelical systematic theology textbook for some time. He presents the doctrine of salvation in a conservative, well-written, fair (to both Calvinist and Arminian persuasions), and comprehensive manner (e.g., current theological conceptions of salvation, the objective and subjective aspects of redemption, as well as a discussion of the means and extent of salvation). Must reading for the serious student.

Fletcher, David, ed. *Baptism and the Remission of Sins: An Historical Perspective*. Joplin, MO: College Press, 1989.

This volume contains chapters by scholars from both the instrumental and the non-instrumental churches of Christ. The first chapter gives an overview of the history of baptism up through Martin Luther; the second chapter explains the radical change in baptismal theology inaugurated by Zwingli in the sixteenth century; the next several chapters deal with specific aspects of the doctrine of baptism in Restoration history; the last chapter is a detailed study of the New Testament teaching on the subject.

France, R.T. *Jesus and the Old Testament*. Grand Rapids: Baker 1982 [1971].

A more technical and detailed work. France is concerned with Jesus's quotations from the Old Testament, their text-form and authenticity. Along the way he discusses many important issues. Chapter 3 is excellent on typology. Although demanding, study of the book will be rewarding.

Gaffin, Richard B., Jr. *Resurrection and Redemption: A Study In Paul's Soteriology*. Grand Rapids: Baker, 1988.

This revision of an earlier work by Gaffin is included in this bibliography because it emphasizes an often neglected area in discussions of salvation: the resurrection of Christ. Gaffin competently demonstrates that the resurrection is as key to Pauline theology as is the cross if not more so.

Garrett, Leroy. *The Stone-Campbell Movement*. Joplin, MO: College Press, 1981.

Anecdotal. Delightful reading. Helpful in understanding of the *a cappella* Churches of Christ.

Geisler, Norman L., ed. *Inerrancy: The Extent of Biblical Authority*. Grand Rapids: Zondervan, 1980.

This is a thorough, scholarly treatment of the many issues related to the doctrine of Biblical inerrancy. It is valuable for meeting the many objections often raised against inerrancy. Especially useful is the chapter dealing with the implications of the fact that the original manuscripts of the Bible are no longer in existence.

Geisler, Norman L.; and William E. Nix. *A General Introduction to the Bible*, revised and expanded edition. Chicago: Moody Press, 1986.

In this book, in over 600 pages of text, Geisler and Nix deal in a clear and thorough way with many of the questions discussed only briefly in chapter one. The main sections deal with the inspiration, canonization, transmission, and translation of the Bible.

Green, E. M. B. *The Meaning of Salvation*. Philadelphia: Westminster, 1965.

A basic introduction to the doctrine, written primarily with theology students in mind. Green's strength (and weakness) is his restriction of the discussion to the specific biblical words for "salvation" (*yeshua, soteria,* etc.). While helpful, he betrays a narrow understanding of language. Consequently, some key salvific ideas (Fall, covenant, etc.) are given little or no comment.

Green, Michael. *I Believe in the Holy Spirit*. Rev. ed. Grand Rapids: Eerdmans, 1989.

Probably the best all-round contemporary presentation of all aspects of the Spirit's person and work in Christianity. It deals sanely and irenically with controversial issues.

Goldingay, John. *Approaches to Old Testament Interpretation*. Rev. ed. Downers Grove, IL: InterVarsity Press, 1990.

A very useful and readable discussion of the various ways the Old Testament has been interpreted through the years. Goldingay interacts with scholarship and offers helpful guidelines for interpreting the Old Testament. The revised edition adds a 12 page update on developments in the last decade.

Hasel, Gerhard. *Old Testament Theology: Basic Issues in the Current Debate*. Fourth ed., Grand Rapids: Eerdmans, 1991.

This work has two excellent chapters, V and VI, that consider the important Old Testament issues and offer sound conclusions. The rest of the book is an important contribution to understanding Old Testament theology and is valuable reading.

Hawthorne, Gerald. *The Presence and the Power*. Dallas: Word Publishing, 1991.

Its challenging and inspiring thesis is that Jesus learned human obedience through His dependence on the power of the Holy Spirit within Him, and so should we.

Hoekema, Anthony A. *Created in God's Image.* Grand Rapids: Wm. B. Eerdmans Publishing Co., 1986.

The author writes from the Reformed position, but he neither bores nor angers those who come from differing theological perspectives by weaving a tedious thread through history; his handling of man historically and theologically is refreshing. Particularly helpful is his presentation of the views of leading theologians; his desire to harmonize or reject these views from the standpoint of the Scriptures is the book's strong point.

Kaiser, Walter, Jr. *The Uses of the Old Testament in the New.* Chicago: Moody Press, 1985.

Kaiser is concerned to show that the New Testament uses the Old Testament in a non-arbitrary way, that the New Testament writers had the Old Testament context in mind, and that the Old Testament text has one essential meaning with a reference to both the contemporary and future applications of the text. He classifies the New Testament uses into several useful categories and gives detailed exegetical examples. His arguments are sometimes labored but this is a useful work.

_____. *Toward Rediscovering the Old Testament.* Grand Rapids: Zondervan, 1987.

A plea for the Christian to take the Old Testament seriously. Kaiser shows some consequences of the abandonment of the Old Testament by the church. Then he offers guidelines for understanding the Old Testament in its dual role as theological foundation for the New Testament and as a guide for Christian living.

Leggett, Marshall. *An Introduction to the Restoration Ideal.* Cincinnati: Standard Publishing, 1986.

Written with the person in the pew in mind. Historical, doctrinal, and practical. Usable in study groups. Workbooks and video available.

Lilly, J. P. *The Lord's Supper: A Biblical Exposition of Its Origin, Nature, and Use.* Edinburgh, Scotland: T. & T. Clark, 1891.

In this in-depth treatment, Lilly concentrates more upon tracing the history of the way Christians have interpreted the Lord's Supper than upon what the Bible teaches about it.

Longenecker, Richard. *Biblical Exegesis in the Apostolic Period.* Grand Rapids: Eerdmans, 1975.

A careful examinination of the phenomena of the quotations of the Old Testament in the New. Longenecker studies the exegetical methodology of the New Testament writers and compares it to early Jewish exegetical methods. He finds both similarities and differences. A foundational work though some of his conclusions are widely debated. One of the best resources for information of Jewish exegetical methodology.

McAllister, Lester G. *Thomas Campbell: Man of the Book.* St. Louis: Bethany Press, 1954.

Treatment of person, insights, life, and teaching of Thomas Campbell.

McDonald, H.D. *The Christian View of Man.* Westchester, IL: Crossway Books, 1981.

This book is a must for anyone interested in a summary of the various views of man held by the church down through the centuries. McDonald's greatest strength is his ability not only to summarize theologians' and philosophers' views but to integrate or reject them on the basis of the testimony of the Scriptures. McDonald condenses a prodigious effort into a small volume, making it

281

very readable.

_____. *Salvation.* Westchester, IL: Crossway Books, 1982.

A concise, popular-level, evangelical treatment of the essential elements of the doctrine of salvation.

McDowell, Josh. *Evidence that Demands a Verdict, Vol. I,* revised edition. San Bernardino, CA: Here's Life Publishers, 1979.

This book, published by Campus Crusade, is an indispensable compilation and explanation of the evidences only summarized in chapter one. Using numerous quotations from many sources, McDowell shows why it is reasonable to accept the Bible's claims to be the inspired Word of God.

Milligan, Robert. *The Scheme of Redemption.* St. Louis: Christian Board of Publication, 1868.

Old, but a good systematic doctrine as perceived by the early leaders of the Restoration movement.

Morris, Leon. *The Apostolic Preaching of the Cross.* 3rd edition. Grand Rapids: Eerdmans, 1965.

A thorough, exegetically-oriented treatment of salvific terminology: redemption, reconciliation, etc. Morris' careful study of "propitiation" is a classic, and alone, worth the price of the book.

_____. *The Cross in the New Testament.* Grand Rapids: Eerdmans, 1965.

A companion volume to the above, giving a book-by-book (New Testament) study of the atonement. This book offers a competent presentation of the substitutionary character of Christ's death.

_____. *I Believe in Revelation.* Grand Rapids: Eerdmans, 1976.

Though this book is probably still out of print, it is still the best single volume dealing with the subject of revelation. Morris very capably and faithfully discusses the Biblical teaching plus many related issues. For anyone desiring to learn more about the subject, it would be worth the trouble it might take to track this volume down in a library or through inter-library loan.

Murch, James DeForest. *Christians Only.* Cincinnati: Standard Publishing, 1962.

Considered the classic history of the Restoration movement. Written by one involved in much of the movement's later history.

Murray, John. *Redemption: Accomplished and Applied.* Grand Rapids: Eerdmans, 1955.

A classic presentation of Calvinism's understanding of salvation. Murray gives a chapter-by-chapter analysis of some of the major "applications" of redemption to the believer's life: effectual calling, regeneration, justification, sanctification — the historic "order of salvation" model which is popular in many Reformed studies of the doctrine.

_____. *Christian Baptism.* Phillipsburg, NJ: Presbyterian and Reformed, 1962.

This volume is a clear example of the false view of baptism instituted by Zwingli, usually known as the Reformed view. Murray himself was a Presbyterian.

Nash, Ronald. *The Concept of God: An Exploration of Contemporary Difficulties with the Attributes of God.* Grand Rapids: Zondervan, 1983.

This is a brief, well-done, conservative philosophical (as distinct from exegetical) defense of the Biblical doctrine of God, in response to attacks by unbelieving philosophers.

Neth, John. *Walter Scott Speaks*. Milligan College: Emmanuel School of Religion Press, 1967.

Handbook on the life and doctrine of the evangelist who popularized the Restoration ideal.

Packer, James I. *Knowing God*. Downers Grove, IL: InterVarsity Press, 1973.

This is a very readable and reverent survey of the Biblical doctrine of God, marred only by its occasional Calvinistic slant.

Paris, Andrew. *What the Bible Says About the Lord's Supper*. Joplin, MO: College Press, 1986.

In a simple and readable style, Paris covers all essential aspects of the Lord's Supper, from the manner of Christ's presence and the Supper's biblical meaning to Communion devotions and meditations for church leaders. Replete with bibliographies on many issues, it contains a wealth of material. This book presents a fuller discussion of the topics that are briefly mentioned in chapter 9 of this book.

Pinnock, Clark. *Biblical Revelation: The Foundation of Christian Doctrine*. Chicago: Moody Press, 1971; currently reprinted by Presbyterian and Reformed.

This volume is not just about revelation; it is also about inspiration and inerrancy. It is a very good discussion of the importance of these doctrines. Pinnock points out very clearly how the very possibility of sound doctrine or theology is dependent upon a Bible that is both inspired and inerrant.

_____, ed. *The Grace of God, the Will of Man: A Case for Arminianism*. Grand Rapids: Zondervan, 1989.

This volume contains fifteen studies by conservative writers who present a non-Calvinistic approach to the doctrines of God, man, and salvation. Included are chapters by two Restoration Movement authors: Terry Miethe ("The Universal Power of the Atonement"), and Jack Cottrell ("The Nature of the Divine Sovereignty").

_____, ed. *Grace Unlimited.* Minneapolis: Bethany Fellowship, 1975.

A collection of essays by a variety of authors, addressing many of the same issues as Murray, yet without the Calvinistic perspective. Restoration Movement scholars Jack Cottrell and James Strauss are among the capable authors of this volume, contending that Jesus laid down his life for all people, not merely the "elect."

Purkiser, G. T., Taylor, Richard S. and Taylor, Willard H. *God, Man, and Salvation.* Kansas City, MO: Beacon Hill Press, 1977.

The authors present a Wesleyan perspective offering a balanced view of man's worth in spite of his failures. The reader would do well to consider the chapter of "The New Testament View of Man" for useful word studies on such topics as *soul/spirit, flesh/body, spiritual/natural, etc.* The authors subsume these words under the general heading, *The Nature of Humanness* and parlay them between New Testament and Old Testament counterparts. There may be too much of a distinction made where synonymous usages occur, but the study is helpful, nonetheless.

Richardson, Robert. *Memoirs of Alexander Campbell.* Cincinnati: Standard Publishing Co., 1897.

Authoritative history of A. Campbell's life and ministry. Voluminous.

Sauer, Eric. *The King of the Earth.* Palm Springs, CA: Ronald N. Haynes Publishing Co., 1981.

Mr. Sauer argues strongly for the harmony that exists between science and Christian faith. He fully accepts the Lordship of Jesus and maintains that only deity could solve humanity's problems. His wedding of science with the inscripturated Word gives great dignity to God and man. A warning is necessary, however, concerning his willingness to accept theistic evolution. He also disputes the account of the universal Flood. It is sometimes difficult to determine if Sauer thinks it is more important to harmonize Christianity with science or science with Christianity. At any rate, the discriminating reader will find this book most helpful.

Shepherd, J. W. *Handbook on Baptism*, second ed. Nashville: Gospel Advocate, 1950. (Reprint of 1894 edition.)

This old but valuable resource is mainly a collection of hundreds and hundreds of quotations from scholars of all backgrounds, all supporting the Biblical view of baptism as believers' immersion for salvation. The quotations are categorized according to topic.

Shires, Henry M. *Finding the Old Testament in the New*. Philadelphia: Westminster Press, 1974.

A standard work which gives easy access to basic statistical material and other facts regarding the use of the Old Testament in the New. Some of Shire's conclusions are unacceptable but his research and appendices are sources of valuable information.

Stevenson, Dwight. *Walter Scott: Voice of the Golden Oracle*. St. Louis: Christian Board of Publication, 1946.

Life and ministry of one of the most colorful leaders of the Restoration movement. Much pathos.

Stott, John. *Baptism and Fullness: The Work of the Holy Spirit Today*. Downers Grove; IL: InterVarsity Press, 1976.

This is a concise and strong defense that the Baptism in the Spirit is the universal and initial experience of all Christians and not a second work of grace (based on I Cor. 12:13).

Strom, Mark. *The Symphony of Scripture*. Downers Grove, IL: InterVarsity Press, 1990.

A delightful book. Strom's aim is to show the unity of the Bible by investigating its major theological themes. He begins in the Old Testament and traces numerous themes into the New, then moves to the New Testament and connects its themes back into the Old. Each chapter has a summary, study questions, and suggested exercises. Strom is easy to read and understand, a good starting point for the Christian eager to learn about the unity of the Bible.

Tozer, A.W. *The Knowledge of the Holy. The Attributes of God: Their Meaning in the Christian Life*. New York: Harper and Row, 1961.

This is a brief but very reverent and very practical study of God's attributes.

Ware, Charles. *Barton Warren Stone*. St. Louis: Bethany Press, 1932.

Life and ministry of the leader of the Restoration movement in the West, including the Great Awakening.

Warfield, Benjamin Breckinridge. *Inspiration and Authority of the Bible*. Phillipsburg, NJ: Presbyterian and Reformed, 1948.

This is a collection of several shorter articles and reviews by Warfield, who was one of the most capable Biblical scholars of the early twentieth century. His detailed studies of the inspiration of the Bible have never been equaled and are still relevant today. The material here is not always easy; some of it deals with the meaning of Greek expressions.

Warren, Virgil. *What the Bible Says About Salvation*. Joplin, MO: College Press, 1982.

One of the "weightier" volumes of this somewhat uneven "doctrinal" series, Warren stresses the restoration of interpersonal relationships as the central key to understanding the Bible's presentation of salvation.

Webb, Henry. *In Search of Christian Unity*. Cincinnati: Standard Publishing, 1990.

Excellent textbook. Scholarly. Comprehensive history of the Restoration movement.

Wells, David. *The Search for Salvation*. Downers Grove, IL: Inter-Varsity Press, 1978.

This is a well-researched and readable survey of contemporary theological approaches to the doctrine of salvation: Roman Catholicism, liberal Protestantism, Liberation theology, and conservative thought. It has, unfortunately, been allowed to go out of print.

Young, Edward J. *Thy Word Is Truth*. Grand Rapids: Eerdmans, 1957.

This book was written in defense of the inspiration and inerrancy of the Bible by a respected Old Testament scholar several years before inerrancy became an issue among Evangelicals. It is a very fine study of the subject.

Editor

Stephen Burris, B.S., M.A., Administrator of Cornerstone Christian School, Camarillo, California.

Authors

John Castelein, A.B., M.Div., Ph.D., Professor of New Testament and Theology at Lincoln Christian College and Seminary.

Jack Cottrell, B.A., M. Div., Ph.D., Professor of Theology at Cincinnati Bible College and Seminary.

Gary Hall, B.A., M.Div., Th.M., Ph.D., Professor of Old Testament at Lincoln Christian Seminary.

Robert Kurka, A.A., B.A., M.Div., D.Min., Professor of Theology and Philosophy at St. Louis Christian College.

Marshall Leggett, B.A., M.Div., M.A. D.D., President of Milligan College.

Robert Lowery, A.B., M.Div., Th.M. Ph.D., Professor of New Testament at Lincoln Christian Seminary.

Tony Newby, B.A., M.A., Professor of New Testament at Ozark Christian College.

Andrew Paris, B.A., M.A., M.Div., free-lance writer in theology living in Cincinnati, Ohio.

Johnny Pressley, B.A., M.Div., Th.M., Ph.D. Associate Professor of Theology at Cincinnati Bible College and Seminary.

Printed in the United States
200016BV00007B/139-147/A